John Reinhardt Werner

A Visit to Stanley's Rearguard at Major Barttelot's Camp on the Aruhwimi

With an account of the river-life on the Congo

John Reinhardt Werner

A Visit to Stanley's Rearguard at Major Barttelot's Camp on the Aruhwimi
With an account of the river-life on the Congo

ISBN/EAN: 9783337245924

Printed in Europe, USA, Canada, Australia, Japan

Cover: Foto ©Andreas Hilbeck / pixelio.de

More available books at **www.hansebooks.com**

A VISIT TO
STANLEY'S REAR-GUARD

AT MAJOR BARTTELOT'S CAMP
ON THE ARUHWIMI

WITH

AN ACCOUNT OF RIVER-LIFE ON THE CONGO

BY

J. R. WERNER

ENGINEER, LATE IN THE SERVICE OF THE ETAT
INDÉPENDANT DU CONGO

WITH PORTRAITS AND OTHER ILLUSTRATIONS

WILLIAM BLACKWOOD AND SONS
EDINBURGH AND LONDON
MDCCCLXXXIX

All Rights reserved

TO

THOSE FRIENDS IN ENGLAND AND SCOTLAND,

WHO, SINCE MY RETURN HOME,

HAVE, BY THEIR KINDNESS AND HOSPITALITY,

AMPLY RECOMPENSED ME FOR THE TOILS AND HARDSHIPS

OF MY SOJOURN IN AFRICA,

THIS BOOK

IS DEDICATED, WITH SINCERE THANKS,

BY THE AUTHOR.

PREFACE.

THE favourable reception accorded to the article entitled "Major Barttelot's Camp on the Aruhwimi" (in 'Blackwood's Magazine' for February 1889) by the press and the public generally, has encouraged me to write out the full narrative of how I first met the officers of Stanley's rear-guard, and the circumstances which led to my visit to Yambuya Camp, in the hope that it will prove of equal interest to my readers.

As this volume is intended for the general public, who, while taking an interest in African affairs, do not care to wade through whole chapters of dry statistics, I have, when speaking of such matters as railways, &c., purposely introduced as few figures as I could, and then restricted myself, as far as possible, to round numbers.

The Arabs occupy, in Central Africa, during the nineteenth century, very much the same position as the Spaniards did in South America and the West Indies during the seventeenth, and carry on the same atrocities. History has in this case once more strangely repeated herself; and the description given by Kingsley in 'Westward Ho!' of the journey of Amyas Leigh and his men over the Caraccas mountains and up the Orinoco, gives a very fair notion of the difficulties of Stanley's last journey. Stanley, however, had, if anything, a worse country to traverse; and his followers, being natives of the Dark Continent, only added to his perplexities.

Times are changed since the days of Elizabeth, and men cannot go out against the Arabs as Queen Bess's buccaneers did against the Spaniards of old; but I hope that, before long, the Arabs will be taught, in one way or another, that the natives of Africa were not created solely for the gratification of their avarice and lust of gain.

I have to acknowledge with thanks the kindness

of Sir Walter B. Barttelot, Bart., C.B., and of Mrs Jameson, for allowing me the use of the photographs of Major Barttelot and Mr J. S. Jameson; also of Captain Coquilhat of the Belgian army, and Mr A. J. Wauters, of the Institut National de Géographie, Brussels, as well as of several other friends who have assisted me with the sketches and photographs utilised in my illustrations.

I cannot conclude without expressing my sincere thanks to Mr William Blackwood, whose kindness to me, when I was still an entire stranger to him, in a distant land, I shall never forget.

J. R. WERNER.

April 20, 1889.

CONTENTS.

CHAPTER I.

ANTWERP TO BANANA.

The Micawber business—The *Saō Thomé*—Down the Scheldt—Passengers for the Congo—Lisbon—Madeira—S. Vincent—Bolama—Principé—S. Thomé—Shooting excursion—" Plenty big bird "—First sight of the Lower Guinea coast—Banana Creek—Waiting for the *Heron* at Banana, . 1

CHAPTER II.

L'ETAT INDÉPENDANT DU CONGO.

The Congo State—Discovery of the Congo—Tuckey's expedition, 1816—Livingstone discovers the Chambezi—Cameron at Nyangwé—Stanley's explorations—The " Association Internationale Africaine "—Stanley's two expeditions, 1879, 1884—Sir Frederick Goldsmid at Vivi—Sir Francis de Winton's governorship—Changes in the Administration—Constitution of the Congo State—General survey of the river, ... 19

CHAPTER III.

UP-COUNTRY TO LÉOPOLDVILLE.

Departure from Banana—Porpoises—Boma—" La Chasse à l'Administrateur-Général "—Dinner at the station—" Palm-oil ruffianism"—Captain Coquilhat—Matadi—Vivi—Preparations for the march— The "dark ways" of native carriers—King Nozo's caravanserai—My first fever—Collapse by the way—"A new fetish"—Lukungu—Carried into Léopoldville—Dr Mense—Causes of fever—View from Léopold Hill—The State steamers—How the *Stanley* was repainted "after many days," . 33

CHAPTER IV.

LÉOPOLDVILLE TO BANGALA.

Station-life at Léopoldville—Ngalyema and his neighbours—Provision-supply at Léopoldville—Yarn of the champagne-bottles—Climate and fevers—"Congo thirst"—The *Stanley's* feed-pump—The Italian expedition—Departure of *A.I.A.*—Winds in the Congo cañon—Scenery between Stanley Pool and Kwamouth—Hospitality of the Kwamouth fathers—The Mississippi pilot—Hippo-shooting—Death of Delatte—Equator—Monotonous scenery—Bangala—Arrival of the *Stanley*—Mata Bwyki, chief of Iboko—Dance and *massanga*-drinking—Departure of the *Stanley*—My quarters in the gun-room—A tropical thunderstorm—First house at Bangala—Food-supply—The Ba-Ngala—Cannibalism, . . 60

CHAPTER V.

THE LOSS OF STANLEY FALLS.

News brought by the *Stanley*—History of Falls Station—Treaty between Wester and the Arabs—Tippoo Tip—Mr Deane wounded on his way up-river to take command—Van Gèle sent out, but invalided to Madeira—Deane goes a second time—Contradictory nature of his orders—The runaway slave—Station attacked—Deserters reach Bangala—Palaver with the Ba-Ngala—We start to relieve Deane—Diversity of sentiments among the people of Upoto—Defective cartridges—Yambunga—Captives restored—War-drums—Orera's misfortunes—Traces of the slave-raiders—The friendly natives of Yarukombe—Captain

Coquilhat's sufferings—Glimpse of Stanley Falls—The Bakumu and their information—Dubois drowned—The Station in ruins—The *A.I.A.* in a fix—We retreat—Samba—Search for Deane—Deane safe at Yarukombe—Skirmish at Yaporo—Attending the wounded—Deane's story—Return to Bangala—The *Henry Reed*—The fearful and wonderful decrees of the *Comité* at Brussels—Departure for Léopoldville—Coquilhat and Deane invalided home—Samba's history, ... 87

CHAPTER VI.

EXPLORATION OF THE NGALA RIVER.

Overhauling the *A.I.A.*—Captain Bayley at Nshassa—Beginning of the rainy season—Start for Bangala—Dissection of a hippo—Hostile natives—Orders to explore the Ngala—The Oubangi-Wellé—Position of Bangala Station—The Oubangi and the Ngiri—Mobeka—Up the Ngala without a guide—Mankula—Village built on piles—Terror of the natives—Rapids—Hostilities with the Saibis—Return—Affair of the hippo—Tornadoes—Arrival of the *Stanley*, . 128

CHAPTER VII.

RIVER-LIFE IN AFRICA.

The missing Houssas from Falls Station—The Langa-Langa—Ikolungu and its chief—Forest of gum-copal trees—H.M. Ibanza of Mpeza—Epidemics in Central Africa—Palaver at Upoto—Curious owls—Return to Bangala—Attacked near Bokélé—A desperate run—Cheapness of human life on the Upper Congo—Bangala diversions "owre the wine"—Lusengi and his news—Another night run—Burning the packing-cases—The Emin Relief Expedition, . 148

CHAPTER VIII.

THE EMIN RELIEF EXPEDITION.

Stanley on the Congo—News from home—The unprincipled Baruti and his awful fate—Stanley and the missionaries—

The *Henry Reed* seized to explore the Loika—A "real mean river"—Chief of Upoto seized as a hostage—Fever—Ngalyema's cow—Léopoldville again—Animal life on the river—Beauty of the Batéké country—'Joyce'—Reminiscences of civilisation—Remarkable effects of home letters when first opened—The hunters' camp on Long Island—Dualla Island—Lukolela—My bull's-eye creates a sensation, . 172

CHAPTER IX.

NEWS FROM YAMBUYA.

Improvements at Bangala—State captives not yet liberated—We start for Upoto — Fireworks *au naturel* — Burning of Upoto—Purchase of slaves at Mpeza—Down-river again—Death on board the *A.I.A.*—Funeral at Lukolela—Shagerstrom's cocktail—The *A.I.A.* strikes a crocodile—The son of Miyongo—Death of Van de velde—Ward arrives with news from the Aruhwimi, ... 197

CHAPTER X.

MAJOR BARTTELOT'S CAMP.

Start for Yambuya — A royal stowaway — War-drums — The Basoko—Scenery of the Aruhwimi—Depredations of the Arabs — Fine timber — Description of Major Barttelot's camp—Salim bin Mahomed—Manyemas—Salim sends his ivory to the Falls—Natives living in canoes—Black "mashers"—Arabs at the Lomami—Large canoes—Raschid's house—His account of the loss of Stanley Falls Station—Yaporo once more—Yangambi, ... 216

CHAPTER XI.

KINSI KATINI.

Arab reports of a large lake—Major Barttelot comes on board at Yalasula—Bwana Nzigé—Present state of Wana Rusari—Walk round the island—Possibility of passing Stanley Falls by means of locks—The Bakumu and Wenya—The crocodile and hippo—Return of Jameson and Tippoo Tip —"Nubian blacking"—Tippoo keeping his accounts— Salim bin Soudi—Her Majesty's birthday—A Manyema child wounded—Tippoo Tip and his followers take passage for Yambuya—A *contretemps* near Chioba Island—A snake on board—Tippoo's method of securing a night's lodging— Arrival of his secretary and garrison—Altering the loads— Difficulties with the Manyemas—"Good-bye"—Leave Yambuya—Terrible news—The *Holland*—News of Deane's death —Salim bin Mahomed arrives from Yambuya—The last of Kinsi Katini—I am taken ill—Ward comes up-river, . 247

CHAPTER XII.

MY RETURN HOME.

A wet journey to Equator—Kindness of Mr and Mrs Banks— News of Major Barttelot's death—Down-country in a hammock—Overtaken by Ward—Jameson dead!—Back at Matadi—The "Devil's Caldron"—Ward catches the mail— Down-river in a schooner—Congo State coinage—Improvements at Boma—Two in a port-hole—Waiting for the *Africa* —To Loanda—Homeward bound—Kotonou—On board the *Biafra*—The Addah shipping-clerk's letter—Sierra Leone —The Canaries—Quarantine at Madeira—Characteristics of English scenery—Home once more! . . . 281

CHAPTER XIII.

THE BISMARCK OF CENTRAL AFRICA.

Tippoo Tip—His first meeting with Livingstone—Cameron visits his camp on the Lomami—Travels with Stanley in 1876—His dress and appearance—Deserts Stanley at Vinya Njara—His own account of this transaction—Raids of Karema and others near Stanley Falls—Tippoo arrives at the Falls in November 1884—Palaver with Van Gèle— Goes to Zanzibar—Deane attacked—Loss of the station— The Arabs left to their own devices for a whole year—Tippoo returns as governor—His feelings towards the Germans —Terms of his agreement with Stanley—He sees the weakness of the Congo State—Advantages of the Arabs—Distrust of Europeans—Tippoo sets to work to strengthen his position and subdue the Bakumu—The original object of the State defeated—Arabs on Lake Nyassa—The African Lakes Company—Futility of attempting to control African operations from Europe—The sort of men required for Central Africa—What the Bakumu think of Deane, . . . 300

CHAPTER XIV.

CONCLUSION.

Inducements to slave-raids—Extinction of the elephant—Improved transport the only effectual means of putting an end to the slave-trade—Ivory bought by the Sanford Company and the Congo State on the Upper Congo—Black and white tusks—Different routes to the interior—The Nile Basin—East coast route—The Tana river—Difficulties of the Congo route—Railway past the Livingstone Cataracts—Proposed bullock-road—African Lakes Company—Portuguese claims—Shall Livingstone's work be in vain? . . . 321

INDEX, ... 331

ILLUSTRATIONS.

MR H. M. STANLEY,		*Frontispiece*
LÉOPOLDVILLE,	To face page	34
MATA BWYKI,	" "	80
FIRST EUROPEAN HOUSE AT BANGALA STATION,	" "	84
MR WALTER DEANE,	" "	88
MAP OF STANLEY FALLS DISTRICT,	" "	106
CAPTAIN COQUILHAT,	" "	112
THE *A.I.A.* AT BANGALA,	" "	134
WEAPONS OF VARIOUS TRIBES,	" "	166
THE *EN AVANT* PASSING ONE PALM POINT,	" "	188
MR HERBERT WARD,	" "	197
TWO PALM POINT,	" "	208
THE *A.I.A.* AGROUND ON A CROCODILE,	" "	210
MAJOR E. M. BARTTELOT,	" "	216
PLAN OF ARUHWIMI CAMP,	" "	227
KNIVES OF ARUHWIMI TRIBES,	" "	240
MR J. S. JAMESON,	" "	246
MY START FOR HOME,	" "	282
MAP OF CONGO AND ITS TRIBUTARIES,		*At end*

A VISIT TO
STANLEY'S REAR-GUARD.

CHAPTER I.

ANTWERP TO BANANA.

THE MICAWBER BUSINESS—THE *SAŌ THOMÉ*—DOWN THE SCHELDT—PASSENGERS FOR THE CONGO—LISBON—MADEIRA—S. VINCENT—BOLAMA—PRINCIPÉ—S. THOMÉ—SHOOTING EXCURSION—" PLENTY BIG BIRD "—FIRST SIGHT OF THE LOWER GUINEA COAST—BANANA CREEK—WAITING FOR THE *HERON* AT BANANA.

WHY I went to the Congo is a question which I have often been asked since my return. I have never yet been able to answer it to my own satisfaction. Perhaps an innate desire for travel had something to do with it; and the opportunity coming, as it did, just when I was free from other engagements, gave a definite direction to my plans. The circumstances which led to my going are as follows :—

In the beginning of 1886, happening to be at Antwerp—where I had passed some weeks, like Mr

Micawber, waiting for something to turn up, in the shape of a vacant post as engineer on board any of the steamers frequenting that port,—I was one day accosted by Mr W. Best (since dead), who asked if I would go to the Congo. Upon my replying in the affirmative, he said he would send my application to Brussels, which he did. Accordingly, a few days later, I received notice, through the agents of the Etat du Congo, to present myself at their offices in Brussels on April 8th. It was past noon on the 9th before I finally left Brussels, with my contract signed, and written orders in my pocket to sail from Antwerp on the 15th of the same month in the *São Thomé*, a Portuguese steamer running from Hull, Antwerp, and Lisbon, to West African ports. I was to proceed with her to Banana Town, at the mouth of the Congo, and thence—by one of the steamers belonging to the Congo State—to Boma, some fifty miles up the river.

I reached Antwerp at 4 P.M., and punctually, at 5 P.M., left for London *viâ* Harwich, in one of the Great Eastern Railway Company's splendid twin-screw boats. I duly arrived in London on the morning of Saturday, April 10th; and though I had a pretty busy time of it getting everything ready, managed to be back in Antwerp on the 14th, when, to my chagrin, I learnt that the departure of the *São Thomé* had, for various reasons, been postponed till the 17th. I had thus hurried over, only to wait two days in, to my mind, the most miserable of all earthly positions—viz., having everything packed and ready, and nothing left to do, yet unable to start, though in hourly expectation of the summons—circumstances under which it is impossible to turn one's mind to anything. I was further annoyed by hearing that the *Saõ Thomé* was to remain sixteen days at Lisbon; and reflecting that I had hurried off without saying good-bye to many of my friends, when—had I only known it in time—I might have spent two more weeks in England, and gone to Lisbon overland.

At last, on April 17th, all was ready,—the *Saõ Thomé* was flying the blue-peter at the fore, and the Congo State flag (a five-rayed gold star on a blue ground) at the main; while aft was the somewhat more intricately designed flag of Portugal. This being the first boat of a regular service between Antwerp and the Congo, a great crowd collected to see her off. Going on a falling tide, we soon left the quay behind—past the docks and forts,—past the dykes holding back the river from the rich pasture-lands of Belgium, till, at Lille Fort, we enter Holland, and the country becomes, if possible, drearier and flatter than ever, while the lofty spire of Antwerp Cathedral gradually vanishes in the dim distance. It is a cold, cheerless day, and I soon dive below, and ransack my baggage for books and papers, but find myself too restless to read, and speedily go on deck again. We stop for a few minutes at Flushing to land the river-pilot: the place is hidden in a damp mist, and some clock is just striking five, bringing to mind tantalising visions of warm, cosy drawing-rooms, with comfortable chairs, and English ladies seated behind tea-trays, ready to dispense the refreshing "bohea" to casual callers. I go in search of a cup of "bohea" for myself, and am served by a Portuguese steward with a black composition which he calls *cha*—whatever that may be: it certainly does not look or taste like tea. In disgust, I adjourn to my cabin, and, rolling myself up in my rug, fall asleep.

I awake with a dryness in my throat, and all the other uneasy sensations that a man experiences when he goes to sleep at improper times and seasons. I find, when I grope my way on deck, that the mist has cleared off; it is quite dark, and we are just in the middle of the Straits of Dover—the two lighthouses showing out boldly on either side before backgrounds of smaller lights. It is, however, too cold to stay on deck long; so I soon descend again, and, rolling into my bunk, sleep soundly till morning.

I was aroused next day by the sudden stoppage of the engines, and found we were lying off Ventnor, Isle of Wight, waiting for the boat to come and take our pilot ashore. This was the last I saw of England; and, after we had weighed anchor, I began to turn my attention to my fellow-passengers. Of these there were seven, all foreigners, and all bound for the same destination as myself. The Baron de Stein and Lieutenant Roget, two Swedish captains, Cronstedt and Shagerstrom, and one Belgian captain, Heuse, were going out, like myself, in the service of the Etat du Congo. Of the other three, Mr F. Hens was an artist, while Messrs Linden and Demeuse were naturalists, going out in search of orchids and other rarities.

The Bay, for a wonder, was calm. I say, for a wonder, because of the general reputation of this much-maligned piece of water. My experience of it, however—and I have crossed it pretty often—leads me to believe that it is no worse than any other part of the Atlantic. It was very misty till the day we arrived at Lisbon, when it cleared, and we had a splendid view of the beautiful castle of Pena, Cintra, perched on the very top of a rocky hill between Lisbon and the sea.

This was my first visit to Lisbon, and, my previous knowledge of that city being chiefly derived from history, I was somewhat surprised to find that the place whence Diaz and Vasco da Gama had sailed to the discovery of the Cape of Storms was more backward in regard to shipping accommodation than any newly developed port in Australia or New Zealand. All the steamers had to lie out in the river ; not a dock or pier was there—not even a quay with water enough alongside to have floated the cockle-shell in which Columbus first crossed the Atlantic. All ships which required repainting had to go to Cadiz in order to be dry-docked, unless, like those of the Empreza Nacional (to which Company the *Saõ Thomé* belonged), they traded to some better-developed port. The *Saõ Thomé* had brought coal from Hull, which we had to discharge here; and we consequently spent a very enjoyable time among the coal-dust for the next ten days. The coal being discharged, she had to take in wine,—an improvement greatly appreciated by the passengers, especially when the wine merchant came on board, and invited us all over to his place on the south side of the Tagus. Accordingly, we took our places, next day, on board a huge lighter, —the sail was hoisted, and off we went across the sunny Tagus. We were duly received by our host as we landed, and conducted round the grounds of the King of Portugal's hunting-palace, and afterwards through immense wine-vaults, which were beautifully cool—coming at last to a small court-yard over which an awning had been placed to keep out the sun.

Here we found a table ready laid for lunch, down the centre of which stood a row of decanters containing no less than twenty-one different kinds of wine. After lunch we returned to the lighter, whose crew had evidently also been lunching, for they were in a decidedly festive condition, and crowded sail on the old tub till she fairly flew.

The great event in Lisbon at this time was the approaching marriage of the Duke of Braganza to the Princess Amélie of Orléans; and the coming event was celebrated almost daily by a tremendous waste of gunpowder, and nightly, by an equal expenditure of gas and rockets. At last, on May 6th, all was ready for departure, and heartily glad was I to be off once more. Before starting, we received a large addition to the passenger-list, mostly Portuguese and French. Among them, however, I presently discovered three or four English and American missionaries bound for Benguela, *en route* for Bihé, a place some 250 miles inland. Two of these, Mr Fay and Mr Currie, had only lately been married, and their young wives were accompanying them to their far-away home. Mrs Currie, I have since heard, soon succumbed to the climate, and paid for her devotion with her life. Mrs Fay is still, I believe and hope, carrying on her good work among the natives of Angola.

Two others, Messrs Swan and Scott, intended to proceed across Africa to a station in Ilala. Mr Scott, however, was compelled by bad health to remain at Bihé; and Mr Swan has disappeared into the interior of the Dark Continent.

Madeira, where we arrived two days after leaving Lisbon, has been so often described, that I will not weary the reader with a repetition of attempts to depict the beauties of this island. No amount of description can do it justice—it must be seen to be appreciated, and not only seen but studied. The first view is apt to be disappointing, especially if one arrives at the glaring hour of noon, when the fierce sun, reflected from every white wall and pane of glass, casts a blinding glare over everything. The finest view I had of the place was on my return voyage, when the steamer arrived and anchored in Funchal Bay by night. I was up and on deck before sunrise, and was rewarded by seeing the island in all the beauty of the changing tints of dawn, and watching the sunlight as it first gilded the hill-tops, and then gradually descended to the pebbly beach in front of the town.

We only remained here some six hours, and then turned southwards for the Cape de Verd Islands. A four-days' run brought us to St Vincent, a barren rocky island, without a single green leaf on it. Even the drinking-water has to be brought over from S. Antonio, a larger island close by, from which come all the food-supplies of the town. The only point in which St Vincent is superior to S. Antonio is its possession of a sheltered harbour; but this outweighs all other considerations, and the town has gradually grown up in spite of the disadvantages of its situation. The barrenness of the place, however, did not deter Captain Heuse, who had been suffering from a slight attack of fever, from landing—preferring to wait here a month for the next steamer, rather than approach the swampy shores of Gambia.

We only stopped here long enough to fill the bunkers with coal, and then left for Santiago, another of the Cape Verd Islands, and a much more fertile one. Two days hence brought us to Bolama, a Portuguese settlement on one of the low islands at the mouth of the Rio Grande, about 120 miles south of the Gambia river. Bolama is, I believe, only the port of Bissao, which is on another island, a little to the north; but as the arm of the river on which it stands has not water enough for large steamers, the latter all go to Bolama. This place, which, like all Portuguese settlements in Africa, is very dirty, consists for the most part of native huts, the greater number of the Portuguese living at Bissao. There were, of course, a church and a hospital, the latter pretty full. The whole place had a dead-alive sort of look, as if doomed to extinction, and only waiting the inevitable end—the only things which seemed to enjoy life being the monkeys, parrots, and insects. I afterwards learnt from one of the West African Telegraph Company's agents that Bolama and Bissao are among the most dreaded of West African stations, situated, as they are, right in the centre of a group of low-lying malarious islands.

We left this place after several hours' delay; and passing out through the Bissagos islands by a more southerly channel than the one by which we had entered, were soon tossing about in a westerly gale which quickly disposed of the greater part of the passengers. After the steaming atmosphere of Bolama, the fresh Atlantic breeze was delightful; and Captain Shagerstrom and myself remained on deck, in the lee of the companion, to enjoy it, till the seas began to wash right over the poop, when we disappeared below. A six days' run brought us to Principé, or Prince's Island, in the Gulf of Guinea—a regular little paradise to look at, with its forest-covered peaks and little town nestling at the far end of a long, deep bay, with steep hills behind and on either side of it—a beautiful situation indeed, had the island been in a temperate latitude, instead of in something under 2° north. The town, however, is close and hot as an oven: not a breath of fresh air can reach it, unless the wind is due east, and blowing straight into the deep bay, at the far end of which stands the now half-deserted town. To walk through the streets and see the decaying houses and churches, one would think it some ruined city, long forgotten and lately rediscovered, instead of being, as it is, an old Portuguese colony, which, under wiser management, might have covered the whole island with flourishing plantations of cocoa and coffee. The heat was fearful; and we were all greatly relieved when evening arrived, and we steamed out of the narrow cañon where we had been lying all day.

Early next morning the *Saõ Thomé* dropped her anchor opposite the town after which she was named, and Demeuse and myself went ashore. Demeuse took his gun, and we wandered off into the woods, to see what was to be had in the way of game. We strolled about for some time, seeing nothing but a few small birds not worth wasting powder and shot on. The forest is not so thick as at Principé; and there are plenty of cocoa-nut palms and papaw-trees about, besides numerous banana-plants. Not having provided ourselves with lunch, we satisfied our hunger on some ripe bananas which we came across, and were thinking of returning, when we met a solitary native, who was at last made to understand what we were after, and undertook to show us some birds. Several were soon pointed out, perched among the dense foliage, and scarcely distinguishable by our unpractised eyes; and one or two of them had been bagged when another native turned up, and a great consultation ensued between the two blacks, both of whom cast dubious glances at us as we stood watching them. At last they arrive at some decision, and our guide, approaching us, gives us to understand—helping out his meaning by signs—that the other one knows where there is "plenty big bird—

good for cat;" and off they both go, down a narrow glade. We follow them for nearly three-quarters of an hour, through dense forest and across a small stream or two, till we reach a little clearing in which are two or three huts, with several women and children standing about. A few words pass between our guides and one of the women, and then, making signs to us to follow quietly, the former glide off down a narrow path leading to a large grove of cocoa-nut trees at the bottom of a valley, and we after them, in a state of subdued excitement, expecting a turkey at the very least. Suddenly one native stops, and looks cautiously up, and then both stand still, pointing at the same object. We both approach on tiptoe—Demeuse with his gun to his shoulder taking aim upward: all we can see is some huge black thing in the middle of a mass of palm-leaves. Demeuse, seeing nothing definite, pauses and whispers to me that it must be a large bird, and that he had better put in heavier shot. Fearful of losing our prey, I reply, " Both barrels ;" and, as he still hesitates, looking undecidedly at the huge shadowy outline, I add, " Fire!" Bang go both barrels at once—something drops—we stoop to examine it, and a shower of soft lumps, seemingly of slimy mud, descends on our heads and necks, and puts us to ignominious flight. We are recalled by a delighted shout from the natives, and burst into a roar of laughter as they advance towards us holding up several black objects. Demeuse had fired into a cluster of sleeping bats—creatures regarded by the natives as a great delicacy. Demeuse attempted to explain his sudden flight by remarking, in broken English, " I thought I shot de debil!"—which one of the natives emphasised by adding, " Good for eat!"

Our two guides were now highly delighted at the result of the stratagem, by which they had procured some sixteen or seventeen large dog-headed bats. Having no firearms, they do not, under ordinary circumstances, find it easy to get at these animals; and they now walked straight back to the huts in order to prepare their dinner. Hungry as we were (it was now evening), Demeuse and I declined to partake of this dainty meal, and having regained the road, made our way slowly back to the town, only to find that the last boat had put off, and there was, apparently, no means of regaining the steamer that night. After walking about for some time, we found that some of the steamer's crew were also still ashore, and these, being Portuguese, soon managed to discover some natives owning a large canoe, who agreed to take us out for a consideration. We therefore all crowded into the old log, and set off just as the sun was disappearing below the horizon. The canoe was very full, and a heavy sea was running, but this did not deter the Portuguese sailors, who were in a decidedly jovial condition, from quarrelling for the paddles; and we several times came so near being upset, that Demeuse tied his gun to the canoe, and both he and I loosened our boot-laces and coat-buttons in readiness for a swim. As the bay swarmed with sharks, this was not a pleasant prospect; and we were quite content, on reaching the ship in safety, to postpone our ablutions for the present.

We stayed one day longer at Saō Thomé, and then left for Banana. Coming on deck on the morning of May 29th, I noticed that the sea looked black as pitch. We were still nearly 100 miles out at sea, and the colour of the water, which, astern, was lashed by the propeller into a blackish-green foam, gave me anything but a favourable impression of the country we were going to, and I began to form mental pictures of low, stinking mud-banks, and endless mangrove-swamps. About noon we came in sight of a high, wooded coast, with bright-looking sands, and reddish cliffs showing here and there between them and the dark-green trees above.

A gap in the hills showed where the Congo (which, from the colour of its water, we had already designated the sewer) empties its huge volume into the ocean. Nearly in the centre of the gap—seemingly floating on the water—were some white specks, which the captain of the *Saō Thomé* pointed out to me as the roofs of Banana Town. As we approached, these specks resolved themselves into houses, still apparently standing on the water,—for, beyond, we could see Banana Creek, where two or three sailing-vessels were lying at anchor. Nearer still, and we could see the long sandy spit on which the houses stand, and groves of young cocoa-nut palms—evidently only lately planted, for they were not yet as high as the houses. Then, one by one, the different factories ran up their flags, and soon the ensigns of England, France, Holland, Portugal, and, last but not least, the Lone Star banner of the Congo Free State, put a little life and colour into the scene. We pause for a few minutes to pick up a pilot, who has come out in a boat to meet us, and then, taking a wide sweep to the south to avoid Stella Bank, which, owing to the exertions of the Dutch (in erecting groins to collect the sand, without which precaution the whole point would probably be swept away by the current), is gradually forming round the extreme point of the peninsula on which Banana stands, we steam slowly into the creek, and drop our anchor in front of the house from whose staff flies the blue flag with the golden star. A boat carrying this flag, and rowed by niggers dressed in imitation of British blue-jackets, and singing "One more river to cross," is soon alongside, followed by another, with a flag whereon I make out the words "Congo Hotel." I am presently introduced to Mr Hâkanson, the chief of Banana Station, and go ashore in his boat. The State station at Banana having been only recently established, there was not room for all the new arrivals in the one house as yet finished. Mr Hâkanson therefore took me to the English factory, and introduced me to Mr Fraser,[1] of the British Congo Company, who made me very comfortable in his station for the two or three days I remained at Banana. Why the place should be called Banana is a question for future generations to dispute about—for, when I landed there, I could not find a single banana-plant in the whole settlement. The whitewashed wooden houses and stores and clean-swept courtyards of the English and Dutch factories looked very refreshing, after the dirty and dilapidated Portuguese towns at which we had touched on the voyage out. The heat, however, was very great, and the glare of the sun on the white roofs awful, though a group of young cocoa-nut palms at the Dutch factory gave promise of future shade.

Next day, on going round to the Free State station, I found that the *Belgique*, one of the State steamers, was going up to Boma with the mails. Hearing that she had formerly been the pleasure-

[1] Mr Fraser died at Banana in August 1888, a few weeks before I reached the coast on my way home.

yacht of the King of the Belgians at Ostend, I walked down to the pier to have a look at her. Lying alongside the pier, and loading bamboo, was a dingy, dilapidated twin-screw boat of some 30 tons, decks an inch thick in dirt, and funnel all on one side. Truly a pleasant prospect, I thought, if I am doomed to spend my time out here in a boat like this. She presently cast off, emitting a great deal of noise and vast clouds of steam, managed to get under way, and soon disappeared round Boola Mbemba Point, on her voyage to Boma.

I was to wait for the arrival of the *Heron*, a screw-steamer of 114 tons, now at Gaboon, whither she had gone in order to have her bottom re-painted, as there is no dry dock on the West African coast; but the tide at the Gaboon river has sufficient rise and fall to leave a vessel like the *Heron* high and dry, if she be drawn on to a sand-bank at high water.

As the *Heron* was the largest steamer owned by the Free State, I could only hope she might be in a better state of cleanliness and repair than the *Belgique*. She did not arrive for two days, which I spent in lounging about the beach watching the sand-crabs. They lie in the sun at the mouth of their holes, into which they instantly disappear when any one approaches; and so timid are they that even the least motion alarms them, and they will vanish on the instant.

In the next chapter, before proceeding with the account of my journey up the river, I intend to summarise very briefly the history of the State in which I was to pass the next few years of my life. As this may be found rather dry reading, I shall make it as short as I can—and it can always be skipped, if desirable.

CHAPTER II.

L'ETAT INDÉPENDANT DU CONGO.

THE CONGO STATE—DISCOVERY OF THE CONGO—TUCKEY'S EXPEDITION, 1816—LIVINGSTONE DISCOVERS THE CHAMBEZI—CAMERON AT NYANGWÉ—STANLEY'S EXPLORATIONS—THE "ASSOCIATION INTERNATIONALE AFRICAINE"—STANLEY'S TWO EXPEDITIONS, 1879, 1884—SIR FREDERICK GOLDSMID AT VIVI—SIR FRANCIS DE WINTON'S GOVERNORSHIP—CHANGES IN THE ADMINISTRATION—CONSTITUTION OF THE CONGO STATE—GENERAL SURVEY OF THE RIVER.

THE Congo river, the *raison d'être* of the Congo Free State, was, until the beginning of the present decade, nothing more than a name to the majority of Europeans. Few, except members of geographical societies, or others who had some special interest in the subject of African exploration, could have definitely stated the course of the great river. When Stanley returned from one of the most extraordinary explorations on record—the tracing of this river to the sea in 1877—the Congo was, of course, in every one's mouth; but it was, like all other sensations, gradually being forgotten, when the general interest was suddenly revived by the news that the International African Association, under the presidency of Léopold II., King of the Belgians, had taken the country under its fostering care, and was going to—ah! that was the question. What was the Association going to do? Everything was at first kept so quiet, that Stanley had already been some time on the Congo before it was generally known that he had gone to found a Free State in Africa. Then ensued another brief period of excitement about the Congo, which, however, soon died away; and for two or three years it was seldom noticed by the papers, except when some new tributary was discovered, or some event of extraordinary interest occurred. It was during this period that a friend of the author's presented himself at the Bureau de l'Etat Indépendant du Congo, at Brussels, and offered his services as an engineer, without even knowing where the Congo was. Finding, on his arrival at Boma, that he was appointed to a steamer on the upper river, and would have to march some 235 miles before reaching his destination, he would gladly have returned home again!

Once more—in 1886—attention was drawn to the Congo by the news that it was one of several routes suggested for the expedition sent out to the relief of Emin Pasha; and the interest was kept up when it became known that Stanley had finally decided to go that way.

The mouth of the Congo was discovered in 1485 by Diego Cão, who, by setting up a pillar on the southern side of the estuary, took possession in the name of Portugal. The Portuguese have, in recent times, made this fact the pretext for claiming the whole of the coast between St Paul de Loanda and the Congo mouth,—though they had never founded any settlements in the northern part of this region.

For over three hundred years the river's course above the falls of Yellala was utterly unknown. It was supposed to come from the north-east: there was even a theory—seriously supported as lately as 1816—that it was the lower course of the Niger. Tuckey's expedition in that year did little or nothing towards solving the problem, and its disastrous results discouraged further attempts in that direction.

In 1867, Livingstone, in the course of his last exploring journey, discovered a large river flowing westwards, called by the natives Chambezi, and said to rise in the Chibalé Hills, in the country of Mambwé. Tracing the downward course of this river, he found that it entered Lake Bangweolo, and issuing thence, flowed north under the name of Luapula, and passed through another lake, Moero. Having ascertained this by personal observation, he learned from native report that, still flowing northward, it was joined by an important tributary, the Lualaba, by which name—according to the curious

African fashion of transferring to the main stream the name of every affluent which enters it—it was thenceforth known. He last saw this river at Nyangwé in Manyema, whence—as is well known— he was forced to return to Ujiji. Convinced that he had met with the upper course of the Nile (though, as his diary shows, he was sometimes assailed by doubts and suspicions that it might, after all, turn out to be the Congo), he once more, after his meeting with Stanley in 1872, left Ujiji, with the intention of reaching Katanga by a circuitous course round the south of Lake Bangweolo, striking its head-waters, and following it down to the sea. But it was on this journey that death overtook him, at Chitambo's, in Ilala.

Cameron, in his expedition across Africa, reached the Lualaba near Nyangwé, August 2d, 1874, but had to relinquish his plan of following it down, owing to the impossibility of obtaining canoes. Finding the altitude of this river at Nyangwé to be less than that of the Nile at Gondokoro, he came to the conclusion that, as it could not possibly be the Nile, it must be the Congo.

The expedition which finally determined the course of the great river left England August 15th, 1874, under the command of H. M. Stanley. The detailed history of this exploration may be read in 'Through the Dark Continent.' On his return home, in January 1878, Stanley was at once brought into communication with the King of the Belgians regarding the further opening up of the regions whose existence was thus, as it were, for the first time revealed to Europe.

It will be necessary here to state that, some time previously, an association had been formed, under the auspices of King Léopold II., for the purpose of developing the hitherto almost untouched resources of Africa, and finding new markets for European produce in that little-known continent. This was known as the "Association Internationale Africaine." The news of Stanley's successful expedition turned the attention of this body to the Congo basin, and the best means of gaining access to it. In November 1878, Stanley was invited to Brussels, to furnish information on the subject to the representatives of the Association. It was then resolved to raise a fund for the equipment of an exploring expedition, which was to obtain accurate statistics with regard to the resources of the country; to build three stations on ground leased or purchased from the natives; to launch a steamer on the upper river, and to keep open a communication between the latter and the sea. The subscribers to this fund were called the Comité d'Etudes du Haut Congo, and included in their number representatives of the English, French, Belgian, Dutch, and American nations.

Stanley, on being intrusted with the direction of

this enterprise, proceeded to Zanzibar to enlist native workmen, and, returning by way of the Red Sea and Mediterranean, reached Banana in the *Albion*, August 14th, 1879.

The steamers — which had been brought from Europe in portable sections—having been put together, proceeded up the river to Boma, and thence to Vivi, where the first station was established. Between February 21st, 1880, and the same date in the following year, a waggon-track was made from Vivi to Isangila, past the first half of the cataract region, and the two steamers *Royal* and *En Avant* conveyed along it, with immense labour and difficulty. The boats were then launched, and carried the expedition, by instalments, along the navigable reach of water between Isangila and Manyanga. At the latter place Stanley was prostrated by a severe attack of fever, which nearly proved fatal, but recovered, and pushed on to reconnoitre as far as Stanley Pool, which he reached about the end of July. Here he found a representative of M. de Brazza, who claimed that his master had taken possession of the northern bank in the name of the French nation, having, it was alleged, bought the land from a chief named Makoko. Stanley, after entering into friendly negotiations with several chiefs—among whom was Ngalyema of Ntamo— returned for one of the steamers (the other was left at Manyanga), and completed the transit by December 3d. After many difficulties, a definite understanding with the natives was at last arrived at, and the station of Léopoldville founded at Ntamo.

In April 1882, after building a house, and laying out gardens, &c., Stanley started for the Upper Congo in the *En Avant*, leaving the station in charge of Lieutenant Harou. On this occasion he only proceeded as far as Mswata, where he established a station, and then returned; but soon afterwards, starting once more, he passed Mswata, and ascending the great eastern tributary, the Kwa, discovered Lake Léopold II. After circumnavigating this lake, or rather marsh, he was taken ill, and compelled to return to Europe, reaching Vivi, on his way to the coast, July 8th, 1882.

Here he found Dr Peschuel-Loesche, a German traveller, who had come out some months before, ostensibly to explore the Loango district, but in reality with sealed orders empowering him to take Stanley's place, should the latter be disabled by accident or illness. He was thus able to leave matters in Dr Loesche's hands, and depart for Europe with a mind at ease.

The Comité d'Etudes had, in the meantime, transferred its work and authority to the Committee of the "Association Internationale du Congo."

On meeting this committee, in October 1882, Stanley represented to them that the Congo territory in its present condition was utterly valueless, and must remain so, unless a railway were constructed through the Cataract region, from Vivi to Stanley Pool. He further pointed out that this railway could only be made remunerative if the country were organised as an independent state under European management, so as to secure to traders and settlers the advantage of a permanent and stable government.

He once more started for the Congo, in November 1882, on the understanding that a competent official should be sent out to represent him on the lower river, during his absence in the interior. Sir Frederick Goldsmid was accordingly despatched in this capacity, but not till some time had elapsed.

Meanwhile, on returning to Africa, Stanley found that the work had nearly gone to pieces in his absence. Dr Peschuel - Loesche, meeting with difficulties in the discharge of his duties, had thrown up his post, and returned to Europe; while, of the subordinate officers, scarcely one had been managing matters in a satisfactory way. To reorganise the stations under competent chiefs was the work of some time; and it was not till May 1883 that he was able to leave Léopoldville, in order to complete the exploration of the upper river. On this trip he ascended as far as the Mohindu (or Buruki), and founded Equator Station at its mouth. Returning to Stanley Pool, he started on his final voyage of exploration, passed the Aruhwimi, where he came upon the traces of Arab slave-raiders, and reached Stanley Falls, December 1st, 1883. Here a station was founded on the island of Wana Rusari, and left in charge of the Scotch engineer, Binnie.

Sir Frederick Goldsmid had arrived at Vivi in the course of the year 1883, and had — besides effecting a great improvement in that station — made an inspection of the country as far as Isangila. But, before the end of the year, he returned to Europe; and Stanley, arriving at Vivi in April 1884, found everything in a deplorable state of neglect.

At the beginning of this year, the late General Gordon was asked by King Léopold to undertake the office of Governor-General of the new State. He consented, and had already made arrangements for leaving, when his plans were entirely changed by the ill-fated request of the British Government that he should attempt the pacification of the Soudan.

The post was then offered to Colonel Sir Francis De Winton, who reached Vivi in June 1884. Stanley, who had remained on the Congo till the arrival of the new Governor, then returned to Europe, and did not again visit Africa till 1887, when he went out in command of the Emin Pasha Relief Expedition.

At the Berlin Conference, held in 1884-85, the International Association of the Congo had its boundaries and its rights as a sovereign state clearly defined, and its flag was formally recognised by the principal European Powers.

Sir Francis De Winton remained in office as Administrateur-Général till February 1886, when he returned to England, leaving the Vice-Administrateur-Général, M. Camille Janssen, in charge. It was about this time that a change took place in the management of the State—the details of which are as yet but imperfectly known to outsiders—by which it was transformed from the "*International* Association of the Congo" into the "Etat Indépendant du Congo," which is entirely under Belgian control. Since that time all the responsible posts in the State have been filled by Belgian officials — mostly lieutenants in the army. In September 1886, M. Janssen was promoted, by royal decree, to the full rank of Administrateur-Général—a title which was, in April 1887, exchanged for that of Governor-General. In February 1888, M. Ledeganck went out to Boma with the appointment of Vice-Governor-General— M. Janssen returning to Brussels, where he succeeded to the duties of General Strauch, who, ever since the founding of the Free State, had been at the head of its European administration, and retired from office in July 1888.

At present the constitution of the Etat Indépendant is somewhat as follows: Its head is the King of the Belgians, with the title of "Roi Souverain"; but the executive power is vested in the Governor-General (resident at Boma), subject to the instructions of the Committee at Brussels, and assisted by an inspector-general, a secretary-general, and one or more directors, all nominated by the king. He presides over a council (*Comité consultatif*), composed, besides the officials just mentioned, of the "Juge d'Appel," the "Conservateur des titres fonciers," and a certain number of members—not exceeding five—to be appointed by himself.

The State is divided into eleven districts: Banana, Boma, Matadi, Cataracts, Stanley Pool, Kassai, Equator, Oubangi-Wellé, Aruhwimi-Wellé, Stanley Falls, and Lualaba. In each of these a Commissaire de District represents the central administration.

The Governor-General's edicts have the force of law; and he is even empowered, in case of urgency, to suspend a royal decree by proclamation.

Having thus brought down the history of the Free State to the present day, I will conclude this chapter by a short general survey of the river, which—in conjunction with the map—will help to make the subsequent narrative clearer.

The course of the Luapula (here called Luvwa),

after leaving Lake Moero, seems to be about due north. It is then joined by the Lualaba (or Kamolondo), coming from the south-west. This river—heard of, but not seen, by Livingstone, and called by him Young's River—has its sources, according to Capello and Ivens, in Katanga, about 8° south, and is by some authorities looked upon as the main stream of the Congo. After the confluence the river enters the unexplored Lake Lanji, and thence flows, roughly speaking, first in a north-west direction past the Arab settlement of Nyangwé, and then due north to the equator, where it throws itself over the seven cataracts of Stanley Falls. North of the equator it makes a great bend, flowing westward and then south-westward, and crossing the Line again in long. 18° E. For about a mile below Stanley Falls the river flows between high banks: it then enters a large plain, some 800 miles in extent, the width of its bed varying from 2½ to 5 miles. It is so full of islands, that only at three or four points is there an uninterrupted view from bank to bank. The misleading statement (without mention of the islands) that both banks are seldom visible at the same time, has given rise to mistaken and exaggerated ideas of the size of the river. This great plain is covered for the most part with dense tropical jungle, abounding in rare and valuable forms of plant-life. At Iboko, on the right bank (in lat. 2° N., long. 19° E.), is the station of Bangala (a corruption of Ba-Ngala, the name of a tribe inhabiting Iboko and the surrounding country). At the equator was formerly another State station (Equateurville), but it has been transferred to the Sanford Trading Company. Here is also a station belonging to the American Baptist Missionary Union; while at Lukolela, about 100 miles lower down, the English Baptist missionaries have established themselves. Before reaching Lukolela the Congo is joined by the Oubangi, the largest and most important of its tributaries, now shown to be identical with the Wellé-Makua, explored by Dr Junker. About 150 miles below Lukolela the level banks rise into hills, and the stream becomes narrower, while its volume is increased by the influx of the Lawson river, and the Kwa, or Kassai, which is nearly as large as the main stream. Near the mouth of the Kwa were two French Roman Catholic mission-stations, since withdrawn—one belonging to the Société d'Alger, the other to the Société du St-Esprit. From here to Stanley Pool the hills, covered either with forest or tall grass, increase in height till they are almost entitled to the name of mountains, and at the same time encroach upon the river-bed till, just before reaching Stanley Pool, it is so narrow that the current seems to have been, as it were, turned on edge to pass through it, and runs like a mill-race.

Suddenly the ranges retreat on either side, and, curving round to right and left, enclose the beautiful sheet of water known as Stanley Pool. Close to the entrance of the Pool, on the left (or south-east bank), is Kimpopo, where a Methodist mission has lately taken up its quarters; and at the other end, just at the point where the river leaves it, is Nshassa, with the stations of the Sanford Exploring Expedition and the Baptist Missionary Society. Opposite Nshassa, on the north bank, is the French port of Brazzaville.

Rounding Kallina Point, we enter the Ntamo rapids, and come in view of Léopoldville, standing midway on the slope of Mount Léopold. Here the river enters upon a series of cataracts, which ends at Manyanga; then follows a reach of 88 miles, which can be navigated with tolerable facility; and then the Congo flings itself over the last terrace of the Central African table-land, the top of which is at Isangila, and the bottom at Vivi. At Vivi, the narrow cañon through which the pent-up waters have been flowing begins to open out a little, but it does not gain much in width till Boma is reached. The magnificent estuary by which the Congo discharges itself into the sea is a noticeable point, when contrasted with the deltas characteristic of the other three great African rivers.

CHAPTER III.

UP COUNTRY TO LÉOPOLDVILLE.

DEPARTURE FROM BANANA — PORPOISES — BOMA — " LA CHASSE À L'ADMINISTRATEUR - GÉNÉRAL " — DINNER AT THE STATION — " PALM-OIL RUFFIANISM"—CAPTAIN COQUILHAT—MATADI—VIVI —PREPARATIONS FOR THE MARCH — THE "DARK WAYS" OF NATIVE CARRIERS — KING NOZO'S CARAVANSERAI — MY FIRST FEVER—COLLAPSE BY THE WAY—"A NEW FETISH"—LUKUNGU —CARRIED INTO LÉOPOLDVILLE—DR MENSE—CAUSES OF FEVER —VIEW FROM LÉOPOLD HILL—THE STATE STEAMERS—HOW THE *STANLEY* WAS REPAINTED "AFTER MANY DAYS."

ON the evening of May 31st, the *Heron* arrived from Gaboon, and early the next day I went on board, and started up the Congo. As we steamed out of Banana Creek and round Boola Mbemba Point, a shoal of porpoises rose almost under our bows. Out came our rifles, and for the next half-hour we had pretty sharp practice at the creatures, which kept alongside, evidently enjoying the fun as much as we did. A porpoise is, if anything, rather more difficult to hit than a sand-crab; and although there were four or five of us firing away

C

at the same time, we did not succeed in bagging one. Several hours' steaming past low, gloomy-looking mangrove-swamps brought us to Kissanga, on the south bank, where we stopped to deliver *one* letter to some men in a canoe who came off from the shore; and then, crossing to Ponta da Lenha, on the north bank, we left a more respectable mail for the Dutch and Portuguese factories at this place. After leaving it, the thick forest gradually gave place to grassy plains; and after passing the beautiful island of Matebba, with its feathery palm-trees, we came in sight of Boma, where we arrived about 6 P.M.

I had scarcely landed when I was told that the Administrator-General wanted to see me at the Sanatorium — a building originally put up as a hospital, but now used as the headquarters of the Administrator-General and his staff. It stands on the top of a plateau a mile and a half from the river. On asking how to reach it, I was told to follow the "main road." The biggest road I could see was a footpath through the grass, which I accordingly followed—and soon found out what a main road is in this country, by losing myself among the tall grass, and finally falling into what seemed a bottomless pit. I landed on the sand and stones at the bottom of a dry water-course, covered with dirt, and with my trousers split right across the back—truly a nice state in which to appear before

LÉOPOLDVILLE. JULY 1888. TAKEN FROM THE BEACH.
FROM A SKETCH BY MR F. HENS.

To face page 34.

the Administrator! It was now quite dark, and it took me about half an hour to find my way out of this muddle—when, having got hold of a native to show me the main road, I at last found the Sanatorium. Here I saw the Administrator-General, who, after laughing at the state I was in, gave me instructions to proceed by the first boat to Vivi, where I was to be fitted out with tent, &c., for the journey to Léopoldville, as I had been appointed to a steamer on the Upper Congo.

I got back to the station somehow, and found myself just in time for dinner, which consisted chiefly of goat-soup, goat's meat, and (tinned) potatoes. After dinner, Portuguese wine and Schiedam (Dutch trade-gin) were brought in; and it was 3 A.M. before the party finally broke up. I was shown a room and a mattress, which, as the station was very full, I was to share with another gentleman. My baggage was all on board the *Heron*. I flung off my hat and boots, and laid myself down on the mattress, but, alas! not to sleep; for the mosquitoes, taking advantage of the absence of my mosquito-curtain, pretty nearly ate me up. When the bell rang at 5 A.M., I was only too glad to get up, wash, and go for a constitutional before breakfast, which took place at six.

The stations on the Lower Congo were at this time in a state of lawlessness and confusion worthy of a Far-West mining-camp in the "days of 'Forty-nine." The headquarters of the Government were just being transferred from Vivi to Boma, and the consequent disorganisation was taken advantage of by those restless spirits who always follow in the wake of new enterprises, and who, as soon as discipline is relaxed, immediately break out into all sorts of excesses, leading others after them. Collected here, on the 110 miles of the Lower Congo, in one of the worst climates of the whole world, were some 200 Europeans, most of them adventurers, capable, if well managed, of accomplishing any enterprise under the sun. Many of them had arrived while Stanley was away on the upper river, and, finding no one with sufficient authority to set them to work and keep them at it, had at once followed the dictates of their own sweet wills, and proceeded to get into mischief. The result has been graphically described by Stanley in his work, 'The Congo and the Founding of its Free State,' and need not be repeated here. By the time of Sir Francis De Winton's arrival, Stanley had restored something like order; and while Sir Francis remained, things surely if slowly improved. Then came the transfer of headquarters, in the midst of which Sir Francis went home, and mischief once more became rampant.

I had, before coming to the Congo, travelled in various parts of the globe, but nowhere had I seen such hard drinking, night after night, as that which went on at the Lower Congo stations about this time. It was not the bottle that was passed round, but whole cases were ordered in by the man who called for drinks, and every one present helped himself to as many bottles as he chose. When a steamer left for Vivi or Banana, it frequently happened that the only provision taken for the day by the captain and engineer was a demijohn of rum, and, on the boat's arrival at her destination, the said captain and engineer would be the first men to go ashore, leaving her to be tied up by the native crew. On one occasion, a steamer lying at anchor off Vivi, with no one on board but her engineer and a black man, broke loose from her moorings and was carried down-stream. The motion awoke the engineer, who coolly proceeded to get up steam, and, with the help of the native, brought her back to her place before any serious consequences had ensued. The steamers were, as I have said, in a very dirty condition, and everything in a general state of neglect.

As the *Heron* had to return to Banana, and the *Belgique* had gone on to Vivi, I was compelled to wait until the latter came back. Towards the evening of June 1st she arrived, bringing down Captain Coquilhat and Bishop Taylor—the latter an American missionary who had come out to start a new mission on the Kassai. To avoid the mosquitoes, I slept that night on the deck of the

Heron; and, as she was anchored some little distance from the bank, managed to secure a fair amount of sleep. Next morning I had my baggage taken on board the *Belgique,* and about 10 A.M. we left for Matadi. The State station at Boma is lower down the river than the trading factories; and we passed in succession the British Congo Company, French (Daumas, Beraud, et C$^{ie.}$), Portuguese, and Dutch compounds. Then came a large, flat-topped rock, rising some 50 or 60 feet sheer from the river, on the top of which were the buildings of the French Roman Catholic Mission. Beyond this, again, standing back from the river, on a mound, is the two-storeyed house, inhabited by the chief of Messrs Hatton & Cookson's factory, into which Stanley was carried, when he arrived, weary and sick, after his awful journey across the Dark Continent.

A few miles above Boma the river emerges from the narrow gorge in which it has run since leaving Léopoldville. The current here runs with tremendous force, and we were obliged to keep well out from the shore on account of rocks. Captain Coquilhat, who was bound for the upper river, was on board, and from him I learnt many details as to what was in store for me. We reached Matadi at 6 P.M., and there found Captain Shagerstrom, who had come up a day ahead of me, and was waiting for carriers. He introduced me to Baron Rothkirch, a German, who was detained by the same circumstance; and we walked up together to the station, where Mr Maloney, the chief, had a substantial dinner waiting for us.

Early the next morning, Captain Coquilhat, whose men were waiting for him, started on his march, and I returned on board the *Belgique*, in order to cross to Vivi and fetch my tent, campbed, and other necessaries. The *Belgique*, as I mentioned above, was a twin-screw steamer, but had lately been so neglected that it was only possible to go astern with one of her engines, the reversing-lever of the other being lashed in a go-ahead position. In this state we crossed Vivi rapids, and arrived safely at Vivi beach, where we waited in the cool verandah of Mr Ulf's house, while a messenger went to bring down donkeys for us to ride up to the station.

On reaching the top of the plateau, I was met by Mr Legat, who informed me that Mr J. Rose Troup, the chief, was down with fever. I had to remain here some days, so Mr Legat first showed me my quarters and then introduced me to Mr Casement, who had charge of the stores, and who now proceeded to supply me with provisions (in West African parlance "chop") and all the necessary paraphernalia for a long march up-country.

Vivi Station — the native town from which it takes its name is mentioned by Tuckey as Banza

Bibbi—is now a thing of the past. Its situation, on the corner of a jutting hill, which at first seemed to be eminently healthy, has proved the reverse. Cold winds blow with extreme force up the confined gorge of the Congo, at the entrance to which it is placed; and chills are, on that river, as fruitful a source of fever as malaria. Matadi has taken the place of Vivi, so far as a starting-point was necessary for the caravan-road, and the buildings of the station have mostly been transferred bodily to Boma.

Next day Mr Troup, having got over the fever, came out of his room, and sent for me to inquire how I was getting on with my preparations. He was looking very ill, and was evidently much shaken by the attack. On Monday, June 7th, I returned to Matadi to get my carriers and complete my arrangements.

My first care, after securing my stores—consisting of two boxes of "chop," cooking utensils, camp-bed, tent, and lantern—was to get rid of all European trunks and portmanteaus, and have my worldly goods made up into packs of some 60 lb. each: 65 lb. is the regulation load for a *pagazi*, but it is better to be on the safe side; and the lighter the load, the less chance of its being suddenly dropped—most likely in some inconvenient place, such as the middle of a stream. I had some things soaked and spoiled in this way.

At last my men were mustered—seven carriers, and two Houssas to serve as escort, besides my interpreter, who also acted as gun-bearer. We started at 7 A.M. on the 10th of June 1886, and then my sorrows began.

Baron Rothkirch and Captain Shagerstrom started at the same time, with their respective carriers; but, owing to the nature of the country, we soon got separated, and had to shift each for himself. The so-called road was a path about 9 inches wide, bounded on either side by a dense jungle of cane-like grass that was never lower than my shoulders, and sometimes rose to a height of 16 or 20 feet. After leaving Matadi, this path—indeed it does not deserve the name, being only the bed of a torrent strewn with huge boulders—passes over two hills, which looked to me almost vertical. It was a marvel to me how the carriers contrived to keep their footing; but they walked bolt-upright, carrying their loads on their heads with seeming ease. However, having been warned that they would attempt to practise on the ignorance of a *mundélé*[1] new to the country, I looked after them as sharply as I could; and, in fact, it was not long before I saw a burden cast down, and its bearer afflicted with a most conspicuous and demonstrative shivering fit. I had to walk up to him and remonstrate by means of the long staff which every white

[1] White man.

man in this country carries, and which certainly, on every application, effected a marvellous cure.

We did not march above nine miles on the first day. I made the mistake of walking at the head of my caravan, which, from the nature of the path, had to proceed in single file, and, as a consequence, had every now and then to walk back, say a quarter of a mile, to cure an attack of sickness somewhere in the rear. By the time I caught sight of the Livingstone Inland Mission Station at Mpallaballa,[1] it was 5 P.M., and I was so exhausted with heat and thirst that I left to the Houssas the task of bringing up stragglers, and made at once for the house, where I received a hearty welcome. By 6.30 my carriers had not arrived—which was serious, as my tent, bedding, and chop-boxes were in their hands. I had tea with the missionaries, but there was not a room in the house they could offer me; and I was fain to seek the hospitality of the black potentate of the district, one Nozo, who has built a hut, rather more elaborate than most dwellings in those parts, for the entertainment of the travelling *mundélé*. His majesty presented me with the key, and ordered one of his subjects to show the way with a lantern. I found two beds, but only one of them furnished with a mosquito-curtain, and that being already occupied by Captain Shagerstrom, I made myself comfortable in the other. Certainly

[1] Since handed over to the A.B.M.U.

we might have been worse off, and very often, in later times, we looked back with regret to the night we had spent in King Nozo's caravanserai. Nearly two years afterwards Captain Shagerstrom remarked, with reference to that subject, "Jolly good beds those—I wish we had them here."

By 6.30 next morning, the men had dropped in by twos and threes—having lain down to sleep here and there by the wayside—and we got them all started an hour later. This time, taught by experience, I brought up the rear, and had the satisfaction, on reaching camp in the evening, of finding them all there before me. Baron Rothkirch and Captain Shagerstrom were already putting up our tents, and counting the loads, so I turned my attention to preparing dinner, and, for an amateur cook, succeeded pretty well. The next three or four days were simply a monotonous repetition of the first two—endless marches through long grass, over hills, and across water-courses, now coming to a village, now to a market-place, where we stopped to purchase fowls, bananas, or any other eatable we could find. Now and then we reached a hillside whence we could get a view over miles and miles of broken country. About the middle of the fifth day I was suddenly seized with pains in my legs, and before we arrived in camp at night I discovered what Congo fever is like. With the assistance of the Houssas I got my camp-bed and tent up, and, rolling myself in the blankets, turned in. Next morning I was no better—in fact, seemed to be worse; so Baron Rothkirch decided to go on to Lukungu, for which station he was bound, and send back a hammock for me. My tent having got torn, the Baron, before departing, took it down, and substituted his own, and then he and Shagerstrom took all the loads and started, leaving me with six men to carry my camp-gear when I should be able to proceed, or the hammock arrive for me. One of these men I had engaged as my "boy"[1] at Banza Manteka. I have had a great many boys since, but he was the only one I ever knew who in any way bore out the character for faithfulness of which one hears so much in connection with African servants.

Two days later, feeling rather better, I determined to make a start, and go to meet the promised hammock from Lukungu. My boy got my camp-bed, tent, and chop-box all ready, and the carriers set off, while I slowly followed. I had eaten very little, as the fever was still on me, and I had no appetite, and, in consequence, found myself much weaker than I had imagined. However, I managed to keep up for some three or four miles, when, as I was walking along a narrow path on the side of a steep hill, on which the grass had been burnt, affording a splendid view

[1] African equivalent for servant.

of the surrounding country, I began to feel queer, the view faded into dim distance, there was a rush as of two passing trains—a crash—and I knew no more. My next sensations were rather peculiar. When I came to myself I was lying on the hillside, where a low, scrubby bush had arrested my fall some ten yards below the path. My boy was kneeling beside me, gazing anxiously into my face, while a little lower down the hill lay one of my carriers, bound hand and foot with his own waist-cloth and that of my boy. Both of them were completely innocent of clothing, and covered with dust and scratches. Raising myself up, I asked what all this meant: for all answer my boy held a small looking-glass (which he extracted from a bag slung over his shoulder) before my face, and, ill as I was, I could not help laughing at the sight I presented. I had seen, in several villages I had passed through, wooden idols or fetishes, whose faces were plentifully bespattered with kola-nut, which the natives chew into a paste and then spit over the idol.[1] In falling, I had cut my face in several places, and now, streaked with blood, and covered with sand and dust, I could very well have set up as an amateur fetish.

On inquiring why the carrier was tied up, I learnt

[1] Hence the native saying—"Nkishi ampa mumbana makazu"— "A new fetish requires plenty of kola-nut,"—*i.e.* "A new machine wants plenty of oil."

that, on seeing me fall, the men, thinking I was dead, had dropped their loads and run away, and that this one had been intercepted by my boy, and tied up to prevent his following the rest. Some water having been fetched from the bottom of a ravine close by, I washed the dirt from my face, and regained the path, where I saw that my tent and camp-bed had been flung down, as well as a tin box in which I carried a few necessary clothes, to which I had luckily added an Ashantee hammock. This I now extracted, and my boy having hidden all my loads in the long grass, cut a pole, to which he tied the hammock, and, releasing the only remaining carrier, made him take the other end, and I was thus carried towards Lukungu. We had not gone very far when we met twelve men with a hammock, sent to look for me by Mr Dannfelt, chief of Lukungu station. Into this I was transferred and carried on, my boy returning with eight men to recover the tent and other things. Next day I arrived at Lukungu, just as Captain Shagerstrom was leaving for Léopoldville; and for the next three days I hardly left my tent, as the fever still obstinately clung to me, and defied all my attempts to get rid of it.

On the fifth day after arriving at Lukungu, I was able to proceed—starting about 3 P.M. with twelve carriers, six of whom were Zanzibaris. Next day, just before reaching Lutété — where the Baptist Mission has a station — I met Mr Herbert Ward, who was going down to Boma. Lutété proved to be tolerably full of white men for the time being, as, besides myself and two or three others going up for the State, there were two expeditions halting there : one, consisting of Captains Bove and Fabrello, sent out by the Italian Government, on its way up river ; and the other, a German expedition under Dr Wolf, homeward bound from the Kassai. I only stopped here one night, and then went my way—to meet with another attack of fever two days later. This time, however, I had plenty of men, and the Zanzibaris soon rigged up my hammock, and, placing me in it, started for Léopoldville. How long it took to get there I had not at the time the least notion, as I lay in that half-insensible state when one is careless of life or death,— only waiting, with a vague longing, for the end, one way or another —I did not care which. When night came, the Zanzibaris set up my camp-bed and laid me on it, putting up my tent over me, and brought me food, from which I turned in disgust. I was actually only two days and two nights in this state, but it seemed much longer. On the morning of the third day, one of the Zanzibaris came and roused me with the news that we should be in Léopoldville before noon ; and, some two hours after we had started, he came to the side of the hammock and pointed out Stanley Pool in the distance. I raised myself to look, but the blinding glare was too much for my eyes, and I lay back till, roused by hearing voices around me, I found myself in Léopoldville Station, being lifted out of the hammock and carried into the house, where a white man (whom I soon discovered to be Dr Mense) was busy arranging my camp-bed and blankets. Having made my entry into the station after this fashion, I soon began to recover under the care of Dr Mense, than whom a kinder and better doctor never existed. His greatest pleasure was to minister to the sick—not only by prescribing medicines, but by devising every possible comfort, and even luxury, for the benefit of his patients; indeed he never seemed happy unless he was doing good to some one. A man would need to be very far gone if he did not soon begin to revive under Dr Mense's treatment; and accordingly, I was soon able to crawl out of my room and look round.

I was puzzled about the fever, which I could not attribute to chills, as I had been warned at Matadi not to stand about in damp clothes after the day's march, and had, in consequence, been careful always to put on an extra coat as soon as we halted. As for malaria, I had been up among the mountains, between one and two thousand feet above the sea, and had always understood that malaria never rises to such a height. Dr Mense informed me, however, that my fever was the result of exposure to the sun. A long day's march under a tropical sun is, it seems—if it does not first result in sunstroke—as fruitful a source of fever as any other.

It is somewhat amusing, in reading Stanley's works, to contrast the ideas of Africa to be gathered thence, with the popular notion of that continent, as a vast, steaming swamp, given over to fevers, venomous reptiles, and nameless horrors of all kinds. This applies chiefly to his latest work—for, in truth, much of 'Through the Dark Continent' is depressing reading enough, though even there the uplands of Manyema, and the glorious cultivated plains of Uganda and Unyoro, come in for their full share of praise. If we may believe the great explorer, Africa is, if not a paradise, at least quite a tolerable place to live in; and it is only the folly and ignorance of white men in general, and newcomers in particular, that cause all the disease and death of which one hears so much in Europe.

The truth is, one must remember that Stanley has spent the best years of his life in Africa, that to it he owes his name and fame as an explorer, and for its sake has undergone hardships and dangers innumerable; and that, in consequence, the " Sphinx of the Nations" is to him, one might almost say, as a child.

But even allowing for Stanley's prepossessions in

favour of Africa, one must admit that there is less now than there was ten years ago to deter Europeans from going to live there. The climate, certainly, is more injurious to them than that of their own country, but all tropical regions are terribly enervating to Europeans, and Central Africa labours under the added disadvantage of the great difficulty experienced in obtaining good food. A man who comes to the Congo must not shut his eyes to the fact that he *is* in a tropical climate, or try to live as he would in Europe. He must remember that the sun is far more powerful, and that, after having been for some months exposed to it, he is less able to resist the sudden changes of temperature to which he is sure to be subjected. As Stanley says, people think a great deal too much about malaria, and not enough about other causes of fever. When I first announced to my friends that I was going to the Congo, "malaria" was dinned into my ears from morning till night, though no one seemed able to tell me precisely what it was—one man, indeed, saying he believed it was a kind of fever. During the first two years of my stay in the country, I had several slight fevers, and one or two bad ones; but not one of these can I attribute to malaria. The first attack was the worst. In the course of the ten days that followed it, my opinion of Africa went down to zero. Had Stanley been writing a prophecy concerning my arrival at the Pool, he could not have described it more exactly than when he says, speaking of Europeans on their way up country : " Some of them, under the fiery impulse of getting on, on, and on, will march their fifteen miles per day, and on arriving at the end of their journey, they will turn round and deliberately curse the land, the climate, and the people."

I started with a great notion of getting on, and walked, if not fifteen miles per day, at any rate more than I ought to have done, after lolling for six weeks about the decks of an ocean steamer. On arriving at the Pool, carried in a hammock, and with just enough sense about me to know that I was still alive, I did curse the country and the climate most heartily, and vowed that, if I ever regained strength enough to bear the journey down to the sea, I would get out of Africa as quickly as I could.

As soon as I was well enough, I took a walk to the top of Léopold Hill. Half-way down this height is a kind of terrace cut out of the hillside, on which the station buildings stand, whence a road leads down, through a banana-plantation, to the beach, and the stores and workshops necessary for the steamers. This hill was pretty steep, but the view at the top amply repaid the climb. It was one of the noblest I had ever seen. I could never do justice to it in a description, were I to try for a year; and even standing on the hill with it before my eyes, I felt as if I could not see enough of it.

Below me lay Léopoldville and the native town of Ntamo—I could look right over them to the baobabs marking the site of Nshassa—and beyond, the broad Pool, with its sandbanks and islands; while, to the north-east, the whitish gleam of Dover Cliffs showed plainly above the dark forest of Bamu (or Long Island); and a little to the east, a gap in the hills indicated where the Congo poured its volume of waters into the Pool. Turning to the south-east, the eye is arrested by Mabengu, lately christened Mense Mountain, in honour of Dr Mense, who ascended it just before leaving for home, which he did March 13th, 1887, to the great regret of all Europeans on the Congo. On the south side of the Pool, a broad grass-covered plain extends from Nshassa to Kimpopo, and back inland as far as the mountain-ridge of which Mabengu forms part. This plain, consisting of a rich black soil, will, I hope, in the dim future—when the long-talked-of railway is completed—be covered with plantations of coffee, rice, and sugar-cane. Some portions of it are inundated by the river during a rainy season of unusual severity; but the greater part is high and dry at all times, and only wants the grass cleared away to be ready for cultivation. To the west, the mighty Congo sweeps round the foot of Léopold Hill, and over the reef which forms the first rapid of Ntamo cataract. In the middle of the cataract are two or three rocky, tree-covered islets, between which the river roars in one mass of boiling foam. Just above the islands is seen one of the mouths of the Gordon-Bennett river, which, emerging from the dark forests of the north bank, flings itself headlong over a lofty cliff into the Congo. Eastward of the Gordon-Bennett, the high wooded bank extends to the village of Mfwa. Here, on a commanding height, the French tricolor waves from the station of Brazzaville, right opposite the rocky promontory, now called Kallina Point, after an Austrian lieutenant who, in 1883, lost his life while attempting to round it in a canoe. This point juts boldly out into the stream, its cliffs rising perpendicularly out of deep water, and diverts the strong current which dashes itself against its upper side, towards the centre of the river, thus forming, under the lee of the cliffs, a return current of almost equal strength. A new-comer ascending the river in a canoe, and keeping, as is always done, close inshore, would not see the broken water beyond the point till his craft was well under the influence of the return current, and being carried, at a speed of three or four miles per hour, right into an opposing current, running at the rate of six or seven. The sudden shock and lurch which follow are almost certain to upset the canoe ; and then the best swimmer would need more than human strength to keep his head above the chaos of cross-currents and whirlpools which sweeps him away towards Ntamo falls. I remember, during my school-days, making a rash attempt at diving through the open sluice of one of the locks on the Medway. The river, not above twenty yards wide at the spot, was running, through a sluice of about two feet six by five feet, into a basin of say twelve feet broad and ten deep. Diving too low, I was caught in the return current, and whirled several times head over heels before I could struggle into calmer water, with a force such as I never wish to feel again. Compared with this trifling instance, what must be the force of current of a river which, after a course of nearly 3000 miles, throws, on an average, about 2,000,000 cubic feet of water out of the Pool, through a channel from one and a half to two miles wide, below which a sudden fall of ground forms the cataract of Ntamo? It is true that canoes can and do go up and down round Kallina Point, manned by experienced native boatmen; but even these are often thrown back several times before they contrive to cross the stream into the calmer bay beyond. Many a time, when rounding the point in the State steamer, have I seen the water thrown up, on either side of her bows, into a great wave, higher than the gunwale, as the plucky little launch charged the current—and wondered how any canoe could possibly live in that stream.

Such is Stanley Pool; and had it been situated in Europe, and blessed with a better climate, it would long ago have been as full of tourists raving about its beauty as Naples, Nice, or Mentone. But civilisation would spoil a spot like this. It is its mighty, lonely grandeur that enhances its beauty, and cultivation would for ever destroy the undisturbed solemnity of nature which surrounds it.

Having taken a good look round from the top of Léopold Hill, I descended to the station, and repaired to the house of the chief — Baron von Nimpsch, Commissaire de District for Léopoldville — to receive my orders. These were to take myself and belongings to Bangala in the steamer *A.I.A.* ("Association Internationale Africaine"), to which I was appointed as engineer. I was also instructed to report myself to Captain Coquilhat, as he was Commissaire de District for Bangala, and I should in future be under his orders. After doing this I made my way down to the beach, where the steamers *Stanley* and *A.I.A.* were lying in the quiet baylet, and the *En Avant* out of water undergoing repairs. The latter (which, it may be noted, was the pioneer steamer of the Congo Free State) was destined to be most unfortunate as regards these repairs. She lay on shore for months, waiting for a new crank-shaft to her engine (the original one having mysteriously disappeared during her transport from Matadi), and at last, when the Emin Pasha Relief Expedition ascended the river, was taken away by Stanley as a lighter in tow of the *Henry Reed*. By the time the *Henry Reed* returned to Léopoldville (some four months later) the crank-shaft had arrived; but the boiler-tubes were still missing, and only appeared in about two months more—when the *En Avant*, after eighteen months' inactivity (at least in her capacity of steamer), once more started up the Congo, whose waters her bows had parted five years ago, when, as the first "smoke-boat," she astonished the natives of Bangala and the Aruhwimi.

Standing in a group near the *En Avant*, I found several engineers and captains discussing the possibility of supplying, with the limited means at their command, an essential part of the *Stanley's* gear, which had not arrived with the rest, and the want of which was now delaying the expedition destined to start for Bangala and Stanley Falls.

One of this group, on seeing me, left the rest, and coming towards me, announced himself as Captain Anderson of the *Stanley*, and then introduced me to the other gentlemen present, among whom was Captain Delatte, of the *A.I.A.* The latter boat—a launch of about ten tons—was lying alongside the *Stanley*, having just been repaired and painted. Her speed had been much increased by taking out her engines and boilers, and substituting those of the *Royal*, which, being of wood, was now no longer fit for the hard service on the Upper Congo. A sun-deck had also been added, which covered the boat nearly from stem to stern, greatly adding to the comfort and safety of travelling during the middle of the day.

By the side of the *A.I.A.* lay the *Stanley*, a stern-wheeler of 27 tons. This steamer had been specially built by Messrs Yarrow, of Poplar, for transport to the Upper Congo. She had been brought up in sections on iron waggons, put into the water and bolted together, had then made her maiden voyage up the river, and now hung like a millstone round the necks of the authorities at Léopoldville. In going up the Kassai, a hole had been knocked in her bottom, and most of the paint rubbed off her on sandbanks; and now she had to be taken out of the water to be repaired and repainted.

As she was too large to be incontinently hauled up high and dry, like the *En Avant* and *A.I.A.*, the only thing to do was to construct either a slip or a dry dock. The engineers in the service of the State were quite able and willing to do one or the other; but the Congo Free State is an institution in which every one knows the engineers' work better than the engineers themselves. There is no superintending or consulting engineer,—orders come from the chiefs of departments for such and such a thing to be done, without the said chiefs knowing whether it is feasible or not; and the man appointed to execute the work has often great difficulty in getting men enough allowed him to carry it through.

So it was with the *Stanley*. A great deal of discussion took place at the upper end of the dinner-table as to what could be done—ending in an order to build a slip. Huge logs of wood, large enough to construct a slip for a 500-ton steamer instead of a 30-ton one, were shortly afterwards fetched over from the north bank for this purpose. The work of constructing this slip was progressing steadily, if slowly, when some one suggested to the chief of the station that a dock would be finished more quickly. A huge hole was accordingly scooped out of the bank, and all the men in prison turned out and put to dig in irons. For some unknown reason, this dock also was shortly after abandoned, and the *Stanley* went unpainted for more than a year, till at last the Compagnie du Congo pour le Commerce et l'Industrie, having decided to place a steamer on the upper river, sent out a company of engineers, carpenters, and blacksmiths, under a competent superintendent. A slip was at length constructed, on which the *Stanley* was drawn up and repaired.

Beside the *Stanley* lay the *Henry Reed*—another stern-wheeler, belonging to the A.B.M.U., but now chartered by the State; and beyond that, drawn up on the beach, the hull of the poor little *Royal*, originally built as a pleasure-launch for the King of the Belgians, and by him presented to the International Association of the Congo; now—after doing some of the hardest work that ever steam-launch did, on the rapids between Isangila and Manyanga, as well as between Stanley Pool and Stanley Falls—utterly dismantled. Here her remains still lay when, two years later, I passed through Léopoldville for the last time; all sound timbers having been removed to repair the other boats, and only the rotten ones left—to be broken up by the weather, and bit by bit carried to the sea, by the river on whose waters she had once so proudly floated.

CHAPTER IV.

LÉOPOLDVILLE TO BANGALA.

STATION-LIFE AT LÉOPOLDVILLE—NGALYEMA AND HIS NEIGHBOURS—
PROVISION-SUPPLY AT LÉOPOLDVILLE—YARN OF THE CHAMPAGNE-
BOTTLES — CLIMATE AND FEVERS — " CONGO THIRST " — THE
STANLEY'S FEED-PUMP—THE ITALIAN EXPEDITION—DEPARTURE
OF *A.I.A.* — WINDS IN THE CONGO CAÑON — SCENERY BETWEEN
STANLEY POOL AND KWAMOUTH—HOSPITALITY OF THE KWAMOUTH
FATHERS—THE MISSISSIPPI PILOT—HIPPO-SHOOTING—DEATH OF
DELATTE — EQUATOR — MONOTONOUS SCENERY — BANGALA — AR-
RIVAL OF THE *STANLEY*—MATA BWYKI, CHIEF OF IBOKO—DANCE
AND *MASSANGA*-DRINKING—DEPARTURE OF THE *STANLEY*—MY
QUARTERS IN THE GUN-ROOM — A TROPICAL THUNDERSTORM—
FIRST HOUSE AT BANGALA — FOOD-SUPPLY — THE BA-NGALA—
CANNIBALISM.

AT Léopoldville every one has to rise early, breakfast being served at 6 A.M., after which all proceed to their work till 11.30, when lunch is ready. After lunch comes the *siesta*, and then, till 2 P.M., the station is as quiet as the City of London on a Sunday. At the latter hour we turn to again till 5.30, when every one washes off the dust of the day's labour. Dinner comes on at 6 P.M., and nearly all have retired beneath their mosquito-curtains by 9—to smoke and read (provided that the materials for such diversion are forthcoming) themselves to sleep. Thus the routine goes on day after day, seldom varied unless by the arrival or departure of caravans or steamers. On Sundays breakfast is on the table at 7 A.M. for such as like to get up for it, but scarcely any one turns up before lunch, unless bent on a long walk or shooting excursion.

On the second Sunday after my arrival, Ngalyema, chief of Ntamo, tired of the even tenor of his way, treated us to a little characteristic diversion. Having had a difference with one of his neighbours, he proceeded to attack him, but was driven back to his own town, which was set on fire by his enemies. Standing on the lofty terrace on which the station is built, we had a splendid view of the whole affair. Baron von Nimpsch despatched a hundred Zanzibaris with rifles to restore order, which they soon did by marching straight for the town. Both parties incontinently fled at their approach; but the grass-built town, once lighted, was not easily extinguished, and continued to burn half through the night, casting a grand, weird light over the broad waters of the Congo.

On the lower river every one had congratulated me on being sent up-country, for two reasons : first, they said the climate was better; secondly, fresh food (in the shape of goats, fowls, &c.) was reported more plentiful, so that we should not be compelled to depend on supplies of tinned meat from Europe. But, unluckily, it has been proved at Léopoldville that the supplies, whether native or imported, are not equal to the demand. The Europeans in that station have several times been reduced to *chikwanga* (a preparation of manioc—the native substitute for bread) and yams, as no more goats or fowls were to be had in the district, and the provisions from Europe had been delayed *en route*, owing to a scarcity of carriers. Soon after my arrival at Stanley Pool things began to look very bad, as the chiefs of transport had great difficulty in getting carriers. There were at this time from twelve to fifteen white men in the station, besides about thirty Zanzibaris and Houssas in the service of the State; and at the two mission-stations some six white men, with their servants and native workmen, whose numbers I do not know. At Nshassa, seven miles distant, is another State station with two or three white men, a Dutch trading-house with two, and another mission-station with four or five. Opposite Nshassa is the French station of Brazzaville, with at least three or four more, and their workmen and servants. All these have to be supported on goats, fowls, &c., purchased from the natives, and naturally the supply gave out under so enormous a drain—the people of the district having taken no pains to provide supplies to meet this extra demand. At last things reached such a pitch that work had to be stopped, and the men sent out with supplies of beads, cloth, and brass wire to scour the country in search of food. Some of them have told me how they would watch the natives preparing their manioc (which is a work of time, as the roots have to be steeped for some weeks after digging, in order to get rid of the poisonous juice), track them to their huts, and watch day and night outside the doors till the *chikwanga* was baked and ready, when they would at once begin to bargain for it. The whites fared somewhat better, as long as the supplies of tinned goods from Europe lasted; but these, too, at length began to give out, and every one was prophesying a return to the good old times of *chikwanga* and yam, when a small caravan arrived and staved off the evil day.

Long before this, however, the chief had thought it better to put every one on short allowance. Among other rations, Portuguese wine was issued at the rate of half a bottle per man per day. Each man had to send his "boy" to the store with his bottle every other day, and of course there was a rush for the big bottles. The storekeeper, instructed by the chief, refused everything larger than a champagne-bottle; and as the second officer in charge of the station superintended the issuing of rations in person, there was no chance for any man to get more than his share. This did not please the engineers, who decided, at a council held in the mess-room of the *Stanley*, that half a bottle per day was not enough; and forthwith a collection of empty bottles began to accumulate in the engineers' store, and experiments were instituted to find out whether the capacity of any one of them exceeded that of the rest, but with very unsatisfactory results. At last some one suggested the device of blowing out the bulge in the bottom of the bottle, so as to leave it nearly flat. No sooner said than done. Not only was the bottom flattened, but it was found possible by means of heat to slightly stretch the bottle itself, so that, though it appeared very little larger than an ordinary champagne-bottle, it would hold nearly half as much again. The trick remained undiscovered till the engineers had all finished their term of service, when the ingenious deviser of the scheme, being the last to depart for Europe, left his bottle to the second in command, with a hint to keep his eyes open for the future.

As to the climate, volumes have been written on African climates, and I do not wish to add to the already over-abundant literature of the subject. A European is naturally out of his element in tropical countries, so it follows, as a matter of course, that he cannot expect his health to be as good as it would be in more northern latitudes.

For the rest, a great deal depends on a man's constitution and habits. Some men go in for slight periodical fevers; others for occasional more violent attacks at irregular intervals; others, again, take their fevers all in a lump. Some seldom or never touch quinine; others cannot keep on their legs without a daily dose. Some can drink an enormous quantity of liquor and never seem the worse for it; others have their temperature raised to an alarming extent by the mere taste of wine. I have known men who, throughout their whole stay in Africa, were troubled, every other week, with intermittent fever (lasting about two days), go home to Europe, get well and strong, come out again, apparently acclimatised, and keep pretty well afterwards. Others have spent two or three years, in very good health, seldom troubled with fever or anything else, and then suddenly collapsed with a severe attack of malarial poisoning. One must pay the toll of the tropics in some way, either by instalments or in a lump sum. Few, very few, escape; and those who manage to spend two or three years in Africa without fever, will usually suffer for it when they get to colder latitudes, or make it up afterwards on their return to a hot climate. At least, such is the result of my observations. There was only one man of my acquaintance who, so far as my knowledge of him went, had entirely escaped illness, and he was in the habit of swallowing large doses of quinine every morning. I subsequently heard a report that he had, many years before, suffered from a severe attack of fever in India. Stanley, in his latest book, 'The Congo, and the Founding of its Free State,' goes very fully into the subject of climate and disease, and seems to think chills and carelessness more productive of fevers than malaria. The nights, at some seasons of the year, are certainly chilly, and even cold—especially on the high uplands of Mpallaballa and Lutété; and cold winds—or winds that feel cold for that latitude—blow strongly up river. One morning, shortly after my arrival at Bangala, I awoke, feeling sick and ill, and sent my boy to inform Captain Coquilhat that I was not well enough to turn out. The captain, soon afterwards, kindly came to my room to see how I was, and after several questions, sent out an order to the store for two more blankets for me, saying that the nights at that time of year were very cool, and that my fever had been caused by getting chilled while asleep.

As to liquor, there is no doubt that many men out here do ruin their health by excessive drinking; but the saying that stimulants were made for use, and not for abuse, applies to Africa as well as to all other parts of the world, and I think that many others, chiefly missionaries, ruin theirs by a mistaken and exaggerated abstinence. Every one becomes more or less anæmic after a short residence in this climate, and anæmia, in a country where good nourishing food is scarce, usually produces a strong desire for stimulants. This, combined with the heat, may be put down as accounting for the far-famed "Congo thirst."

Many steady young men, fresh from Europe, and inexperienced in tropical climates, feeling themselves growing weak and enervated, give way to this craving, and thus injure their constitutions and ruin their prospects; while others, who are strict teetotallers, will often be prostrated by sickness, when the timely use of a little wine would have kept up their strength. I never, during my whole life, felt such a desire for strong drinks as during two or three months in which—owing to my duties having kept me a great deal exposed to the sun— I was more than usually anæmic; and perhaps it was as well for me that I was in a country where wines and spirits were very scarce.

When the country is better opened up to trade, and the railway and steamship companies enable Europeans to obtain home luxuries and plenty of nourishing food, things will become very much what they now are in India, and the vague terrors of life in Africa will disappear before the magic influence of steam. When splendidly appointed steamships perform the journey from Liverpool to Boma in fifteen days, and rush up the estuary of the mighty river, with their passengers lounging under double awnings in luxurious chairs, with iced drinks by their side, and are whirled away to the grander beauties of Stanley Pool and Batéké within twenty-four hours of their landing at Matadi : when this time comes — and as the surveys for the railway have already been made, let us hope it is not far distant—then will the "Dark Continent" become light, and the "open sore of the world" be healed, for the iron horse will open the way for civilisation, and before the advance of civilisation slavery must fall.

It was nearly three weeks after my arrival at Léopoldville before the steamers were ready to start for Bangala and Stanley Falls. As the delay was caused by the non-arrival of a piece of the *Stanley's* new feed-pump, Mr Walker, the engineer of the steamer, decided, after waiting a long time, to make a new piece. There being no lathe nearer than Boma, 250 miles away, the whole thing had to be cut out of a solid piece of iron, with hammer, chisel, and file. At last the work was done ; and one night, when every one was seated at dinner, discussing the approaching departure of the steamers, a boy gave Mr Walker a note from the chief of the station, announcing that the long-missing piece had just arrived, having been discovered at Lukungu, and sent on.

While this had been going on, the two Italian

captains, Bove and Fabrello, had arrived at Léopoldville, as well as most of the stores for Bangala and
the Falls; so it was finally decided to make a start
at the end of the week, and all the available men
in the station were sent to scour the country round
for dead wood, to be used as fuel for the steamers.
Accordingly, at 8 A.M. on July 18th, the *A.I.A.*
left Léopoldville, having on board Captain Delatte,
Lieutenant Dhanis, and myself, besides a crew of
nine Zanzibaris, and two boys. The *Stanley* was
to follow us next day. We were soon out of sight
of Léopoldville, and through the strong current
round Kallina Point, and, passing the Dutch factory
and Baptist Mission Station, called at the State
station of Nshassa, and then steamed away across
the eighteen-mile length of Stanley Pool. Kimpopo station was not at this time occupied by any
Europeans, so Captain Delatte hugged the sand-
banks round Bamu island, and before night we
were well up the deep gorge out of which the
Congo rushes like a mill-race, to spread out into
the broad expanse of the Pool. Between this and
the mouth of the Kwa (Lower Kassai) the river is
very narrow, varying from three-quarters of a mile
to a mile in width, and rushing along at the rate
of from 6 to 8 miles an hour, at the bottom of a
deep gorge, the hills on either hand rising to a height
of over 4000 feet. The winds, which nearly always
blow up river, after passing over the broad surface

of Stanley Pool are confined in this narrow gorge, and become exceedingly strong, especially in the months of August, September, and October, when the opposing stream of water is forced up into huge waves, rendering it next to impossible for the light-built open steamers at present in use to proceed. They very often have to lay up all day waiting till the wind abates, which it nearly always does about 4 P.M., to rise again with the sun in the morning. Delatte, who had been up and down the Congo for nearly three years, knew the river thoroughly, and was well up in all the dodges of crawling round the edges of sandbanks, and getting the advantages of slack-water and return currents; so we made very good progress. He had only five months more to stay in the country, and talked nearly every day of his return home. Poor fellow! he was never to see his home again!

Being now in good health, I began to look about for something to shoot, and shortly after leaving the Pool sighted an antelope; but these animals are far too shy to be approached in a steamer, so I turned my attention to a monkey which sat grinning at me from a neighbouring tree, and favoured him with a shot, but the monkey calmly grinned on.

The scenery between Stanley Pool and Kwamouth is grand, and really worth seeing. It is very much like that on the Rhine between Bonn and Mainz, only on three or four times as large a scale; and the towering hills are covered with dense tropical forests and long grass instead of vineyards, while gaunt, bare rocks take the place of ruined castles. For my part, I infinitely prefer the lonely, savage grandeur of this part of the Congo to anything the Rhine can show. On the second day we came to Lissa market, where we stopped for an hour to enable the men to buy food. Just above this is the narrowest part of the river, which is here barely three-quarters of a mile wide. The north bank slopes precipitously down to the water's edge, forming in some places sheer cliffs 50 to 60 feet high. Dense forests clothe the hillsides, while the tops are nearly all bare of trees, and in the rainy season covered with long grass, which is burnt when it dries up, after the cessation of the rains. The south bank is not so steep, and has only patches of low scrub in place of the grand forest of the north side. This is, however, relieved by large groves of *Hyphæne* palm, which look very beautiful. Just at the upper end of this narrow reach are two pretty little islands, called by Stanley Pururu and Dualla islands. The latter—the lower one—is entirely covered with bush and scrub; but Pururu, the larger of the two, has only its lower half clothed with forest, the upper being covered with a splendid grove of *Hyphæne* palm. After passing these islands, the river gradually widens.

On the third day we passed Mswata, a now deserted station of the State, and towards noon arrived at Kwamouth. Here there was also formerly a State station, now handed over to the French Roman Catholic Mission, and occupied by two *pères* belonging to the Société du St-Esprit. We stopped here for lunch, and on our departure the hospitable fathers gave us a supply of onions and lettuce, which were most welcome, as vegetables can at present be grown only in a few places in this benighted land, Kwamouth being one of the favoured spots. We then crossed the mouth of the Kassai, a few miles higher up the Congo, and stopped at another newly established French mission, belonging to the Société d'Alger. Some eighteen months later these missionaries transferred their stations to French territory, and Kwamouth has again become a station of the State, while the site of the Société d'Alger's Mission is occupied by some Belgian priests.

Here two *pères* in white robes came out in a canoe to guide us to a safe landing-place, as the banks of the river were here very rocky, and having received their mail, walked up to the station with Captain Delatte and Lieutenant Dhanis, inviting me to follow—which I did, as soon as I had put the engine and boiler right for the night, and indulged in a wash. I found, on reaching the station, that the missionaries had not yet got their house built, and were living in tents. They had, however, by some means or other, come into possession of an antelope, and had a table set out in the open air, by the light of a big wood-fire and a full moon; and, for the second time since landing in Congo, I enjoyed a piece of really good fresh meat. Antelope is like very tender, juicy beefsteak; while goats—the quadrupeds most frequently eaten here—are always as tough as leather.

We left here next morning, and passed on to Chumbiri, where we spent another night,—and then on again, up the now widening Congo to Bolobo—from which place we crossed to the north bank. After passing Two-Palm Point, a few miles below Bolobo, the river widens to four miles—the centre of the channel being choked up with islands and sand-banks. We had a man always stationed in the bow of the boat with a long pole, with which he kept trying the depth of the water. Up to Two-Palm Point, the pole had shown deep water all along, except when we approached the shore; but now it was always finding bottom, and slows and stops became frequent. Mark Twain's Mississippi pilot would answer very well for the Congo, —only the Congo, besides being much larger than the Mississippi, is wild and unknown, and one has to feel every mile of one's way.

The hills, too, gradually disappeared in the distance; and as we threaded our way towards the north bank, the country, though still pretty and park-like, became a monotonous flat. The low grass-covered islands and banks in this part of the Congo are the favourite haunts of the hippopotami; and I frequently saw from ten to twenty of their huge heads appear above water, only to vanish more quickly than they had appeared, when they saw our rifle-barrels gleam in the sun. After wasting several cartridges in trying to hit one, I came to the conclusion that, next to sand-crabs and porpoises, a "hippo" is the most difficult animal to shoot. Two or three days later, when Dhanis and I had taken our rifles to pieces to clean them, we suddenly came upon two of the great brutes, high and dry on shore. They looked like enormous grey beer-barrels on short, stumpy legs, with a huge head at one end. Yet, in spite of the shortness of their legs, how they *did* run, when the little steamer came snorting up!

When we did succeed in mortally wounding one, he nearly always fell over the edge of a sand-bank into deep water, and so was lost. I hit one standing on a sand-reef half-way out of the water, and thought myself sure of him; but when struck he jumped clean out of the water, cleared the bank, and landed with a tremendous splash in the deep stream. Another, at which Dhanis was aiming, suddenly opened his huge mouth, and received a Martini express bullet, like a Holloway's pill, clean down his throat.

Crocodiles afforded better sport, as they were not

so timid, but their armour-plated backs were very hard; and sometimes my ball would ricochet off their scaly sides and go spinning along the water, like the flat stones with which schoolboys play at ducks and drakes. About 4 P.M. we reached a place where there were several dead trees, and stopped for the night in order to cut fuel. Having landed the woodcutters, and made everything right, we then—the captain, Dhanis, and myself—sat down to dinner, and soon after it was over I turned in, being very tired. I should explain that there are no cabins in the *A.I.A.* Our sleeping-places were at the stern of the boat, the captain's being farthest aft; our mosquito-curtains were fastened up to her sides, and our camp-mattresses reached right across her, as she is only six feet in the beam. Captain Delatte was in high spirits, and kept playing tunes on a melodeon we had with us; talking, in the intervals, of his home at Brussels, and his delight at soon seeing it again. Presently he poured out three glasses of Portuguese wine, and handed one to Lieutenant Dhanis, and the other (under the mosquito-curtain) to me. I tasted it, and passed it out again, with the remark, "It's too strong; put some Congo in it!" He added a little water, and said, "Hang it, man, it's pure water!" and I never heard him speak again; for, soon after, I turned over and went to sleep, with the strains of "Myosotis," which I had asked him to play, ringing in my ears. Next morning, instead of being called by him as usual, I slept on, till roused by Lieutenant Dhanis, who came to me, with a white, scared face, asking, "Where is the captain?" "I don't know," I replied. "I believe he's in the Congo," said Dhanis. Of course I was up like a shot. Sure enough, there was the captain's bed— his clothes, boots, hat, all lying beside it; his mosquito-curtain untorn showed that nothing unusual had taken place; and he could not have got ashore without awakening either Dhanis or myself, as the boat was anchored with her bow to the bank. We questioned the men, but none had seen or heard anything save occasional splashes in the water— which no one on the Congo ever heeds, as crocodiles and hippopotami may be heard splashing all night long. How it happened will never be known till the day of judgment; we could only come to the conclusion that he had got up in the night, fallen over the stern of the boat, and gone down (being unable to swim) without a cry — perhaps never even rising to the surface a second time, as the current is very strong. We searched the sand-banks for miles down the river, and promised large rewards to the natives for finding the captain's body, or any traces of him, but in vain. It is very seldom, if ever, that any traces have been found of a white man drowned in the Congo.

We were compelled at length to proceed, having

orders to reach Bangala before the *Stanley*. Though neither Lieutenant Dhanis nor myself had ever been on the Congo before, we had with us a Zanzibari who had been all over the river with Stanley, and knew the channels pretty well, and he now acted as our pilot. The day after Delatte's death we left the grass country for the forest region, and stopped for the night near the deserted site of Lukolela Station. Four days later we arrived at Equator Station, where we found Mr Eddie, of the A.B.M.U., in fairly good health, and leaving him the same day, reached Bangala in about four days more, having, ever since our departure from Lukolela, steamed through the same flat, monotonous, forested country. I do not say there is no beauty in this region, for there is; but it takes a little time to get used to the dense jungle, and one's eyes must become accustomed to distinguish one shape of leaf from another before he can appreciate it. This needs more leisure and comfort than one can at present command on the Congo: besides, when viewed through the jaundiced medium of African fever, no country seems pleasant, and I daresay many a man would fail to see any beauty even in far-famed Sydney Harbour if his temperature were a few degrees above normal. An artist usually picks out the grandest or loveliest scenes for his pictures, and people in Europe take a series of the views they see in books, string them together in imagination into one long, impossible landscape, and then are disappointed with the reality.

It was nearly 7 P.M. on August 1st—just fifteen days after leaving Léopoldville—that we reached Bangala, and my first view of the place was not enchanting. All I could see before me, in the dusk of an African evening, when I stopped the boat, was a steep mud-bank, with a house of the same material at the top. I was tired, hungry, and ready to fall asleep on my feet, and it was not particularly cheering to find that not a spare room was to be had at the station. However, I slept soundly enough, in spite of the mosquitoes, wrapped in my blanket, on a native mat under the mess-room table.

Next day, as we were seated at lunch, a shout of "Sail, oh!" from the Zanzibaris announced the arrival of the *Stanley*. As she was bringing up representatives of the Swedish and Italian Governments, Captain Coquilhat had ordered a military reception; and accordingly, as she steamed up to the beach in front of the station, the Houssas and Zanzibaris, drawn up in line, fired a volley from their rifles, followed by a salute from the two mountain Krupp guns belonging to the station. On the bridge of the steamer stood Captain Coquilhat and Lieutenant Dubois in full uniform, with the two Italian captains and Baron Schwerin, also in uniform, while the deck of the boat was crowded with Houssas and Zanzibaris. Captain Coquilhat, the founder of this station, was warmly welcomed by the Ba-Ngala, who pressed round him in hundreds to get a shake of his hand, and then went off for a great drinking of *malafu*[1] and *massanga*,[2] to celebrate the arrival of the *Stanley* and the return of "Mwafa,"[3] as he was called by them. In the evening the members of the Italian and Swedish Expeditions, as well as the officers of the *Stanley*, came up to the station to dinner. After we had finished, and were all seated round the table talking, one of the mess-boys came in and told Captain Coquilhat that Mata Bwyki,[4] the chief of Iboko, had come to see him; and in walked one of the biggest black men I had ever seen. He was three or four inches over six feet, and had a fine well-developed figure, though he now looked shrivelled and wiry with age (he was reported to be eighty-four or eighty-six), and had lost one eye, which gave him a very one-sided expression. He was said to have fifty wives, several of whom now followed him, bearing native chairs and stools, as well as sundry large pots of *massanga*. The scene which now ensued was worth coming all the way to Africa to see. The huge old cannibal stalked in, smeared over with camwood-powder and palm-oil, wearing a tall leopard-skin cap, which added another foot to his stature, and with a long pole in

---

[1] Palm-wine.'   [2] Fermented juice of the sugar-cane.
[3] "The Eagle."   [4] "Lord of many Guns."

one hand, and walking up to Captain Coquilhat, who was dressed in the full uniform of "Capitaine d'Etat-Major de l'Etat Indépendant du Congo," enfolded him in his arms. From this bear's hug Captain Coquilhat emerged with great red patches over his blue coat and gilt facings, and "Le Roi des Ba-Ngala" turned his attention to the rest of the company, who were doubtless as glad as I was to escape with a shake of his huge paw, without undergoing the same ceremony as the captain. When he had gone the round of the table, his wives brought the *massanga*-pots, and Mata Bwyki began to pour the stuff down his throat by quarts at a time. He was a tremendous toper, and could consume enormous quantities of his favourite beverage.

His death, which took place about two months later, was an occasion of great excitement amongst the Ba-Ngala. It is their custom, on the death of a chief, to kill as many slaves over his grave as the said chief had wives during his lifetime. Cannibal feasts were doubtless also indulged in, but this has been disputed. Now Mata Bwyki had fifty wives: fifty slaves had therefore to be provided for the sacrifice—one by the parents of each wife.[1] This great massacre was, however, happily averted by the officer in command of the station, who,

[1] The slaves were probably substitutes for the wives, who would perhaps themselves have been sacrificed in former times.

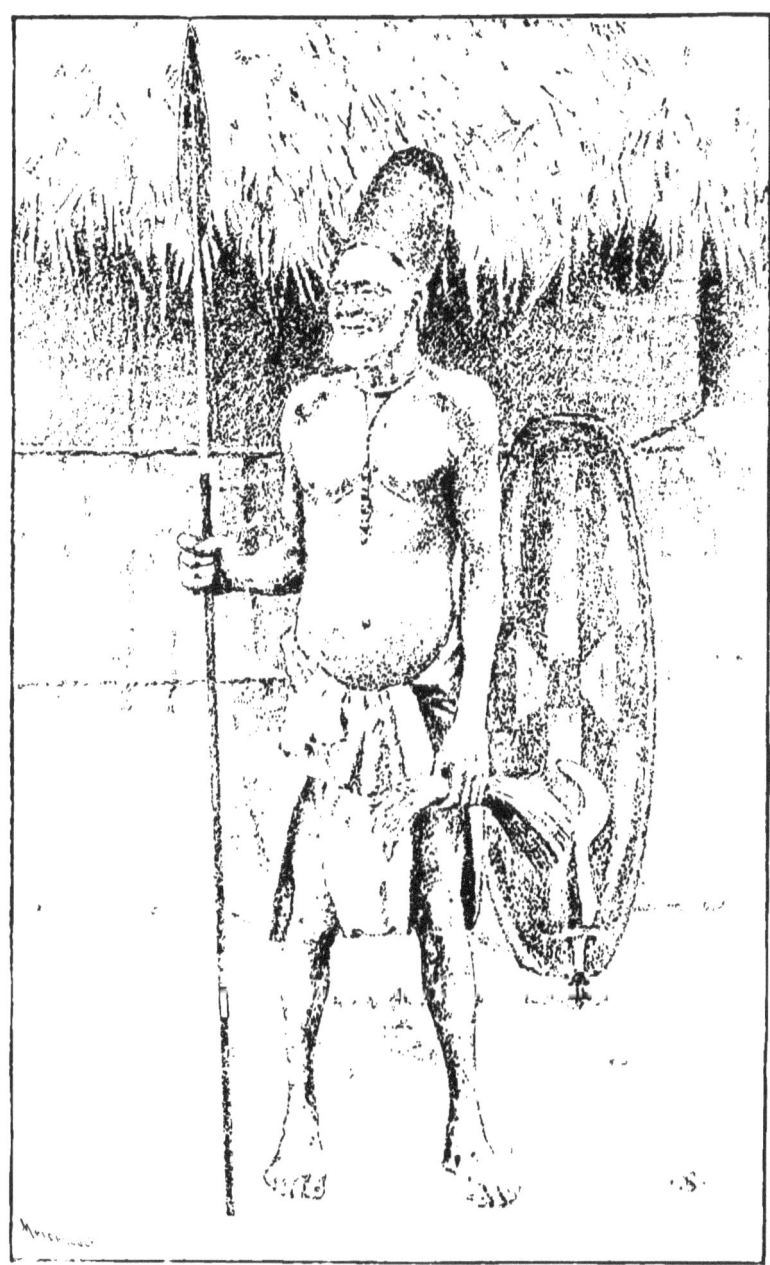

MATA BWYKI.
FROM A PHOTOGRAPH TAKEN BY CAPTAIN COQUILHAT.

To face page 80.

hearing of Mata Bwyki's death, prepared a huge coffin lined with red *savelist*, and—having persuaded the Ba-Ngala that, as Mata Bwyki had been the *mundélé's* friend, it was only appropriate that the white men should bury him—nailed him safely up in the box, and interred him with all due honours, such as the firing-off of guns, &c., over his grave. The Ba-Ngala were, however, not to be done; for we found out, a long time afterwards, that they had sacrificed ten slaves in another village. Still, this was better than killing fifty. Another custom of the Ba-Ngala is to cut open a dead man, and examine his liver and kidneys, to see if he has been poisoned. I am not aware whether this was done in Mata Bwyki's case.

This huge savage had developed a remarkable affection for Captain Coquilhat; and I afterwards heard that, when he was dying, he kept asking when the latter (who had gone to Stanley Falls) was coming back, as he wished to see him. Perhaps even this hardened old warrior and man-eater had a presentiment of death, and, knowing nothing of the world to come, wished to see the only person on earth whom he considered superior to himself. Who knows?

After the *massanga* was finished, Mata Bwyki left in order to superintend a grand dance which was going on in the village, *au clair de la lune*.

We all followed him to a clear space in the centre of the village, where there was a large fire, which two or three men kept feeding with dry palm-fronds, so as to make a blaze. In front of this fire were two rows of natives, one of men and the other of women; and on the other side was the band, consisting of three or four huge tom-toms, from which several men were extracting a fearful noise. The dusky figures of the Ba-Ngala, flitting backwards and forwards across the firelight, as they went through the complicated figures of a native dance, formed a very pretty sight; and the moon, (which was nearly full) shining through the fronds of the palm and banana trees around, gave a very Macbeth-caldron-business effect to the whole scene, the combination of moonlight and smoke having very much the effect of the gauze screens used in theatres to make the ghost in "Hamlet" appear and disappear when wanted.

After staying two days to get a good supply of dry wood for fuel, the *Stanley* left for the Falls, the two Italian captains and Baron Schwerin going with her, as well as Lieutenant Dubois, who was appointed to Stanley Falls Station.

I now began to think of shaking down into my new quarters. Two new houses were being built, but as these were as yet but half finished, and the house we at present inhabited was very full—being only constructed to hold two Europeans and their stores — I had to make myself at home (for the present, at least) in the gun-room, while Lieutenant Dhanis was relegated to the provision-store. For more than a month I slept on a bedstead formed of two planks supported at either end on a barrel which, on examination, I found to contain charges of powder for the two Krupp guns; while boxes of cartridges, cans of turpentine, and a goodly variety of inflammable materials, were in close proximity. Reading in bed was, of course, too dangerous a proceeding to be indulged in under these circumstances; and even taking a naked light into the room would have been a hazardous experiment had I not made myself acquainted with the position of the various items, and carefully covered up the most dangerous. One night, while a regular tropical thunderstorm was raging, Captain Coquilhat entered and advised me to come outside till the storm was over, as he was afraid I might get shot by the lightning igniting the cartridges; but as the danger was about the same in any part of the house—since the barrels of powder would have blown the whole station into the middle of the Congo—I could see no advantage in a change of quarters, but preferred remaining comfortably in bed where I was, so thanked him and went to sleep. I had slept in too many strange places lately to be kept awake by the chance of being blown up.

This house had been built by Captain Coquilhat

when he was left here by Stanley in January 1884, and considering the limited tools at his disposal, it does him great credit, for it has successfully resisted all attacks of the natives—the cannibal river-pirates, whose fleet of war-canoes tried to bar Stanley's passage in 1877. It is built of "wattle and daub," the woven branches, supported by firm upright posts, being plastered over with the clay of the country, which becomes extremely hard when baked in the sun, and renders the whole fireproof. The ceiling is formed of logs laid right across from wall to wall, with an eight-inch layer of clay spread all over them; and over all is a roof of palm-leaves, supported on pillars standing at a distance of eight feet from the walls, and forming a verandah all round. This roof can be set on fire and burnt right off—indeed, I believe this has happened— without injuring the rest of the building in the slightest degree; and thus the great native weapon —fire—is rendered harmless. The windows are small, barred, and placed very high up; and so long as ammunition lasted, three or four white men could hold the place against all the tribes on the Congo. The two doors are the weak point, but could, in case of need, be defended by the two Krupp guns.

The new houses were being constructed on the same principle, but were larger, and in a better position—being situated on higher ground, 200 or 300 yards down the river.

FIRST EUROPEAN HOUSE AT BANGALA STATION.
BUILT BY CAPTAIN COQUILHAT.

To face page 84.

Bangala was at this time pretty well off for fresh meat, fowls and goats being plentiful and cheap. But this state of things did not last very long, and, as at Léopoldville, the supply could not keep pace with the demand, when the number of Europeans in the station increased. Long before my time was finished there was hardly a fowl to be had in the neighbouring villages, and the chief of the station had to send men a journey of two or three days to get any. The supply of goats held out longer, but even these grew scarcer and dearer at last. About 150 had been preserved for their milk, but even these were beginning to meet their inevitable fate before I finally left the station on my way home.

The Ba-Ngala are a fine race physically, tall, powerful, and splendidly formed, — the women being the handsomest I have seen in Africa. Their dress is scanty, consisting, for the most part, only of a waist-cloth for the men and a short kilt of grass for the women. They cicatrise their arms, shoulders, and busts in patterns by cutting the skin and injecting some irritant. Sometimes the result looks very well; but in other cases the process is not successful, and raises huge unsightly lumps of flesh.

That the Ba-Ngala were cannibals, Captain Coquilhat had ample proof during the first few months of his residence among them. One day a canoe came down the river and stopped just in front of the station; and from this canoe the natives brought several large pots, which were found on inspection to contain portions of human arms and legs. Before I had been in the place three weeks, I was one night aroused by a great shouting and beating of tom-toms. On inquiring the cause of the row, I was informed that the Ba-Ngala were celebrating some event with a feast of human flesh. One old chief, I was told, had about twenty wives, and had been known occasionally to kill and feast off one of them. This chief, when I saw him, was a much milder-looking man than Mata Bwyki; and had the latter been the same way inclined, I am afraid his fifty wives would scarcely have sufficed to keep him going.

CHAPTER V.

THE LOSS OF STANLEY FALLS.

NEWS BROUGHT BY THE *STANLEY* — HISTORY OF FALLS STATION — TREATY BETWEEN WESTER AND THE ARABS — TIPPOO TIP — MR DEANE WOUNDED ON HIS WAY UP RIVER TO TAKE COMMAND — VAN GÈLE SENT OUT, BUT INVALIDED TO MADEIRA — DEANE GOES A SECOND TIME — CONTRADICTORY NATURE OF HIS ORDERS — THE RUNAWAY SLAVE — STATION ATTACKED — DESERTERS REACH BANGALA — PALAVER WITH THE BA-NGALA — WE START TO RELIEVE DEANE — DIVERSITY OF SENTIMENTS AMONG THE PEOPLE OF UPOTO — DEFECTIVE CARTRIDGES — YAMBUNGA — CAPTIVES RESTORED — WAR-DRUMS — ORERA'S MISFORTUNES — TRACES OF THE SLAVE-RAIDERS — THE FRIENDLY NATIVES OF YARUKOMBE — CAPTAIN COQUILHAT'S SUFFERINGS — GLIMPSE OF STANLEY FALLS — THE BAKUMU AND THEIR INFORMATION — DUBOIS DROWNED — THE STATION IN RUINS — THE *A.I.A.* IN A FIX — WE RETREAT — SAMBA — SEARCH FOR DEANE — DEANE SAFE AT YARUKOMBE — SKIRMISH AT YAPORO — ATTENDING THE WOUNDED — DEANE'S STORY — RETURN TO BANGALA — THE *HENRY REED* — THE FEARFUL AND WONDERFUL DECREES OF THE *COMITÉ* AT BRUSSELS — DEPARTURE FOR LÉOPOLDVILLE — COQUILHAT AND DEANE INVALIDED HOME — SAMBA'S HISTORY.

Towards the end of August the *Stanley* unexpectedly reappeared, having accomplished the up-journey to Stanley Falls in the remarkably quick time of twelve days. After staying four or five days at that place, she had made the return trip in seven days. The news she brought was not reassuring. Mr Walter Deane, commander of the Falls Station, had been fighting the Arabs; and although hostilities had been brought to a close on the *Stanley's* arrival, the captain and officers of the steamer were of opinion that the Arabs would again attack Mr Deane, as soon as he was left alone with only one other European (Lieutenant Dubois) and eighty black men, of whom only forty were Houssas, and the rest undisciplined Ba-Ngala.

In order to understand this—one of the most heroic struggles against slave-traders on record, and worthy to rank with the defence of Khartoum by General Gordon—it will be necessary to take a short survey of the history of Stanley Falls Station.

Had Mr Deane been well supplied with arms and men when he was sent to his dangerous post, and been allowed to act on his own responsibility, instead of being hampered by contradictory orders from Europe—which only reached Stanley Falls some six months after they were written, when the state of affairs at that post had completely changed—the Arabs would never have gained a footing west of the Seventh Cataract, and the natives of the Aruhwimi would still be living in their villages, instead of being scattered through the forest and decimated by the slavers.

In December 1883, Stanley, having made ar-

MR. WALTER DEANE.
THE DEFENDER OF STANLEY FALLS STATION.

From a Photograph.

rangements with the Arabs, and obtained from the natives of the district a site on the island of Wana Rusari, left Binnie, the engineer of the *Royal*, to build a station, and departed for the coast, taking with him several confidential slaves of the Arabs, in order to show them the white men's settlements and their mode of trading.

Binnie remained alone at Stanley Falls till July 1884, when he was relieved by Captain Hanssens, who brought up the Swedish Lieutenant Wester, and the Belgian, Amelot, to take his place. Binnie, who had during his stay at the Falls been on very good terms with both Arabs and natives, returned down river with Captain Hanssens. In October of the same year, Lieutenant Wester made a treaty with the Arabs, by which they bound themselves not to descend below the Seventh Cataract of Stanley Falls, or enter the Free State territory, either to fight, trade, or seize slaves or ivory. The division-line west of which the Arabs were not to come was to be drawn north and south through the Seventh Cataract, and peace was to be kept between Arabs and white men. This treaty was signed by one of Tippoo Tip's sons, and also by Karema and Kajumba—the former of whom was at Yaporo when Stanley came up to found the station. The natives round the station were also parties to this treaty, *and placed themselves under the protection of the State flag.*

Hardly had this treaty been concluded, when the Bismarck of Central Africa, Tippoo Tip, chief of all the slave-raiding gangs between Tanganika and the Lualaba, arrived upon the scene with a large force, and informed Wester that he had been sent by Said Barghash, Sultan of Zanzibar, to prevent the Arabs from disposing of their ivory to traders coming up the Congo. The confidential slaves taken down river by Stanley had made good use of their five senses, and their report had reached the ears of the Sultan through Tippoo Tip, who was much too sharp an Arab not to try and obtain for himself the profit to be gained from the enormous quantities of ivory of which his men had told him on their return. Finding out, also, from these men (for an Arab, while seeming to be utterly indifferent to all that passes round him, will miss nothing), the exact strength of the Power he had to deal with, he probably represented to the Sultan that, if this new enterprise of Stanley's were allowed to succeed, the trade of Zanzibar would be ruined. It seems pretty certain that Said Barghash had supplied Tippoo with men and goods; but whether this was for the purpose of driving the Europeans from Stanley Falls, or whether the Sultan had really given him the instructions he alleged, still remains, as far as I can make out, a mystery to the public.

Tippoo completely ignored the treaty Wester

had concluded with the other Arabs, and declared himself ready to fight; but Wester, not being strong enough to risk hostilities, let things take their course until he should have an opportunity of communicating with the Administrator-General at Boma; and Tippoo, finding he was not interfered with, promised not to attack any of the State stations.

In January 1885, Captain Van Gèle arrived at Stanley Falls with supplies for the station, and had a long palaver with Tippoo Tip, in which the latter (probably on the same principle on which the Pope, in 1493, divided the unexplored part of the world between Spain and Portugal) claimed the whole of Africa, from Zanzibar to Banana, on behalf of Said Barghash, who had sent him to make a report on it, and prevent the Arabs from sending their ivory down the Congo. All that Van Gèle could do was to try and gain time. He succeeded in getting from Tippoo Tip a promise to recall his men, and then left for Boma, to report on the state of affairs to the Administrator-General.

The decision of the authorities was to fortify the Falls station so strongly that it would be in a position to resist any attack; and, in June 1885, Mr Walter Deane left Léopoldville with a company of men, to take command. Just below the mouth of the Aruhwimi is a long narrow branch of the Congo, called the Monongiri channel, on the banks of which lives one of the most piratical tribes of the whole river. These people represent in Africa the Thugs of India, and will never attack except from behind, or in the dark, and then only in superior numbers. Mr Deane, in passing through this channel, was overtaken by night, and obliged to camp; when, at midnight, the natives suddenly attacked him, and killed several of his men, almost before he knew that anything was wrong—as they had crept up quietly through the bushes, and speared his sentries. Deane himself received a wound in the thigh, and a spear right through the calf of his leg, and pulling this spear out of the wound, defended himself with it till his gun was brought to him. According to my Houssa informant, he killed the man who had thrown it with his own weapon.

This wound compelled him, on arriving at the Falls, to leave the command to Wester, and return down-stream to Léopoldville, where he reported that Tippoo had so far kept his word that the Arabs had withdrawn to the country east of the Seventh Cataract, and that no raids had taken place. In December 1885, Van Gèle arrived at Stanley Pool from Brussels, to take command of an expedition to the Falls, but was prostrated by so severe an attack of bilious fever that he was obliged to leave Africa to regain his health, and Deane, though still suffering from the effects of his wound, consented to remain another year on the

Congo, and return to the Falls till either Van Gèle was restored to health or some one else appointed in his place.

He left Léopoldville in the *Stanley* in December 1885, with Lieutenant Eycken and forty Houssas, and, after picking up forty Ba-Ngala at Iboko, in January, he reached the Falls about the middle of February 1886. It was, I believe, on this journey[1] that he was again treacherously attacked, while buying provisions from the natives of Mpeza—who, tempted by the sight of quantities of brass wire, beads, &c., suddenly began throwing spears at Deane's men, in order to create a panic, during which they could possess themselves of the coveted goods without paying for them. Deane, shouting to his men not to fire, advanced without his gun, in order to try and arrange matters peaceably. He would probably have succeeded, had not a little dog he had with him taken offence at the threatening attitude of the natives, and rushed at them. The result of this was a shower of spears, one of which passed through the edge of Deane's boot, and another through his trousers, pinning him to the ground. His men then commenced to fire, and he remained in that position till his gun was brought him, when, to use his own words, he " lost his temper

[1] I had this account from Mr Deane himself, and then understood that he was at the time on board the Baptist Mission steamer *Peace*, so cannot give the exact date when it happened.

and let fly." The spears, fortunately, had not wounded him.

At the beginning of 1886, then, Mr Deane took over the command of Stanley Falls Station. The spirit of his orders was, that he was to afford protection to the natives, to do all in his power to prevent raids and put down the slave-trade, *and to keep on good terms with the Arabs*. These orders —while hampering Deane, and preventing his using his own judgment as to whether it would or would not be better to shelve the question of protecting the natives till he was strong enough to drive out the Arabs—left those in authority a loophole of escape from all responsibility in the matter. Had Deane kept on good terms with the Arabs, he could not possibly have afforded protection to the natives; whereas it was a manifest impossibility to protect the natives without offending the Arabs, who were all on the look-out for a *casus belli*. The disastrous result of Deane's attempt to carry out these orders to the letter is only too well known; and I have heard him complain bitterly of being put in a position in which he was not allowed to act on his own judgment. His orders were such as to admit of two diametrically opposite interpretations: he was not properly supported, and did not receive the men and ammunition promised him in case he should be forced to fight. Yet, when all was over, and he had all but sacrificed his life, he was greatly blamed for the way in which he had acted, and as good as told that he had adopted the worst possible course.

In June 1886, the Baptist Mission steamer *Peace* reached Léopoldville, bringing from Stanley Falls Mr Baumann, a member of Dr Lenz's expedition, who had been taken ill and left behind at Stanley Falls, and Eycken. The latter was in a dying condition with dysentery, and did not live long after his arrival. She also brought despatches from Mr Deane, who announced that Tippoo had gone to Zanzibar, and that relations with the other Arabs were becoming somewhat strained.

From Mr Charters, the engineer of the *Peace*, I had a rough account of the events that had occurred at the Falls since February, up to the time of the steamer's departure. All had, it seems, gone fairly well till a few weeks before the *Peace* arrived, when a woman came to Mr Deane and asked his protection against the Arabs. Deane, having no positive proof of ill-treatment, wished to send her back, but eventually allowed her to remain in the station till her master came to claim her, which he did shortly afterwards. Having failed to ransom her, Deane allowed him to take her away, on condition that she should not be flogged or otherwise ill-treated for asking his protection.

A few days later the woman returned to him, covered with wounds,[1] on which he refused to give her up unless she returned to her master of her own free will. He, however, offered a ransom, which was again rejected. While matters were in this state, the *Peace* arrived, with Messrs Grenfell, Charters, and Eddie on board. Bwana Nzigé,[2] Tippoo Tip's brother and deputy, at a palaver where the three missionaries were present, again demanded the woman from Mr Deane, who replied that she must choose for herself, and that, although he was willing to keep on friendly terms with the Arabs, *as an Englishman he would not, and as an officer of the State he could not, give her up.*[3] Bwana Nzigé then asked if Deane wished to risk his head, and the latter replied that he did not consider his head in any danger, and was well able to take care of it himself. Bwana Nzigé departed in a rage, and shortly afterwards the *Peace* left for Léopoldville, taking away Baumann and Eycken, and leaving Deane entirely alone among his enemies, with only forty half-disciplined men and forty utter savages to depend on in case of attack. No more was heard of affairs at the Falls

---

[1] When Deane himself, after his rescue, related the story to me, he told me the woman had been tied up for two or three days, receiving a hundred lashes each day.

[2] "Master Locust."

[3] His own words were, "As an Englishman *I will not*, and as an officer of the State *I cannot*, give her up."

till the *Stanley* returned to Bangala, August 30th, 1886.

As before stated, I had arrived in Africa towards the end of May in the same year, and first met Captain Coquilhat at Boma—he having left Belgium some two or three months before me. Captain Van Gèle's health not allowing of his immediate return to his post, Captain Coquilhat received orders to take command *pro tem.* of the Falls, in addition to his own station of Bangala,—and was intrusted by the Administrator-General with the necessary powers. These orders were shortly afterwards followed by another, relieving him from the command of the Falls Station, which was left entirely to Mr Deane.

Captain Coquilhat was not aware till the return of the *Stanley* that Deane was short of ammunition, as the latter's request for cartridges had gone direct to Boma. Consequently, when the *Stanley* left Léopoldville in July, she only took as many as were considered necessary for her own protection.

Just before her arrival at the Falls, hostilities had broken out in earnest, the Arabs having seized on one of the women belonging to the station, and fired on some of the Houssas sent by Deane with a message to Bwana Nzigé.

On the arrival of the *Stanley*, a few days later, the Arabs offered to make peace, and the captain of the *Stanley*, having left Deane about 300 Snider cartridges—all he could spare—came down to Bangala, and reported the state of affairs to Captain Coquilhat.[1] Hamberg, the engineer of the *Stanley*, told me his opinion was that the Arabs would again attack the station, as he had seen numerous large parties of their men continually arriving in canoes. His fears were only too well founded. On September 3d, the *Stanley* left Bangala for Léopoldville. Two or three days later, I had retired to my bed on the top of the powder-barrels, and gone to sleep, when I was disturbed by the barking of some dogs. Being pretty sleepy, I merely struck a light and glanced at my watch to see if it was near dawn. Finding it only a little past midnight, I was turning over to go to sleep again, when I was thoroughly aroused by hearing Captain Coquilhat—whom I knew to be very ill—come out of his room and begin talking to some one, half in English, half in Kiswahili. My first thought was that the Arabs,

---

[1] It was fully a year later, after Mr Deane had been to Europe and returned again to the Congo, that I heard all the foregoing narrative of what occurred after his arrival at Stanley Falls, in February 1886, from his own lips. When I started up river with Captain Coquilhat to Deane's relief, I was in utter ignorance of the real position of affairs at the Falls; and as the captain was at this time very ill, I learnt very little until Deane became strong enough to tell me. Even then, the time I was with him before he left for Europe was too short for him to give me the narrative in full. Captain Coquilhat, in his work, 'Sur le Haut Congo,' has given a very full account of the history of Stanley Falls Station from first to last. I would advise any one who wishes to understand the whole affair to read this work.

having disposed of Falls Station, had descended the river; and, like a shot, I seized my revolver, and in a moment more was standing, in my *pyjamas*, behind Captain Coquilhat at the front door. Seeing only two or three Houssas, who were talking calmly to the captain, I was beginning to feel rather ashamed of my alarm, when I heard something about white men arriving next day. Captain Coquilhat continued his questioning—though I did not catch much more, as the Houssa he was speaking to was not very well up in English—and then, turning to me, informed me that Falls Station was probably lost, and that, as I would be of no use that night, and should probably be worked hard enough next day, I had better return to bed. Being very tired and sleepy, I obeyed, and was soon in a deep slumber, whence I was aroused at daylight by a confused tumult of voices. Running out, I found Captain Coquilhat in the midst of a group of Houssas, among them several in red shirts, who did not seem to belong to the station. The captain was eagerly questioning, through an interpreter, a half-starved, miserable-looking nigger, who had been bound hand and foot, and only just released, and was hardly strong enough to return answers to the questions put to him. This poor wretch, I discovered, was a prisoner taken from the Arabs, and had been so ill-treated by the Houssas on their way down that he only lived till next day. I soon became aware that there were ten Houssas from Stanley Falls in the station, and Captain Coquilhat came and told me that these ten men and the forty Ba-Ngala had come down by themselves, and that their original statement—that the white men were following them —was untrue. He then ordered me not to leave the house, while he went with Messrs Baert and Dhanis into the village to try and find out the truth from the Ba-Ngala. In about an hour he returned with two or three men, carrying some bales of cloth and rolls of brass wire, and, informing me that the Houssas had deserted Deane, ordered me to bring out the spare anchor-chains of the *A.I.A.*, and put them in irons. As the chains were not at hand, I brought out some rope, and nine of the Houssas were promptly bound hand and foot, in a circle, round the trunk of a palm-tree, and some men with guns set to guard them. The tenth, who was the corporal, Mahomed Tenné—the man whom I had heard talking to Captain Coquilhat in the night— was handcuffed to one of the posts supporting the roof of the mess-room; and a court-martial was at once formed, consisting of Captain Coquilhat, Lieutenants Baert and Dhanis, myself, two Zanzibaris, and two Houssas, to try him for desertion. It now came out that not only had Mahomed Tenné, his nine men, and the Ba-Ngala, deserted Deane, but they had also plundered the station store, and that there were, in the village, Snider rifles and bales of goods, which they had brought down in the night. It could not be definitely ascertained whether Deane and Dubois had left the station, or were still holding out; there seemed to have been a general *sauve qui peut* among the Ba-Ngala, and contradictory reports came from every witness.

The court-martial was brought to an end, and a palaver held with the Ba-Ngala, in which the latter refused to give up the goods they had brought down from the Falls. Things now began to look serious, and a row with the Ba-Ngala seemed imminent. The two Krupp guns were turned round from the river with their muzzles towards the village, and some men set to work the ramrods in and out, in order to make the natives think they were loading them. At last the Ba-Ngala yielded, and the guns and other goods were returned, and then we saw from what they brought in that some great disaster must have happened, and that the two Europeans, if not already dead, must be holding their own at a very great disadvantage. It also came out that the Houssas and Ba-Ngala had attacked a village on their way down river, and captured eight women and children. These were also handed over to Captain Coquilhat.

I had in the meantime been getting the steamer ready, and, on the 11th, Captain Coquilhat and myself went on board with thirty-two men—nine of whom were deserters from the Falls. The corporal, Mahomed Tenné, was put in irons and chained up inside the house,—Captain Coquilhat giving orders that he was not to be released till we had returned from Stanley Falls and his guilt or innocence was proved. We only took three Zanzibaris, and these because they were the only men who knew how to work the steamer. There were also three Ba-Ngala, one of whom, named Dua, afterwards attached himself to the station in the capacity of interpreter; the rest of our men were Houssas.

The *Stanley* had brought up from Léopoldville a whale-boat 30 feet long. This was now lashed alongside the little *A.I.A.*, and both boats were heavily loaded with arms, men, ammunition, and provisions. We also took on board the eight women and children captured by the Ba-Ngala, as Captain Coquilhat intended, if possible, to restore them to their homes. These, together with ourselves and our two boys, made a total of forty-four,— no light load for our little steamer. It must be remembered that, at this time, Captain Coquilhat's orders were to leave the command of Stanley Falls entirely to Mr Deane; and that, although he had been for some days suffering severely from dysentery, he did not for a second hesitate to act on his own responsibility and good judgment, and started off with only thirty-two men — some of whom were not to be depended upon—to the rescue of his brother officers at the Falls.

We reached the strongly fortified village of Ikolungu on the second day, and Upoto on the sixth or seventh. As we passed the latter place, we were much surprised to find that, while in one village the natives appeared friendly, and invited us to come and buy food, their neighbours got up a furious war-dance, and waved spears and shields at us. Captain Coquilhat told me his opinion was that the Houssas and Ba-Ngala had attacked some of these villages as they passed down the river, and that he would stop and inquire into the matter on his return, as he could not depend on the Snider cartridges on board being good. Up to this time I had heard nothing about the bad cartridges, and it was not till some days later that I realised the full gravity of the situation, and learnt that many of the cartridges Mr Deane had had at the Falls had failed to explode, and that, before leaving Bangala, the Houssas had come to Captain Coquilhat and declared themselves ready to do anything he wished, provided he would give them good cartridges. Some of these cartridges were undoubtedly bad in themselves, as they were in their original air-tight soldered cases till I took them out for use, and looked perfectly good—and yet missed fire by the dozen. I believe the defect was in the caps, as, after our return to Bangala,

I extracted some of them and placed them on an anvil, and they failed to explode when struck with a hammer. The majority, however, had become damp through having the air-tight cases cut open for examination at Boma, and then being re-packed in wooden boxes without re-soldering the zinc cases. When, a few days later, on nearing the Falls, I opened case after case, and found the zinc lining cut and the cartridges covered with verdigris, I felt very much like shooting all the cartridge manufacturers and packers in creation.

Some days after this we arrived at Yambunga, a village standing on an island. This being the place whence the Houssas had captured the women and children, Captain Coquilhat restored them to their friends, and the natives made him a present of goats and fowls. This was a very gratifying exchange, and left us a little more room in the crowded boats.

On September 22d, twelve days after leaving Bangala, we reached the mouth of the Aruhwimi, and became familiar with the boom of the great war-drums, used by the tribes round Stanley Falls as more civilised nations use the electric telegraph.[1] That the country was now thoroughly aroused was

[1] These drums can be heard for a distance of about two miles. Before I understood the Ba-Ngala language, Dua used to indicate to me that we were approaching a village by imitating the action of beating one of these drums loudly or softly, according to the distance we were from the place.

evident, for these drums boomed almost continuously day and night. Dua, who had previously been in this country, was now constantly employed in shouting questions to the natives, to which they returned very contradictory answers, some asserting one thing and some another. Comparing one statement with another, the information received seemed, on the whole, to amount to this—that Deane had beaten off the Arabs, and was holding out; but this, from what we already knew, we could scarcely believe. Captain Coquilhat's boy, Katembo, who was a native of these parts, also tried questioning the people, but with no better success.

I had at this time a very fat, porpoise-like boy, who came from a village a little above the Aruhwimi. This boy acted as cook, and had orders from Captain Coquilhat to extinguish the fire every night, after he had finished cooking our dinner. One night, about the time we were passing the Aruhwimi, he had the fire still alight, with a pot of boiling water on the top, and the captain ordered him to extinguish it. He threw a little water on the fire, and, as the captain walked away, stooped down, and tried to blow up the embers into a flame again. Happening to look round, and seeing how his orders were being obeyed, Captain Coquilhat returned, and the boy, in his hurry to escape, upset himself on the top of his fire and the pot of boiling water. With one bound and a yell he leapt overboard, and lay howling in about two feet of water. Captain Coquilhat, fearing he might get drowned, called out to me, and with the help of three or four Houssas I hauled him into the steamer. He was fearfully scalded, and in rolling about in the water, had got the burns covered with sand, which must have given him terrible pain. I then cleaned his wounds, and dressed them with oil. So much for the burning; now for the result. A few days later we came to Orera's native village; and the inhabitants, seeing him lying in the bow of the steamer—his black skin piebald from the scalding he had received—wanted to buy him of Captain Coquilhat for culinary purposes, on the plea that he was fine and fat, nearly dead, and already half-cooked!

Ever since we left Bangala, Captain Coquilhat had been getting worse instead of better. He could eat nothing but a little soup, and I began to fear he would not be able to hold out till we reached Kinsi Katini.[1] As we approached the Falls, we discovered plenty of traces of the slave-raiders—whole villages burned to the ground, and the natives living in canoes, hidden along the wooded banks or on the islands in the river, besides the tales told us everywhere of the cruelty of the Arabs—tales of wanton murder,

[1] The Zanzibari name for Stanley Falls.

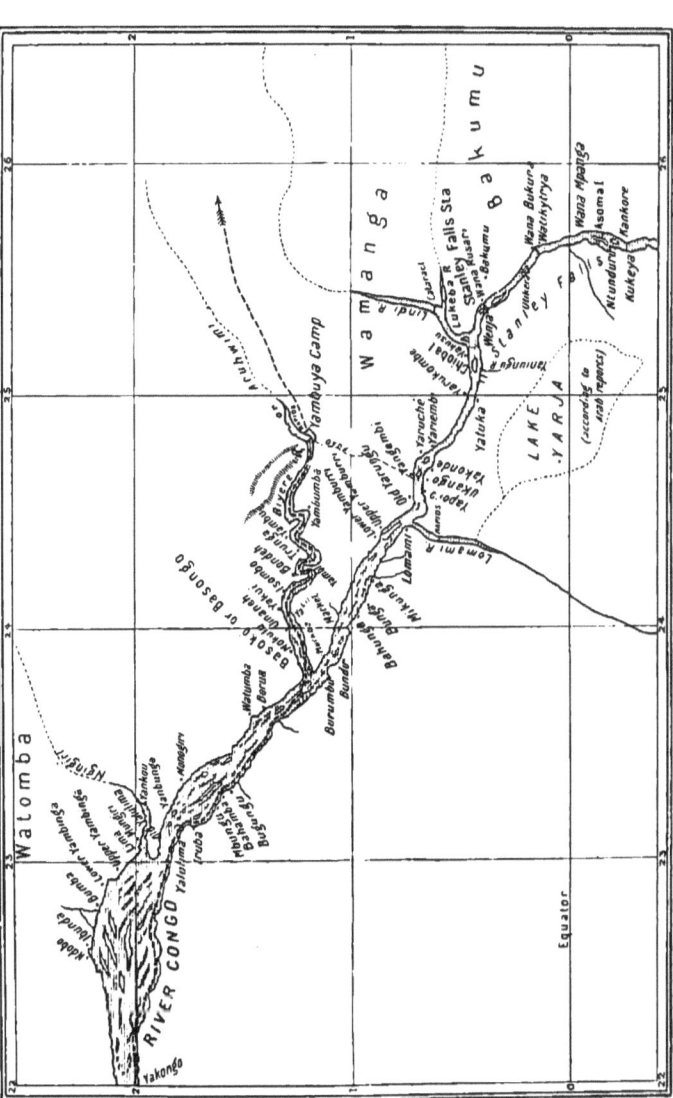

MAP OF STANLEY FALLS DISTRICT.

This Map is after Mr Stanley's, in his book, 'The Congo and Founding of its Free State;' by kind permission of Messrs Sampson Low & Co.

and women and children flogged to death in sheer brutality.

Soon after passing the Lomami we came on an Arab camp at Yaporo, and were saluted with a shower of shot; but as we were quite out of range, it took no effect, and being in haste to reach the Falls, we reserved our reply for a future occasion, and passed on. Next day we passed several villages, but the natives were shy and frightened, and would not sell us food. At last, having passed all the islands, and reached a part of the Congo where it ran between high banks in one united stream, we came to Yarukombe. Right opposite, on the south bank, is another village called Yatuka. As the natives of Yarukombe seemed disposed to be friendly, Captain Coquilhat stopped here, and made the chief a large present. About three hours after leaving this place, when passing Chioba island, we suddenly struck a rock right in the centre of the channel, but did no damage beyond a slight dent in one of the bow-plates of the whale-boat.

On the morning of September 26th, we steamed past the mouth of the Lukebu, and approached Stanley Falls. Captain Coquilhat was so much worse, that I thought he could scarcely live more than two or three days longer, and what made matters still more distressing was the fact that I could do nothing for him. As we neared the Falls he roused himself, and taking his captain's coat and cap from his box, put them on, in order that, if he met Bwana Nzigé, or any other Arab chief, he might appear in his official capacity. He then lay down, and so weak did he seem that I hardly thought he would be able to stand up again. Shortly after this, one of the men caught sight of Falls Station, and I, as I had been instructed, went to the captain and informed him of the fact. In an instant he was on his feet, opera-glass in hand, eagerly inquiring if we could see the flag of the State, and for the next three or four days he seemed to have taken a new lease of health, and in fact kept up till Deane had been rescued, and we were safe out of the Arab territory, running free for Bangala, when he was once more prostrated. It was not till two years later, when I myself was suffering from dysentery, that I realised the tremendous force of will Captain Coquilhat possessed, and the awful effort he must have made to rouse himself to his duties in the way he did.

We only caught a glimpse of the station, for we had to steer for the opposite side of the river in order to avoid some rocks, and soon lost sight of it. Here some Bakumu natives came out of the bush, and informed us that the station had been burnt, and that one of the two white men had been drowned while trying to escape. On being asked which one, they replied that it was the one who had come up with the *Stanley*, and we knew that poor Lieutenant Dubois, who had not been four months in Africa, was gone over to the majority.

As we steamed round the next point, our worst fears were confirmed. The blue flag with the golden star no longer floated over the island of Wana Rusari, and blackened patches of ground were all that remained of the station of which Captain Shagerstrom said, when talking about it a year later, that "there never was such a station, and never will be such a station on the Congo again."

When within 500 yards of the island, we suddenly grounded on a sunken reef of rocks, and, as if this had been a preconcerted signal, a crowd of men, among whom we could distinguish many white-shirted Arabs, came running down to the shore and began firing at us. We were within twenty yards of the north bank. Captain Coquilhat, ordering all the men into the water to push the steamer off, jumped up on the sun-deck with two or three of the best shots, and began to return the fire of the Arabs. Then followed a *mauvais quart-d'heure*. The boat would not move; so, as there was plenty of steam, I sent my fireman and greaser into the water to help the other men, and filling up the magazine of my Winchester rifle, I went to the engine myself, and, turning the steam full on at the boiler, worked her with the reversing lever with one hand, while I held my Winchester to my shoulder with the other, and now and then, as I got a chance, let go a snap shot at the Arabs. Fortunately for us, they were too far off to do us any damage. Had they been any nearer, the chances are that none of us would have come out alive, as nearly all our men were in the water trying to push off the boat, and could not have defended themselves. At last she began to move, and I hastily pulled the reversing lever to put the engines astern. The valves refused to move, so I gave the links a kick with my foot: the engines went astern, but the forward valve-rod jammed, and could not move far enough, so that it bent the eccentric rod, but luckily not enough to disable us. However, we were not yet clear, for no sooner were we off one rock than the current forced us on another. This occurred three times, but we managed to get clear at last, and, turning tail on the Arabs, steamed away down to where we had seen the Bakumu, who informed us that Deane was hiding from the enemy in the bush. One of these Bakumu, named Samba, who had been in the station with Deane, came on board to help us to search for him. By Samba's aid we traced his camps down as far as the junction of the Lukebu with the Congo: there we lost all trace of him, and as it was getting dark, were obliged to camp for the night. Next day we learnt from some Bakumu that he had bought a canoe and was gone—down river, said some; up the Lukebu, said others. Captain Coquilhat decided on the down-river course as the most likely one, and off we started, searching first one bank and then the other— occasionally blowing our steam-whistle (as we had done all the previous day), in case Deane might be out of sight in the dense jungle;—now chasing a solitary frightened native in a tiny canoe, in order, if possible, to get some information from him; now pausing for a few seconds while Samba, whose eagle eye had detected the smoke from a camp-fire in the jungle, shouted questions to, and received answers from, invisible Bakumu and Wenya, and then again running for a mile or two without seeing a sign of life. The little *A.I.A.* seemed to appreciate the necessity for haste as much as we did, and she never steamed better. I gave her all the steam I could, and her cranks became almost invisible as they flew round, while the fireman, having very good wood, kept the steam up to blowing-off point. We knew Deane had a good twenty-four hours' start, at least, and were afraid that he would reach Yaporo and be attacked by the Arabs before we could come up with him. Even supposing he managed to pass Yaporo in safety, there were hostile natives below; and once he reached the broad part of the stream, with its numerous channels and islands, how could we ever hope to find him? It would be like looking for a needle in a haystack. And how could a man who, as we learnt from Samba, had been thirty days in the bush, living on what he could pick up, possibly get safely over the 500 miles that separated him from Bangala, without goods to purchase food from the natives, or arms to defend himself against the cannibal tribes who had twice before treacherously attacked him?

The speed at which we were going soon began to tell on the engines, and finding the bearings were getting hot, I turned on cold water from the service-pipes. They were just cooling down again when I heard a knocking, the meaning of which I knew only too well: one of the connecting-rod bolts had become slack, and I should be obliged to stop. We were again approaching the village of Yarukombe, and I went to Captain Coquilhat and told him we must pull up for a few minutes or break down completely. Just at this moment, Samba, who had been shouting to some natives, turned and spoke to the captain, who then asked me if I could not keep on a little longer, as Deane was reported to be at Yarukombe. We had still over a mile to go, but I determined to risk it, and going to the engine, stood with my hand on the stop-valve, in case anything should break. The knocking of the loose rod was awful, and I expected the cylinder-

CAPTAIN COQUILHAT.

cover to give way every second. Captain Coquilhat, becoming alarmed at the noise, came and asked me if I thought the engine would hold out. I replied, " It must." Just then a shout from our men drew my attention to a canoe which had put out from Yarukombe, in which were two or three red-shirted Houssas. In response to Captain Coquilhat's questions, one of them called out that Deane was alive and safe at Yarukombe. Greatly relieved, I slowed down, and the canoe came alongside. On board was the Houssa sergeant-major, who had been with Deane, and who now, as we slowly steamed up to the village, told us that the latter was lying in a hut, very sick, and hardly able to move. As soon as our bows touched the bank Captain Coquilhat was ashore, and mounting the steep slope to the village ; while I—leaving to the men the task of getting out the anchor—set to work to put the engine right, for which I had already got out the tools. This did not take long; and then, leaving one of the men to clear up and put away the tools, I began to prepare a bed for Mr Deane, who was presently carried down by the Houssas, under the direction of Captain Coquilhat. He was alive, but that was about all, and it was some minutes before he could get strength enough to speak. All the clothes he had on consisted of a piece of blanket tied round his loins, and he was covered with sores from sleeping night after night

H

on the hard ground. A little Madeira wine (of which Captain Coquilhat had a case among his private stores) soon revived him, however, and the chief of Yarukombe having come on board, a palaver was held, at the end of which Captain Coquilhat gave the chief ten percussion-muskets (all he had on board) and several kegs of powder, and promised that he would return and bring him a hundred more muskets, and that the Arabs should be driven out.

The sergeant-major, three Houssas, and four boys, who had remained faithful to Mr Deane, now came on board, with all that the latter had saved from the station. The inventory of these articles was a very short one. A watch, a pair of opera-glasses, a pair of boots, a revolver, and six cartridges, were all he possessed; while the sergeant-major had brought away a Martini rifle.

Samba having decided to accompany us to Bangala, we started again about noon; and as we had to pass the Arab settlement at Yaporo, we made ready for a fight. All the cartridges were sorted out, and the good ones distributed to the Houssas. The boxes and bales of cloth were piled up along the sides of the steamer, and, thus cleared for action, we prepared to make it as hot as possible for the Arabs. As we neared Yaporo, we could see men in long white shirts running about, as well as a crowd of black figures, evidently in a state of great excitement. Deane, who had wonderfully revived since coming on board, now asked for his revolver. As it had been in the water, and was pretty rusty, I oiled it up, and replacing the cartridges with some of my own, handed it to him. He at once raised himself on his elbow, saying that, if he was too weak to use a rifle, there was no reason why he should not shoot with the revolver, if we approached near enough. As we neared the Arab camp they opened fire long before we were within range; but we soon let them have enough, and they disappeared behind trees, whence they kept up a pretty hot fire, while all we could do was to watch till a head or arm emerged, and then "draw a bead on it."

Once or twice a gleam of white among the grass showed that a shot had told, and an Arab received a dose of lead. About the centre of the village the Arabs had planted numerous canoes upright in the ground, and, standing inside them, fired at us through holes cut in the bottom. Captain Coquilhat had intended to storm and burn the place, and accordingly, on reaching the upper end, we had slowed down. Leaving the engine in charge of the greaser, I had taken up my Martini, and was having good practice at snap-shooting, as now and then I caught sight of a white-turbaned black head protruded from behind a tree, when the man at the wheel got a shot (apparently) through the jaws, and, letting go, fell to the bottom of the boat with a tremendous outcry. The *A.I.A.* swung round, end on to the shore, and received a raking fire fore and aft, which wounded Captain Coquilhat and twelve others, and would have been still more destructive had he not, with his wounded arm, seized the wheel and brought her round on her former course. Just at this juncture the Houssas, having exhausted their stock of cartridges, came pouring out of the whale-boat into the steamer, with blood-bespattered clothes and faces, asking for ammunition, and I had to turn my attention to supplying their wants. When I was once more free to look round we had passed Yaporo, and Captain Coquilhat was consulting with Deane as to whether or not it would be advisable to accede to the demands of the Houssas, who were yelling for vengeance, and go back and make another attempt to storm the Arab camp, which, as nearly as I could judge, seemed to contain about 200 men. Against these we had only some thirty men, twelve of whom were wounded; and as we now found out, not half the cartridges we had were of any use. In addition to this, we were running short of fuel for the steamer, so prudence was allowed to get the better of valour, and we continued our course down-stream. I now turned my attention to the medicine-chest;—none of the men were killed, and the wounds received were not very serious. Indeed the man at the wheel—as I found, to my great disgust, when he came to me to get his chin dressed—had nothing whatever the matter, except that the skin was scratched by a splinter of lead. The shot that had entered Captain Coquilhat's arm just before he seized the wheel was by far the worst wound of the lot, and it was several days before we could find and extract the lead. We had no means of knowing the loss of the Arabs, but I am certain that several were killed and a good many wounded.

Deane, now he was safe on board, began to pick up very rapidly, though still suffering severely from rheumatic pains in his head. He was a very tall man—quite six feet, if not more—and both Captain Coquilhat and myself being very small, the difficulty was how to clothe him. Luckily I had some rather large-sized *pyjamas*, and with these, and a flannel shirt of the captain's, he managed till we reached Bangala, though the legs of the former articles were too short to reach much below his knees.

Deane's account of the events that followed the departure of the *Stanley*, though one of the most thrilling tales on record, I must necessarily make very brief, as—though I heard it bit by bit on the run down from the Lomami to Bangala—I had so much to do every day, between dressing the men's wounds and looking after the work of the steamer, that I neglected till too late to write it down. Captain Coquilhat, too, now that the excitement was over, was getting perceptibly weaker, and I again began to fear that he would never reach Léopold-ville alive. I myself had kept in remarkably good health, though I was also beginning to feel tired, and to wish for a rest in the station.

Deane had been very much disappointed when the *Stanley* arrived in August without the expected reinforcements in men and ammunition, especially as he thought that the Arabs had seized the woman from his station merely in order to furnish a pretext for a quarrel, and distrusted their professed wish for peace. He borrowed all the cartridges he could from Captain Anderson of the *Stanley*, but these did not amount to more than three rounds for each of his men, and as it turned out when they came to be used, most of them were bad, and would not go off. The day after the *Stanley* left, some natives came and told him that the Arabs were preparing to attack him; and sure enough they did, keeping up the attack for three days. Deane and Dubois, having to fight all day and keep watch all night, were naturally becoming exhausted, and Deane was suffering with severe pains in the head and bleeding from the ears—a result of the continual concussions to which he was subjected while firing off the two Krupp guns at the upper end of the station: a third Krupp at the lower end of the island was worked by Dubois.

On the fourth day, the Houssas, having no more

cartridges, came to him and told him they meant to leave the station. Deane tried to persuade them to hold out, telling them that in thirty days' time help would arrive; but they persisted in their intention, and all he could do was to induce them to wait till night, when he promised to evacuate the station under cover of the darkness. He and Dubois at once set about their preparations. They cut the throats of all the goats, let all the fowls out into the bush, poured some demijohns of petroleum they had in the store over the bales of cloth and other inflammable material, laid a train to the powder-magazine, and, as soon as it was dark, took the breech-pieces, linch-pins, cottas, &c., out of the Krupp guns, and threw them into the river. Everything went fairly well, and had their men had the least pluck or steadiness in them, every one would probably have embarked in safety, and in due time reached Bangala. But no sooner was it dark than some of the men broke into the store, and carried off part of the goods. A panic at once ensued; the Houssas and Ba-Ngala rushed for the canoes and went off down river, without leaving Deane and Dubois, and the eight Houssas and boys who remained in the station, a single vessel in which to escape. About midnight the station was fired, and Deane and Dubois, wading across the narrow channel which separates the island of Wana Rusari from the right bank, took to the bush, and left Kinsi Katini for ever. In clambering along the bank Dubois slipped into the water, and was carried off by the current. Deane sprang after him, and succeeded in getting him on to a rock, which Dubois clutched in a half-unconscious way. Supposing him to be safe for the moment, Deane let go his hold for a few seconds, in order to regain his own footing; and before he could again catch him, Dubois had slipped off and was seen no more. He had left Europe only five months before, and had been but nine days at the station — a brave young fellow, much liked by every one who knew him, swept away without leaving a trace, like poor Delatte of the *A.I.A.*

For the next twenty-six or twenty-eight days Deane wandered about in the bush, moving from one camp to another, to keep out of the way of the Arabs, living on almost anything he could pick up; going at night to the outskirts of villages and cutting some green bananas, or digging some manioc root, which he cooked in an old broken pot found on a native grave. At last he was obliged to eat caterpillars and wood-worms, the latter being fat white creatures about three inches long, and from half an inch to five-eighths of an inch in diameter. The Ba-Ngala esteem them a luxury, but Deane must have been very hungry before he could bring himself to eat them. I have myself often found them in dead trees when getting wood for the steamer, and on one occasion, remembering Deane's experience, got the Ba-Ngala to cook some for me; but, when it came to the point of eating, I backed out, and contented myself with watching the niggers enjoy them.

At last, having reached the extreme end of the peninsula between the Congo and Lukebu, Deane managed to purchase a canoe from a native chief, and set off down river. Some time before this—I believe soon after his escape from the station—he had taken off his clothes, which had got wet, and hung them in the sun to dry. While they were drying, an alarm was raised that the Arabs were upon them, and Deane made off, literally *sans* everything. One of his men had an old blanket, which he tied round him after the fashion of the natives, and in this style of costume he remained till found by us. He did not go very far the first night after buying the canoe, and was camped somewhere just above Yarukombe, when an alarm of Arabs or hostile natives was again raised, and all his men and boys rushed for the canoe, leaving Deane—who was now too weak to stand—lying on the ground. All the means of defence he possessed was his revolver, and the six cartridges with which it was loaded. He afterwards told me he was reserving these six cartridges in case he should be captured by the Arabs, meaning to shoot down the five most important men he could get at, and put the sixth ball through his own head, sooner than fall alive into their hands. He was crawling towards the canoe when a huge native rushed up, and would have speared him had Deane not covered him with his revolver. After dodging about trying to get a chance to throw his spear, the native suddenly paused: Deane, reluctant to waste a cartridge, did not fire; and the native, lowering his spear, came a little closer, and, perceiving who it was, suddenly shouted, "*Mundélé! mundélé!*" This was the chief of Yarukombe, to whom Captain Coquilhat had made a present only the day before. He now explained to Deane that he had taken him for an Arab, and brought him to his village, telling him that a steamer had gone up river, and would be down again in a day or two. To convince him, he showed him Captain Coquilhat's presents, and fortunately induced him to remain till we arrived and rescued him—on exactly the thirtieth day after he had tried to persuade the Houssas not to desert him, by telling them that reinforcements would arrive in thirty days.

We steamed down river, finding no trace of the twenty odd Houssas who were still missing, and on October 3d duly arrived at Bangala. Here we found the *Henry Reed*—the A.B.M.U. steamer, which had been chartered by the State—with Captain Van Gèle on board. She brought orders for Captain Coquilhat to take command of the

Falls — in exact contradiction to his last orders, which directed him to leave the command to Mr Deane. The Falls Station was now no more: and thus ended an ill-advised attempt to direct operations at an isolated post in the very heart of Africa, —over 1500 miles from the nearest telegraph-station,—from headquarters in Europe.

On October 6th the *Henry Reed* left for Equator, and next day I followed in the *A.I.A.*, taking Deane and Captain Coquilhat. The latter, now that his work was done, seemed to sink rapidly into a kind of stupor. At Equator Station, Captain Van Gèle took him up to the house, and by the help of Mr McKittrick, one of the missionaries, succeeded in partially arresting the dysentery. Captain Van Gèle had a whole pile of wood ready cut, from which he directed me to help myself, saying that I had two sick men on board, and must get to the doctor as fast as possible. Thanks to his forethought, I was able to get nearly four days' fuel on board before dark; and next day started for Léopoldville, where I arrived safely on October 15th, and was heartily pleased to see Dr Mense waiting on the beach, ready to take charge of the two invalids—both of whom soon began to recover under his care. Captain Coquilhat was at once despatched to Europe, where, I am happy to say, he arrived all right. But he had had too severe a shaking to recover all at once; and when

I met him at Brussels, more than two years later, he told me that he still had to take care of himself, as he was only just getting over the effects of our trip to Kinsi Katini. Deane's constitution must have been made of steel, for less than a year had passed before he was back again in Africa, and I again had the pleasure of once more meeting the defender of Stanley Falls.

Several times in the course of this narrative, I have had occasion to mention Samba; and as his name will occur in the succeeding chapters, a few words about his history may not be out of place here. He belongs to the Bakumu tribe, who inhabit a stretch of country on the right bank of the Congo, just above Stanley Falls. Some years ago he was sold by these people as a slave to the natives of Yambunga and was bought from them by some traders of Lulanga, who had gone up to Yambunga to purchase ivory. Some time after, he was again sold by them to the people of Irebu, and by them passed on to Chumbiri, only to be again sold to some native trader at Ntamo. He would probably have been passed on in this way till he reached the coast, had not Stanley bought him, and taken him up the river when he went to found Stanley Falls Station. Here he was left, probably to act as interpreter; but he made himself useful in many other ways, especially by his hunting expeditions, from which he always returned with some fresh meat or fish for the station. Shortly after Mr Deane took command of the Falls, Samba, with two Houssas, was out in a canoe above the cataracts. The canoe, drawn into the rapids, was carried over the fall into the roaring channel below. The two Houssas were drowned, but Samba saved himself by swimming, though how he escaped being dashed to pieces on the rocks passes my comprehension. When the station was attacked by the Arabs, Samba proved himself the best fighter among the black men there; and I have several times heard Mr Deane praise his courage and faithfulness. When all seemed lost, and the station had been blown up, Samba provided himself with a spear, and took to the bush; and, though he did not now remain with Mr Deane, continued to supply him with food, and so kept him from absolute starvation. When Deane was obliged to take to a canoe and go down the river, Samba, unaware of the fact, remained behind; and when Captain Coquilhat and myself arrived in the *A.I.A.*, he came on board, and led us from one to another of Mr Deane's hiding-places, only to discover the smouldering remains of his camp-fires. It was Samba who found out from some other natives that Mr Deane had purchased a canoe and gone down-stream; and again coming on board, with his sole earthly possessions—a loin-cloth and a spear (which latter I bought from him, and still have)—accompanied us to the village, where at length we found Mr Deane, and thence to Bangala. Here he still lives, in hopes of some day returning to his people, when his great enemies, the slave-raiding Arabs, have been driven out. Until the authority of the Free State is in some measure re-established in that region, it will not be safe for Samba to show his face there; for he is a marked man among the Arabs, and has done them too much injury to hope for mercy should he fall into their hands. The particulars of his earlier history I had from himself, and only regret that I do not know enough of the native languages to get a fuller account, as it would form a most interesting narrative, and would give some idea of the Congo before it was ever seen by Stanley. He is the only instance I ever met with of a native who showed any gratitude either by word or deed. Freed by Bula Matari, he has faithfully served the State ever since; whereas most natives, on being rescued from slavery by the white man, try to run away, and if successful, perhaps help their former masters to fight against their deliverer. If a native gives a present, he expects to receive ten times its value in return. If you find a man dying by the wayside, save him, and restore him to his people, you will not get a word of thanks from him or his; but he will think you a fool for not tying him up and demanding a high price from his tribe for his release, with the alternative of selling him into slavery if it is not paid. Were all natives such as Samba, the regeneration of Africa would be comparatively easy.

CHAPTER VI.

EXPLORATION OF THE NGALA RIVER.

OVERHAULING THE *A.I.A.*—CAPTAIN BAYLEY AT NSHASSA—BEGIN-
NING OF THE RAINY SEASON—START FOR BANGALA—DISSECTION
OF A HIPPO — HOSTILE NATIVES — ORDERS TO EXPLORE THE
NGALA—THE OUBANGI-WELLÉ—POSITION OF BANGALA STATION
—THE OUBANGI AND THE NGIRI—MOBEKA—UP THE NGALA
WITHOUT A GUIDE—MANKULA—VILLAGE BUILT ON PILES—
TERROR OF THE NATIVES — RAPIDS — HOSTILITIES WITH THE
SAIBIS—RETURN—AFFAIR OF THE HIPPO—TORNADOES—ARRIVAL
OF THE *STANLEY*.

CAPTAIN COQUILHAT, having left orders for me to take the steamer and whale-boat back to Bangala, was carried off on his way to the coast in a hammock, and I turned my attention to overhauling the little *A.I.A.*—as, after her late spell of hard work, she sorely wanted it. Everything was ready for a start by October 23d; so M. Lemarinel (who had, during my absence, succeeded Baron Nimpsch as chief of Léopoldville) decided to send down the cargo to me on Monday, so that I could get away early on Tuesday morning.

On Sunday I walked over to Nshassa Station, then under the charge of Captain Bayley, the best hunter and coolest shot on the Congo. Here also I met Mr Swinburne, the founder of Nshassa Station, who, after serving some five years, or more, with Stanley, had returned to Europe. He was now back again in Africa for the Sanford Exploring Expedition — a new company, formed at Brussels, to exploit the Upper Congo and Kassai.

At this time it was a question whether or not the station of Léopoldville should be removed to Nshassa; and the State having refused to part with the latter place to the Sanford Company, Mr Swinburne was building a station of his own just above the village of Nshassa, in the centre of which the old station stood. As there was no timber round Nshassa, he had to fetch all the materials for his house from Long (Bamu) Island, in Stanley Pool; so, hearing I was down with the *A.I.A.*, he sent a request to M. Lemarinel to let him have the use of the steamer for one day, to fetch this timber over. Accordingly, my departure was delayed for a day; and on Monday I went to Long Island, where I found Captain Bayley in camp, with a huge heap of timber, which I transferred to Nshassa—Captain Bayley remaining behind with a canoe, to try if he could not find a buffalo or an antelope.

On Tuesday I loaded up with a pretty heavy

cargo of brass wire, beads, bales of cloth, and boxes of provisions and ammunition; and on Wednesday, October 27th, I left, saying good-bye to Captain Anderson, who was shortly to start for Europe. The rainy season had begun, and the rain poured down in torrents, beating in under the sun-deck, and as it was no use trying to keep dry, I made up my mind to get wet. In addition to this, we had on board as much cargo as it was safe to carry, and steamed very slowly—so that, all things considered, I did not have a very pleasant start. After stopping for a few minutes at Nshassa to take a letter or two from Captain Bayley, I went on to Kimpopo—where Bishop Taylor's missionaries had occupied the old State station—and as it was getting late, camped there for the night.

Léopoldville had been very short of meat when I left, and two or three fowls were all that could be spared. I had also some difficulty in persuading the natives to sell fowls, and only succeeded in getting two at Kwamouth (given me by the French missionaries), and two at Bolobo. My men, too, had nothing but rice and *chikwanga* (cassava bread) to eat—so that there was a general rejoicing when we came upon a hippo standing in very shallow water, and I managed to bowl him over with a shot behind the ear. We stopped a day to cut him up and dry some of the meat. As he was very heavy, the men could not manage to drag

him up on dry ground; but they got on one side
of him, and the huge brute, being very fat, was
ignominiously rolled along the sand-bank like a
beer-barrel till he was in very shallow water, when
the Ba-Ngala (of whom I had three on board)
ripped him open, and one of them, getting right
into his inside, began to heave out armful after
armful of still undigested grass. By the time he
had finished, the hippo did not look nearly so plump
as he had done before, but was much more handy,
and was soon cut up.

Nothing worth mentioning happened after this
till we were nearly at Equator, when, for some
reason or other, the natives of a village we were
passing suddenly came running out in war-paint,
and, waving spears and shields, invited us to come
ashore and fight them. As we took no notice, but
quietly steamed on, some, more adventurous than
the rest, ran along the bank, and getting into a
large canoe some distance ahead, pushed out, and
tried to intercept us by putting the canoe right
across our bows. As they persisted in keeping
right in our way, my men began to get out their
guns, and I had some difficulty in preventing their
shooting. However, one Zanzibari, who had been
a long time in the country, and could speak
English, seconded me so well that they desisted,
and I turned my attention to the canoe, which
was moving backwards and forwards ahead of us,

keeping right in our course whichever way we turned—the natives evidently thinking we should be compelled to fight them. Putting on full steam, I then took the wheel, and made right for the centre of the canoe. Just at the last minute they tried to avoid us by turning; but I saw their intention in time, and turned too, and catching the canoe fair and square amidships with an awful crash, cut her clean in two. I never saw a more astonished expression than that shown by the faces of these natives, as they disappeared into the water and struck out for the shore. One, indeed, hung for a few seconds on to the whale-boat; but a blow across the knuckles soon made him let go, and we continued our way in peace, arriving safely at Bangala on November 14th, when I handed Captain Coquilhat's despatches to Lieutenant Baert.

These despatches instructed Mr Baert to explore a river called the Ngala, which empties itself into the Congo about forty or forty-five miles above Iboko. To account for the importance attached to this expedition, it will be necessary to explain that at this time the French claimed both banks of the *lower* Oubangi river, which has since proved to be the lower course of the Wellé. Had the Ngala turned out to be—as was thought—an outlet for the upper waters of the Oubangi, the French would probably have had their claim allowed. A few words about the situation of the station will also make matters clearer.

Bangala Station stands on the north bank of the Congo, in the town of Iboko, which forms the centre of a ten-mile line of towns and villages inhabited by the Ba-Ngala tribe. This settlement is surrounded on three sides by swamp, and on the fourth the river Congo cuts off all communication except by boat. According to native accounts, it is possible in the dry season to go some two days' journey inland; and I should think it quite practicable to penetrate as far as the Oubangi: but, as the tribes on the banks of that river are hostile to the Ba-Ngala, I had no means of ascertaining the fact, and I have never been more than six or seven hours' journey in that direction myself. I found the country gently undulating—the rising ground for the most part cleared and cultivated, and the hollows filled with a dense scrub, which, in the wet season, grew out of three or four feet of water, sometimes more. After some three hours' journey inland, all cultivation ceases, and the path runs through one continuous jungle of scrub, there being very few large trees.

When I first arrived at Bangala, the officers in that station had a theory that the Oubangi emptied itself into the Congo by several mouths, one of which was thought to be the Ngala river. This theory was hotly discussed until it proved to be false, and then it was charitably put down as one of Mr Grenfell's mistakes. I myself do not believe that Mr Grenfell ever held that theory, as, from the descriptions I have heard of the Oubangi river, no one who had been up it could suppose that it made use of the Ngala river as an outlet to the Congo. I am sorry to say that I never thought of asking Mr Grenfell when I saw him what his impressions of the Ngala really were. I will presently describe the exploration of the Ngala by Mr Baert and myself, but, before doing so, will proceed to give my reasons for thinking that, instead of the Oubangi supplying water to the Ngala, both the Ngala and the Congo empty some of their water during the greater part of the year into the Oubangi —this water, of course, re-entering the Congo at the mouth of the Oubangi.

In passing up and down the river, between the station and the mouth of the Ngala, I noticed several channels, from 50 to 100 yards wide, into which the water of the main river seemed to flow. These channels are reported by natives to lead into the Ngiri river, a small tributary of the Oubangi, which was explored by Captain Van Gèle, and reported by him to flow east to west. Captain Van Gèle traced its course till he was close to the longitude of Bangala Station, when he was obliged to turn back on account of the stream being choked with weeds and grass. In December 1887, I noticed,

THE *A.I.I.* AT BANGALA.

FROM A PHOTOGRAPH BY CAPTAIN COQUILHAT.

To face page 134.

after a sudden fall in the waters of the Congo, that the water from these channels ran into and not out of the river, from which I concluded—supposing these channels to be connected with the Ngiri—that the waters of the Oubangi were not falling as fast as those of the Congo, and that the latter river was therefore receiving some of the water of the Ngiri, which usually went to the Oubangi.

On November 22d, Mr Baert started in the *A.I.A.*, accompanied by me. As my journal of this trip has been lost, I can only give a very superficial account from memory, and what little information I have noted down on a map of the river which I made at the time, and still possess.

About the middle of the second day, we entered the mouth of the Ngala river, which, for the last five miles of its course, flows almost parallel with the Congo—its width being about 300 yards. After this, it takes a bend towards the north, and just at this bend is a narrow channel, some 60 to 70 yards wide, and about half a mile long, connecting with the Congo. The water in this channel flows out of the Congo into the Ngala river. Towards evening we arrived at Ngombe, a village of the Wabika, whose great town, Mobeka, was a few miles higher up. Up to this point, the banks of the river had been low and swampy, and here they were very little better, the villages being barely above high-water level.

Here we camped for the night—the natives being very friendly, and bringing large tusks of ivory to sell. Next morning we proceeded to Mobeka, a large native town, a little higher up the river, from whose chief, Lusengi, Mr Baert hoped to obtain a guide. In this, however, he was disappointed, as Lusengi wanted to retain the monopoly of the ivory trade on that river, and appeared to think we were going up to buy ivory. He demanded an exorbitant price for several tusks which he produced, and made out all sorts of difficulties and dangers which, he said, would befall us, if we went up the river. The text of all his arguments was, " Buy my ivory —go away home, get more money, and come back to buy more."

We did not finish the palaver that night, so a watch was set, and we turned in. About 11 P.M. Mr Baert got up, and went to see that the Houssa sentinels were all awake. Finding one, who was posted on the sun-deck of the steamer, asleep, he put his hand on his shoulder, and the man—thinking the natives were on him—sprang up, dropped his gun, and, rushing along the sun-deck towards the stern, jumped into the water, whence he was extracted, looking like a drowned cat.

Next day, failing to obtain a guide, we left, and for two or three days more, steamed between low, swampy, forest-covered banks, having a great deal of trouble every evening to find dead wood for fuel, or a piece of ground dry enough for a camp. As I have lost my journal, I cannot be sure of dates, but about the 25th of November we arrived at two villages called Mankula and Iboke—very miserable-looking places, situated on ground that was only two or three feet above the water, and exceeding in dirtiness any that I had previously visited. That we had entered a new country was evident, for the natives had their faces cut and cicatrised in a way that reminded me of the Basoko on the Aruhwimi river; in fact we afterwards had Basoko given us as the name of the tribes on the left bank, while on the right they were called Akoulas. This rule did not always hold good, for now and then we would find a village of Akoulas on the left bank, and *vice versa*.

After leaving here, we continued between the same swampy, forest-covered banks till evening, camping at night on the only piece of dry land we had seen all day. Next day we passed a small village called Mpeza, built on piles, the water, at this season of the year, having overflowed both banks of the river. The place reminded me very much of pictures I had seen of villages on Lake Mohrya, as described by Commander Cameron. The natives here, never having seen a white man or a steamer before, all ran away; so we could get no information from them beyond the name of the village. On the 27th, we saw some low hills on the right bank, and came upon a village called Mputu, where Dua (a native of Bangala, who, having been to Stanley Falls, knew something of the languages used on this part of the river) managed, after a long palaver, to obtain permission for us to land; but this was of little use, as far as buying food was concerned, for the natives were too frightened to sell much to our men. The chief, a very old man, presented Mr Baert with a bunch of bananas, two or three fowls, and a wretched-looking native dog. The latter was declined in spite of Dua's request that he should be delivered over to him, to furnish a meal for the Ba-Ngala who were with us. This village looked as dirty and miserable as Mankula, and the people were evidently cannibals; for I came across a dead tree in the centre of a small open space, round the trunk of which was a seat formed of pieces of old canoes supported on human skulls, while the leafless branches were adorned with many more of these trophies. Salt-making seemed to be the chief occupation of the natives of this place.

After leaving Mputu, the banks became higher, and the river assumed a general north-easterly course, finally turning round to north by west, and then back again to north-east. The natives here all ran away as soon as they caught sight of the steamer, many of them, who were in canoes, jumping into the water and leaving their canoes to drift down-stream. Some of them must have deserted their canoes at the mere sound of the puffing from the steamer's exhaust-pipe—for, several times, on rounding a bend of the stream, we nearly ran down empty canoes of whose owners we could not see a sign. Dua, standing on our sun-deck, and shouting into space, could only elicit a short reply from some invisible native, hidden in the bush, to the effect that we were bad spirits and were to go away. As we persisted in continuing our course, we were presently assailed with arrows made of reeds, with hard wood points; but most of them fell short, and no one was hit. The huts in the villages on this part of the river were mostly of conical form.

On November 30th, we passed two or three small tributaries on the left bank, about 70 or 80 yards wide; and the river rapidly narrowed, till, towards evening, it was barely 60 yards wide, running at the bottom of a valley between two ranges of low hills. Next day these hills gave place to bluffs, and we passed the first rapid, coming shortly afterwards to a tributary on the right bank, about 50 yards wide, which was now about the width of the main river. Shortly afterwards it narrowed down to about 30 yards, and we had to make our way through a succession of rapids, where we had only from 4 to 5 feet of water over the rocks, and round several sharp curves, till we entered a gorge between two vertical bluffs, from 30 to 40 feet high, through which the river rushed at such a rate that our little steamer could only just make headway against it. Rounding a very sharp bend, we came upon a village on the top of the left-hand bluff, the natives of which did not run away, but stood looking down at us. In answer to Dua's inquiries, they gave the name of their tribe as Saibis, and we drew alongside the bank to try and obtain further information. Taking advantage of the halt, I was proceeding to examine the engine, when a crash on the sun-deck, followed by the sharp report of a revolver, made me jump for the wheel, and in a few seconds we were tearing at full speed down the rapids, to avoid a shower of pieces of wood, stones, and arrows from the angry natives, one of whom had for some unknown reason thrown a lump of wood at Mr Baert, who had replied with his revolver. There was now nothing for it but to turn back, as the natives were all up in arms, and war-drums boomed on all sides, arousing the tribes below us, who, having got over their fear of bad spirits, now lined the banks in front of their villages, and showered arrows on us in such numbers that we were several times compelled to use our rifles to drive back the natives. From the fact that the arrows were made of light reeds, with only a hard wood point, we concluded them to be poisoned.

Going with the stream, we soon passed the villages, and came to a stretch of uninhabited country, where we found a clearing used by the natives as a market-place, and camped there for the night. There were two or three roads leading away from this market-place, and a sentry was posted at each of these, while the rest of the men cut wood for fuel, which they brought into the centre of the clearing, and proceeded to chop into smaller pieces. In the middle of the night, we were suddenly aroused by a cry from the sentries that we were attacked by the natives. Up jumped all our men, and bullets began to fly indiscriminately in all directions. Mr Baert and I jumped ashore, and made our way to where three or four Houssas were keeping up a persistent fire into the bush, where they said they had seen something moving. As this happened to be the very spot where we had tethered our goats, Mr Baert soon stopped the shooting—the alarm having merely been a ruse on the part of our sentries, who had been unable to buy meat for some days on account of the hostility of the natives, and got up a sham night-attack, in the hope of shooting a goat in the confusion.

We reached Bangala on December 5th, and a few days later I was off again to Equator Station, with letters, which were to be picked up by the *Henry Reed* steamer when she came up-river, and taken down by her to Léopoldville. When I returned to

Bangala, I found that there had been a row between some of the Zanzibaris in the station and some natives, about a hippo which had been found by the latter, and which the Zanzibaris alleged to have been shot by one of the Europeans. The natives, on the other hand, said that it had been killed with spears; and this seemed to be the truth, for no bullet-wounds could be found. However, it was now too late to patch matters up, for a Zanzibari, having gone into the villages of Mendongé, had got into a dispute with some natives about this hippo, and been attacked and wounded. On hearing this, Mr Baert took a company of Houssas, and starting out early one morning, burnt the village. This was only a day or two before Christmas; and when it arrived, instead of spending it in peace and goodwill towards men, I was steaming about all day in the little *A.I.A.*, with an Express rifle, chasing and knocking holes in all the canoes I could see, in order to prevent the natives landing at the station and burning our houses. At last, after having their villages destroyed, and losing several men, they were glad enough to come and ask for peace; and on the last day of the year the palm-tree was cut,[1] and every one retired homewards—the natives to rebuild their huts, and I to overhaul the *A.I.A.*, which had now had over six months' hard and continuous work, and wanted repairing and cleaning.

[1] The native ceremony on making peace.

We had to wait a month before we could even begin to expect the mail-steamer from Léopoldville; and things began to assume the monotony usual at isolated posts like Bangala. I tried various expedients for relieving this monotony—among others, I bought from a native a small live crocodile, about three feet six in length, and, putting a ring round his loins, in the same way in which monkeys are tied up, chained him to a palm-tree. Close to this I dug a large tank, in which he could swim as far as his chain would allow. I soon, however, got tired of him—for he used to catch unwary fowls that came to drink at his tank; and after eating half of them, he would leave the rest lying in the water, which soon became so foul that the smell was unbearable; so one day I took a knife and a revolver, and avenged the fowls.

On January 22d, 1887, we had a most tremendous tornado, the thunder lasting fully ten minutes by my watch, one peal beginning before the last had stopped. The wind was something awful—palm-trees bent like fishing-rods when a twenty-pound salmon is hooked; and I expected to see the whole station fly away bodily, but it held on. The lightning and thunder were something grand, the whole lasting from an hour and a half to two hours.

January and February seemed to be the months for storms at Bangala, for we had several in succession, between the middle of the former and the end of the latter month, in 1887. These were pretty severe, but could not hold a candle to the cyclone which swept over the station in February 1888. I use the word cyclone purposely, and with the full knowledge of its import—not, as so often happens, merely to designate a tornado or hurricane. It began blowing from the north-east, and the wind increased in strength till it drove the rain-drops against my face like shot. Banana-trees were levelled and fences blown down; every living thing disappeared, and nothing could be heard but the roar of the wind, the patter of the rain, and the creaking of the tall palm-trees, as they bent like reeds before the howling blasts, till I expected to see them uprooted and swept away. The rain was bitterly cold, and I would gladly have got under shelter, but feared that the steamer might break loose, and so was obliged to stand by her. All of a sudden, a great crash made me look up, and I found that the old station-house—which had been built by Captain Coquilhat in 1884, and was now used as a carpenter's shop—had been blown bodily over, and its roof was being carried by instalments into the river. Then came a lull, and I was thinking of going and getting into dry clothes, when the wind began again from the south-west, and was soon blowing as hard as it had previously done from the north-east. This sudden change did more harm than ever, and seriously damaged the thatch on the roofs of the new houses, so that the rain passed through and converted the clay on the top of the fire-proof ceilings into a moist paste. When I entered my room, drops of muddy water were falling on everything, and the whole place was in a fearful mess. This storm was a genuine cyclone, and a great deal more violent than the above-mentioned hurricanes and tornadoes; the wind came first from one quarter, then we had the calm centre, and after that the wind began to blow with equal violence from the opposite direction. Everything in my room was wet and dirty, and the drops of mud and water continued to come through the logs of the ceiling, which creaked with the extra weight. Nothing could be done till the water had all drained off; so, having got into some dry clothes, I hauled my bed into the driest corner of the room, and prepared to turn in. It was only about 7 P.M., but there was nothing else to do, and I felt cold and miserable. Before turning in, I again looked at the roof, the creaking of which was becoming louder. It hardly appeared safe, as some of the logs were getting rotten—the house was a year old—and might give way, letting a few pounds of mud down in the course of the night; but I was too much disgusted with things in general to care about a little extra discomfort, and saying to myself, "It will hold out till to-morrow," I turned in and went to sleep. About 11 P.M. I was roused by a pattering

K

on the top of my mosquito-curtain, and a groaning
and creaking of the logs above my head. Scarcely
half awake, I got out of bed, and going to the table,
struck a match and lit a candle, which I held up to
examine the roof, and see whether the shower of
mud was not nearly over. As I raised the light,
it was suddenly extinguished by the roof coming
down, and I made for the door like a flash of greased
lightning, just as some two tons of wood and clay
descended with a fearful crash, and buried all my
property. I had an almost miraculous escape, for,
just as I cleared the door, I was struck on the
shoulder by one of the descending logs, and hurled,
face downwards, on the verandah. I arose, however, unhurt, and turned to look at my room; the
entrance was completely blocked up, so I opened
the door of the next, whose occupant I knew to be
very ill. He was all right, and his ceiling did not
appear to have suffered, so I went to the room on
the other side, which was occupied by the chief of
the station. I knocked—no answer; I listened,
and could hear no sound. Fearing the worst, I
opened the door, and, on looking in, saw the Com-
mandant du Territoire des Ba-Ngala crawling out
from under his bed, whither he had gone for safety
on hearing the crash. By this time the other
Europeans, and a crowd of Houssas and Zanzibaris,
had come to see what the noise was about, and
with their help I excavated two or three blankets,

and rolling up in them, lay down on the verandah, and slept the sleep of the just.

But it is time to return to the proper course of my narrative. Things went on in a very monotonous fashion until the arrival of the *Stanley* with the mails, about the end of January. She brought up Lieutenant Van Kerckhoven, who was to supersede Lieutenant Baert in the command of the district, and two other Europeans, one of whom, Mr Verhees, was a Belgian gentleman who had come out to Africa on a hunting-trip, but had entered the service of the State at Banana. After stopping two or three days at Bangala Station, the *Stanley* departed for Léopoldville, and we were once more left alone.

CHAPTER VII.

RIVER-LIFE IN AFRICA.

THE MISSING HOUSSAS FROM FALLS STATION—THE LANGA-LANGA—
IKOLUNGU AND ITS CHIEF—FOREST OF GUM-COPAL TREES—
H.M. IBANZA OF MPEZA—EPIDEMICS IN CENTRAL AFRICA—
PALAVER AT UPOTO—CURIOUS OWLS—RETURN TO BANGALA—
ATTACKED NEAR BOKÉLÉ—A DESPERATE RUN—CHEAPNESS OF
HUMAN LIFE ON THE UPPER CONGO—BA-NGALA DIVERSIONS
"OWRE THE WINE."—LUSENGI AND HIS NEWS—ANOTHER NIGHT
RUN—BURNING THE PACKING-CASES—THE EMIN RELIEF EXPEDITION.

WHEN I arrived at Bangala from Stanley Falls, after the rescue of Mr Deane, only seventeen out of the forty Houssas who had formed the garrison of Falls Station could be accounted for. Both Deane and Coquilhat were so ill and weak that we had to hurry on in order to reach Léopoldville and put them under the doctor's care, and could not stop to make inquiries of the natives on the way. Of these seventeen, ten had come down to Bangala bringing the first news of the disaster, and four had been found with Deane. The other three, who had remained with Deane when the panic occurred at the Falls, had afterwards been separated from him and killed by the Arabs, if they did not die of starvation in the bush. There were also at the station a number of women and children—freed slaves ransomed from the Arabs. Of these several had come down with the ten Houssas and forty Ba-Ngala, but the fate of the majority was, like that of the remaining twenty-three Houssas, still a mystery.

On returning to Bangala after Captain Coquilhat had gone home, I learnt from Lieutenant Baert that they had been captured by the natives of Upoto—the very people, in fact, who had invited us to fight them on our way up-river. Upoto is one of a group of towns some six days' steaming above Bangala, and separated from it by an immense, uninhabited, forest-covered swamp, which takes nearly four days to pass through. The Ba-Ngala call the natives of the country round Upoto Langa-Langa, by which name I shall hereafter distinguish them.

Mr Baert had bought back one of these Houssas at an exorbitant price, in order to obtain information from him. This information he had transmitted to Boma, asking, at the same time, for orders as to whether he should ransom the rest, or go up to Upoto, and threaten to burn the place unless our men were given up. At the end of

January 1887, Lieutenant Van Kerckhoven, as we have seen, arrived at Bangala and took over the command; and in the following March, he started in the *A.I.A.* on a visit to the Langa-Langa, to try and liberate the Houssas and women still in their hands. The little steamer was loaded up with brass wire, beads, cowries, cloth, empty bottles, and all the other innumerable articles that pass for money in this part of the world—and off we went. The second day brought us to Ikolungu, a large settlement on the north bank, about four hours steaming above the mouth of the Ngala river. This town stands on a stiff clay bank, and is surrounded by a splendid forest, containing trees from 80 to 100 feet high. When I first saw it—on my voyage up to the Falls with Captain Coquilhat—it was at war with Bangala, and was one of the best defended native towns I have seen on the Congo. Along the river-bank, and round the land-side of the town, were palisades, three or four deep, formed of poles 12 feet long and 2 or 3 inches thick, driven into the ground about 9 inches apart, and fastened together by a horizontal stick lashed along, 8 feet above the ground. Inside them, at a distance of 10 yards, was another set, three deep, and inside that a third set; so that the place—belonging as it did, to a powerful tribe—was able to stand a long siege. The defences on the river-bank, however, have now disappeared, and those on the land-side are in a state of decay; for the palm-tree has been cut between the Wabika and the Ba-Ngala, and Dua, chief of Ikolungu, comes down unmolested to Iboko to sell his ivory to the *mundélé*. All this has been brought about by the Free State; for when the chief of Ikolungu became the blood-brother of the *mundélé* at Bangala, he asked for help to fight the Ba-Ngala, while the Ba-Ngala chief preferred the same request. To all which Captain Coquilhat replied—"Mata Bwyki is my brother, Dua is my brother. If Mata Bwyki and Dua want to fight, I will go into my house and go to sleep till it is all over." So, after a long palaver, the palm-tree was cut, and the war was at an end. The strong current sweeping round the bend of the river at Ikolungu has cut into the bank and carried away the palisades, and they have not been renewed; while Dua has launched his trading canoes, for peaceable traffic with his old enemies. After his last visit I had the pleasure (?) of towing him, his wives and slaves, up alongside the *A.I.A.* The poor little steamer had two other large canoes and a whale-boat to tow as well; but though I growled at the extra strain on the engines, which rendered them more liable to break down, the amusement I had in watching his highness soon dispelled my annoyance; and I cannot help regretting that Stanley did not—so far as I can discover—make his acquaintance, as we have thereby lost a graphic and amusing description. Whenever King Dua took a drink of palm-wine, or ate his meals, one of his wives produced a hard brown nut, about the size of an egg, with one end cut off, and the inside hollowed out. This nut (which I have not succeeded in identifying) he slowly placed on the great toe of his left foot; this done, the palm-wine or food was placed before him, and a slave-boy came and stood behind him with a hand-bell. Every time he took a mouthful of food, or a drink of *massanga* or palm-wine, he rapped the bottom of the canoe with the nut on his great toe, while a tinkle on the bell announced to all whom it might concern that Dua of Ikolungu was eating, or drinking, as the case might be. He went through the same ceremony when smoking, taking a long pull at his pipe for every rap of his toe and tinkle on the bell. I had watched this for some time with great amusement, when the king observing me, offered me a cup of *massanga*, which I accepted; and, not to be behind him in ceremony, before drinking it, turned round and gave some instructions to my fireman. Hardly had I raised the cup to my lips, when a series of short, sharp blasts on the steam-whistle of the *A.I.A.* made Dua jump almost out of his canoe; while I, between laughing and drinking, was nearly choked.

After leaving Ikolungu there is a long stretch of

low country which, during several months of the year, is either covered with water or so swampy that no natives have ventured to establish themselves there. It takes three days, or perhaps a little longer, to steam past this swamp. Stanley has a great deal to say about the beauties of this region, but I must say I was always glad to leave it behind. However, a tree covered with orchilla-weed is indeed a beautiful sight; and a whole forest of trees, with this fleecy, light-green drapery swaying about in the wind, is worth going miles to see. It generally grows on gum-copal trees, and I have myself seen the forest of these trees covered with orchilla-weed described by Stanley.[1] There is also a creeper which winds itself round the trunks of trees like a huge serpent, and having climbed to the branches and spread over them, drops down numberless ropes, which seem to take root in the ground. The main stem is often four, five, or six inches in diameter, and the hangers from half an inch upwards. If you cut one of these stems clean across with a knife, a white milky sap is seen to exude between the bark and the woody centre— this is india-rubber or caoutchouc.

Besides these three articles, which will some day help to pay the dividends of the Congo railway, there are thousands of trees whose beautifully grained timber has only to be brought to Europe

[1] The Congo, vol. ii. p. 87.

to find a ready sale. I have cut up dead rosewood-trees for firewood, out of the trunk of which a log two feet in diameter, and from twenty to thirty feet long, of splendid grain, could have been obtained, after the outer casing of white wood had been cut away; while teak, kingwood, camwood, lignum-vitæ, and African black oak, are only a few out of the valuable woods I have found rotting in the forest, and cut up to feed the insatiable little furnace of the *A.I.A.* But in spite of the beauty and wealth of this part of the Congo, there seems something depressing in being constantly shut in between two high forest walls; and I always feel a sort of relief on coming down to the wide open channels about Bolobo, and running through the park-like scenery of the Congo between that village and the Pool, where it rolls in a single majestic stream through the glorious hilly country of the Bayanzi and Batéké.

After the swamp—continuing our upward voyage—comes the village of Mpeza, also on the north bank, whence the ground gradually rises, till, at Upoto, ten miles higher, it ends in a spur of hills which, running out into the river, forms a reef of rock extending to Rubunga on the south bank, over which the Congo rolls in a kind of mild rapid, quite passable for steamers of light draught, except in one or two channels between the islands near the south bank. It is, however, a dangerous place at low water, the rocks being then only two or three feet below the surface, so that the sounding-pole and lead-line are kept in constant requisition. Mpeza is the first town of the Langa-Langa, and its chief would, by himself, make the fortune of a travelling show. His name is Ibanza—*Anglicè*, the devil; and truly, were I asked to depict his satanic majesty, I think I could not do so more accurately than by a sketch of this chief. His face is one mass of small fleshy lumps raised by some process known only to the natives—rows of these lumps adorning his forehead, cheeks, nose, and chin,—while his hair and beard are made up into a clotted mass with palm-oil. On his head is a leopard-skin hat, in front whereof is fastened a tin plate presented to him by Mr Van Kerckhoven. As this is kept brightly polished, it is well to keep out of its range while interviewing his majesty on a sunny day, in order to avoid the risk of sudden blindness from the dazzling reflection as he nods his head, and, extending his elbows, waves them up and down as if about to fly, at the same time ejaculating *way! way! way! way!*—his form of salutation—after which he claps his hands together, and clasping one over the other, gives a most unearthly grin. Mpeza is one of the dirtiest and most untidy-looking villages on the whole Congo, and were it more civilised, would soon be decimated by disease. But the heaps of dirt and refuse lying about will be swept by the next storm into the Congo—which must in fact act as the great sewer of Central Africa— and in this way, I believe, disease is averted. For to the terrible storms and great waterways of the African continent may be attributed the comparative immunity from infectious diseases, and the absence of epidemics among the aboriginal tribes inhabiting the interior at a distance from civilised communities. The epidemics which have from time to time raged through India and the East seem to be unknown in regions whither neither Christians nor Mohammedans have penetrated. Smallpox I have heard of as brought from Zanzibar by the Arabs to some place or places east of Stanley Falls; but neither smallpox nor cholera is known among the natives west of the Falls. Barbadoes leg, elephantiasis, ulcers, and sores, comprise about all the diseases that have come under my observation. That there are others I do not doubt, but not of an epidemic character. When one considers the general indifference of the natives as regards sanitary conditions, one sometimes wonders that the population of whole villages is not carried off by some terrible pestilence; and the absence of such a scourge I believe to be due partly to the heavy rains and vast rivers which carry off the refuse, and partly to the ants and other insects, and the carrion-eating birds. Nature, when left alone, does her own scavengering; but as civilisation advances, the works of man often interfere with the natural drainage, without providing any substitute; and it is only when the population has been decimated by disease that men's eyes are opened. Europe has had, in the middle ages, many a severe reminder that men cannot live packed in cities like herrings in a barrel; and had it not been for the great plague and fire of 1665-66, London might still be anything but the healthiest city in the world. Epidemics as terrible and fatal as any that have visited India may yet sweep across Central Africa. It was in the half-civilised middle ages of Europe, when man had not yet been taught by science how to replace the means provided by nature for preserving health, that pestilence slew its thousands and tens of thousands—as it does to-day among the millions herded together in Eastern towns, where nature's remedies have gradually retreated before the advance of man. The primitive savage living in his hut, and enjoying fresh air in plenty, has no need of dust-bin or dust-cart. He plucks and dresses his fowl for dinner in front of his door, throwing all rubbish and dirt to one side. The ants from the large hill close by will soon make short work of any meat he may have left on the bones; the sexton-beetle will soon bury what remains out of sight, and the wind and rain wash all feathers and dirt into the river. An African village is always a dirty place, but I have several times noticed a wonderful difference after a tornado, or even a good shower of rain—everything looking quite neat and clean for several days. As civilisation advances, roads are made, the ant-hills get destroyed, and hawks and carrion-birds disappear before the death-dealing shot-gun. The natives congregate together in large towns without any improvement in their sanitary arrangements, where the salutary effects of wind and rain are probably neutralised by the way in which the streets are built; and so things go on till disease is generated, and men fall by hundreds.

Above Mpeza is another large settlement called Bokélé, extending some two miles along the riverbank; and above that, nestling on the lower slope of the range of hills, is Bokuti, opposite which, on an island, is the smaller village of Lulangi. At Bokuti we stopped, and Mr Van Kerckhoven succeeded in buying back three or four women and one Houssa. Finding the natives unwilling to sell the rest, he decided to go on and try again on our return; so we steamed off round the point to Upoto, which occupies a commanding position on the eastern slope of the hills, with a view right across to Rubunga on the south bank. Having steamed to the upper end of the village, we stopped the engines, and the interpreter, Samba, standing up in the bows, shouted aloud, for the benefit of all whom it might concern, the why and wherefore of our coming. We then anchored off a sand-bank, and awaited the commencement of the palaver. Presently several canoes approached us, and Mr Van Kerckhoven having landed on the bank, the ceremony of blood-brotherhood was gone through, and business began. After one or two of our men had been bought back for an amount of brass wire, cloth, beads, &c., of a value equivalent to between £3 and £4 sterling, and the price had been fixed within certain limits, matters began to progress more rapidly. After we had ransomed three or four, we heard from them that eleven of their number had been killed by the natives, and one or two sold away to other tribes. One of these last was already at Bangala, having been bought back from Bukumbi, a village on the south bank nearly opposite Ikolungu. By nightfall we had bought back five Houssas and sixteen women — among them the woman who had been seized by the Arabs from Stanley Falls Station, in order, as Mr Deane supposed, to furnish a pretext for a quarrel, as, when he sent some Houssas to demand her back, the Arabs fired on them. This woman, I believe, escaped from the Arabs, and came back to the station before the night on which it was abandoned.

It was at this place that I saw a very curious

little owl which was brought for sale by some of the Langa-Langa, and bought by Mr Van Kerckhoven. This owl, when its wings were folded, looked as if it consisted of nothing else but a beak and two huge eyes, surrounded by radiating feathers. Its wings seemed to fold up behind the feathers which surround the eyes, and its feet were completely hidden. When standing still, it looked like a small ball of feathers about six inches in diameter, and when walking about it had the same appearance, only a little more animated. Its cry, which was something like "cook-a-look-a-look-a-look," was very well imitated by the Langa-Langa. It was rather a pretty little bird, on the whole, and I was very sorry that it did not live more than a few hours after it came on board the steam-launch.

Next morning, as the Upoto people did not seem inclined to part with the rest of their captives, we returned to Bokuti, where, after some trouble—due to one of the chiefs, who declared that he would fight, but would sell no more of his slaves—Mr Van Kerckhoven succeeded in getting three more women and one Houssa. As these twenty-five people, in addition to our crew and armed force of thirty men, completely filled up the little steamer and the whale-boat, we headed at once for Bangala, where we arrived in four days. This was in March 1887, and the *A.I.A.* was for some time after employed

on other business, in an entirely different direction.
On the 3d of June, with Lieutenants Van Kerckhoven and Dhanis on board, she again reached
Upoto; but as we approached the shore, the natives
ran down with shields and spears, and would on no
account hold any palaver with us, but insisted on
fighting. We steamed down to Bokuti, and finding that there too the natives were hostile, passed
on to Bokélé. When we were about half-way past
this latter place, Samba drew Mr Van Kerckhoven's
attention to several large war-canoes, fully manned
and armed, crossing the channel just in front of us,
while two or three more were lying half concealed
under the bushes on the island. Suddenly the report of a flint-lock musket rang out, and a shower
of slugs across our bows indicated only too plainly
that the natives intended to capture a few more
State soldiers, in order to sell them again to the
mundélé. Two more huge war-canoes emerging
from a small creek behind us, showed that they had
well thought out the affair beforehand, and now
reckoned on having caught us in a trap. However, we had no intention of sitting at their tables,
as Charles Lamb has it, "not as guests, but as
meat." Out came our Martinis and Winchesters;
the men were furnished with cartridges for their
Sniders and Chassepots, and slowing down for a few
minutes, we let them have it, right and left, before
and behind; and then, putting on full steam,

charged straight for the two canoes ahead of us. As we approached, we exchanged our long-range Martinis for the quick-firing Winchesters, and the mighty men of Langa-Langa were soon glad to dive into the river to escape the deadly hail of the repeating-rifles. The whole river-front of the village was lined with savages, in their war-paint and feathers, popping away at us with flint-lock muskets, and brandishing spears and knives; while the occasional sharp crack of a rifle showed that they were still in possession of the Sniders, and a few of the cartridges taken from the captured Houssas. Their ignorance of the power of our rifles was evident from the way in which they held up their shields of plaited cane whenever they noticed a gun pointed at them. I saw more than one poor wretch put up his shield, only just in time to receive a ball right through it and himself as well, and come rolling down the clay bank into the river, dead as a door-nail. We contrived to run the gauntlet and come out scot-free; but as we had only about thirty men with us, while Bokélé could muster some thousands, Mr Van Kerckhoven decided to put a good distance between us as quickly as possible. Accordingly, we ran down-stream by the light of the moon, which was in her first quarter, and gave a fairish light till towards morning, when clouds obscured the sky, and we lost our way, and grounded on a sand-bank. Failing to get off, we anchored where we were; but as soon as the first streaks of dawn showed in the sky, we roused the men, and in half an hour were once more afloat. Having stopped at 8 A.M. to cut fuel, which took us some two hours, we proceeded, and finally, about 7 P.M. reached a good camp, where we prepared to spend the night.

Before continuing my narrative, I will state the reasons which Mr Van Kerckhoven gave for trying to ransom the Houssas. It may be said that such a course would obviously lead—as in fact it did—to attempts on the part of the natives to capture more of the Free State employees in order to sell them again. At first sight the proper course would seem to be, to go up with a strong force to retake them, and punish the offenders. Had this been done (and I believe there was at one time some talk of it), the natives, who are almost as cunning as the Indians of North America, would have heard of the expedition long before it reached their country, and hidden their prisoners away far inland; while the relieving force could have done no more than burn their towns and kill a few dozen savages, with the satisfaction of knowing that, when all was over, the men they had come to save would be beheaded to furnish "funeral baked meats" in honour of the Langa-Langa slain in the fight. Mr Van Kerckhoven knew the native character too well to be unaware of this, and resolved accordingly to remove the men first, if possible, and leave the question of retribution alone for the present. Eleven men had already been beheaded before our first expedition—some of them, perhaps, for trying to escape, others for no earthly reason, unless it might be said that their masters killed them for the fun of the thing; for this is the only way in which I can account for the wanton murder of so many slaves by these savages.

In spite of the munificence of King Léopold in founding the Free State—in spite of all that has been, and is being, done to stop the slave-trade—human beings are almost daily killed like so much vermin within a few miles of Bangala Station. I had often, when passing the villages just above Bangala, noticed groups of poles standing out of water, to the top of which a piece of cloth was tied. I paid no great attention to them, taking them for fetishes of some kind; but one day, happening to ask Mr Van Kerckhoven what they were, I was informed that they were placed to mark the spot where the corpses of decapitated slaves had been thrown into the river. It seems that, at a place called Lusengo, whenever the natives have a great *massanga*-drinking, they cut off the heads of one or more slaves, and throwing the bodies into the river, set up a pole to mark the place, to the top of which is tied the dead man's loin-cloth. I do not know whether the pole is driven through the body of the victim, but imagine that it is, as, during the whole time I have been at Bangala, I have not seen above four dead bodies floating down the river; while above Lusengo I have counted thirty of these poles in less than a mile of river-frontage. I tried to find out from the natives the reason for this slaughter, but never succeeded. They do not deny that they kill their slaves in this fashion, but distinctly repudiate the notion of eating any part of them; yet, for my part, I am inclined to believe that cannibal feasts occur now and then.

The authority of the State has so far prevailed that this sort of thing does not, as a rule, take place in Iboko; but noisy drinking-bouts, which too often end fatally, are far from uncommon. The usual procedure is this: two or three large pots of *massanga* are brought and set down on the ground, and the company gather round them. When they reach the excited stage of intoxication, sticks and knives are produced—the latter, of native manufacture, are very long and sharp—and the play begins. Two men stand opposite one another, each holding a knife in his right hand and a stick in his left, and slashing at the stick held by his opponent till he has succeeded in cutting it through. It may be imagined that, as some very hard hitting is indulged in, and the various couples engaged in the game stand crowded together in a very small space, it is not always the sticks alone which suffer; and the wonder is that so few serious accidents take place. One evening I happened to be in the village during one of these performances, and saw two men, wrought up to frenzy with *massanga* and excitement, fighting with their knives in good earnest. I expected every moment to see them lose their heads, not only figuratively, but literally; and seizing a heavy bludgeon from the nearest spectator, prepared to join in the fray, thinking that a good blow across the wrist would make both combatants drop their weapons. However, before I could get near enough to interfere, up rushed a native girl, who, seizing one of these doughty champions in her arms, slung him across her shoulder, as if he had been a baby, and ran away with him. Though so ignominiously borne off, with his head and arms suspended in air, he still brandished his knife, and yelled Ba-Ngala curses at his adversary, who was so overcome by astonishment that he staggered backwards, and sat down in a *massanga*-pot, thus wasting the staple of the evening's entertainment, and being forced to run for his life to escape the wrath of the disappointed drinkers. It was a plucky feat for a Ba-Ngala woman,—they usually run away as soon as the knives make their appearance. Had that dusky ἄναξ ἀνδρῶν, old King Mata Bwyki, "Lord of Many Guns," been alive, he would have laid about among these brawlers with his royal barge-pole, and quickly secured peace and quiet.

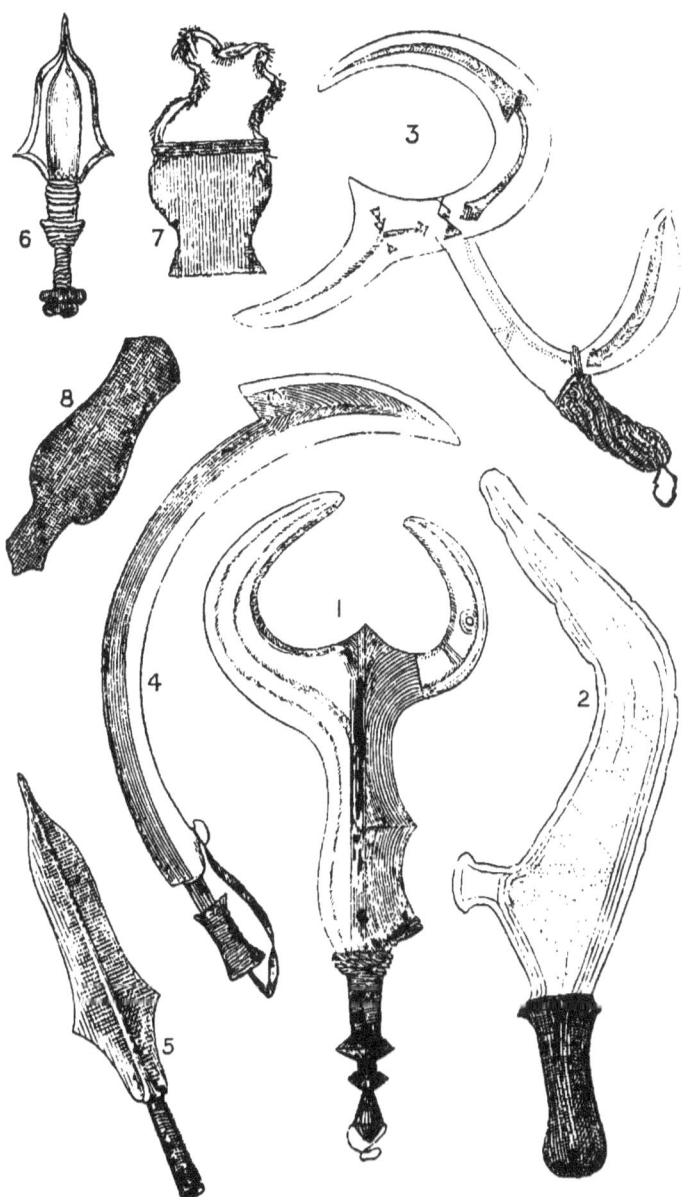

1. Execution Knife used by the Ba-Ngala.
2. Knife of the Langa-Langa.
3. "   "   Ubika.
4. "   "   Aruhwimi.
5. Spear-head of the Lomami.
6, 7. Dagger and Sheath used by the Natives of the Lomami River.
8. Iron used as money at Stanley Falls.

To return to the starting-point of this digression. We had hardly been encamped an hour, and I was just going to sleep, when a large canoe came alongside. It had on board Lusengi, chief of Mobeka who was out among the islands of the Congo in search of a large tree, of which to make a war-canoe. He told us that an expedition of eight steamers had, four days before, passed up to the Falls by way of the south bank. I have already mentioned that this part of the river is choked with islands; and just at the spot where we were anchored, there is one over fifty miles long, in the middle of the stream, so that boats may easily miss each other by passing on different sides. As there were not at that time eight steamers afloat on the Upper Congo, we allowed for native exaggeration; and concluding that an expedition of perhaps three or four steamers and two whale-boats had been fitted out to recapture the Falls, Mr Van Kerckhoven gave orders to start at once, and reach Bangala as quickly as possible, to hear what orders had arrived for the *A.I.A.*

Having been up all the preceding night, I did not rejoice at the prospect before us; but there was no help for it, and I turned to and got up steam again—somewhat consoled by the thought that possibly Deane might again be on his way to the Falls, and it might be my lot to join him there. As the fire had not long been out of the boiler, this was quickly accomplished, and before 9 P.M. we were off, rushing down-stream at the rate of eight miles an hour through the dark night—the moon, hidden by heavy clouds, just giving light enough to impart a dull grey gleam to the water. Mr Dhanis took his place in the bows, with Dua, our interpreter, who, having been up and down with us several times, was supposed to know the road well. He did not fail to keep up his reputation. How he could tell one channel from another, with nothing to guide him but the two dark walls of forest, and the glimmer of grey water between them, I do not know; but only once, during the whole night, did the sounding-pole touch bottom.

On we rushed through the silent night, hearing only the puffing and panting of the engine, and the wash of the water, as it parted before our bows, or was churned into foam by the propeller. Occasionally, as we passed a grassy swamp, the croaking of numberless frogs would come to our ears, or a bird, disturbed from its roost on a neighbouring tree, would fly off with a shrill scream; but beyond this everything was quiet, and black as the grave. Now in a broad open reach, which looked limitless in the darkness; now through a narrow channel, where we could see no outlet through the dense shadows that seemed to bar our path ahead; now brushing against some overhanging bushes, as the steersman, deceived by the obscurity, hugged the shore a little too closely; and then taking a sudden sheer to right or left, to avoid a snag which Dua's cat-like eyes had espied in front. Hour after hour passed: now and then we would get a momentary gleam of moonlight through the clouds; but this was seldom, and we were soon again left in utter darkness. I could hardly keep my eyes open, and, more than once, nearly fell asleep over the engine from utter weariness. In the middle of the night I gave up, and, calling the Zanzibari greaser, lay down and slept for a couple of hours. I got up again about 3 A.M. Mr Van Kerckhoven had relieved Mr Dhanis at the look-out. The engines were working beautifully, and steam had kept up well, so I opened the stop-valve a little more. The palm-oil lamps were beginning to burn low, and everything about the engine was in a dirty greasy state—as, in the dim light, it had not been possible to avoid spilling the oil over it. But we had passed the great swamp between Ikolungu and Langa-Langa, and were approaching our destination, for now and then we could catch a glimpse of villages and banana-plantations. Steam was getting low, and on going to find out the cause, I discovered that we were running short of fuel. I had once before, in a similar case, imitated the Yankees on the Mississippi, and burned a "bacon-ham"; but then I had only a mile to go to reach the station, whereas we were now nearly forty miles from Bangala, and there were not hams enough on board (even had there been enough in the whole region of the Upper Congo), to have kept up steam for four or five hours—the time necessary to do that distance.

I aroused Mr Dhanis: we neither of us liked to stop; so we began tearing the tarred canvas coverings off the bales of cloth, and breaking up all the wooden packing-cases we had on board, and managed in this way to keep going. At last the long night was over, and daylight began to appear. Mr Van Kerckhoven came to ask me whether—supposing the expedition that had gone up river was, as we conjectured, intended for the recapture of Stanley Falls—I could have the steamer ready to start again next day. I replied, Yes; and as we neared the station, I began to get everything ready for cleaning out the boiler, and making the few necessary preparations for an immediate start. Towards 9 A.M. (May 28th, 1887) we came in sight of the station, and perceived the Europeans hastening down to the shore to meet us. As we approached the landing-place, I took out the fire and began to blow the water out of the boiler, in order to save as much time as possible. As soon as I could get a minute to spare, I went to Mr Baert to hear the news, and learned that our race through the darkness had been all for nothing. The boats we had passed did not carry an army for the recapture of Stanley Falls, but the advance column of Stanley's expedition for the relief of Emin Pasha.

CHAPTER VIII.

THE EMIN RELIEF EXPEDITION.

STANLEY ON THE CONGO—NEWS FROM HOME—THE UNPRINCIPLED
BARUTI AND HIS AWFUL FATE—STANLEY AND THE MISSIONARIES
—THE *HENRY REED* SEIZED TO EXPLORE THE LOIKA—A "REAL
MEAN RIVER"—CHIEF OF UPOTO SEIZED AS A HOSTAGE—FEVER
—NGALYEMA'S COW—LÉOPOLDVILLE AGAIN—ANIMAL LIFE ON
THE RIVER—BEAUTY OF THE BATÉKÉ COUNTRY—'JOYCE.'—
REMINISCENCES OF CIVILISATION—REMARKABLE EFFECTS OF
HOME LETTERS WHEN FIRST OPENED—THE HUNTERS' CAMP ON
LONG ISLAND—DUALLA ISLAND—LUKOLELA—MY BULL'S-EYE
CREATES A SENSATION.

STANLEY on the Congo! I exclaimed. Why, I thought he was in America! And who under the canopy was Emin Pasha? and what did he want relieving for? While, as for Tippoo Tip, who, it seemed, was going up as the new Governor of the Falls,—I had indeed heard of him before, but only as one of the marauding Arabs whom we were so anxious to expel from the territory of the State. It must be remembered that, for about four months, I had received no news from the civilised world, in any shape or form; and the whole was naturally a complete puzzle to me.

At length, when all was made fast—it being Sunday, of which, as I was completely tired out, I was heartily glad—I went to the chief's room to receive my mail; and having shouldered the sack which was handed me as my own share, and sought the solitude of my own room, I cut it open, and commenced pulling out the welcome letters and papers. But I was too utterly weary to read; and after vainly attempting to make out the meaning of one of the letters, I gave it up, and using the mail-bag as a pillow, lay down in the middle of the room, and slept till night, when I was awakened by my boy, with the information that dinner was ready. Having revived exhausted nature with some india-rubber-like goat-steak and yams, I returned to my room with a pot of palm-oil; and having rigged up a lamp with this, I once more set to work at my letters, and looked up Emin Pasha—only to be maddened by finding that while I was running down the right bank of the river several friends of mine had passed me on the left! These were men who had been on the Congo when I first came out, and had gone home when they had finished their time—afterwards returning to Africa with Stanley's expedition.

Besides all this, I received a letter telling me that Mr Arthur Jephson, whom I had known at school many years before, had accompanied Stanley, and found, on inquiry, that this gentleman had passed on with the advance-guard. I was, however, consoled by hearing that Messrs Troup and Ward were still at Léopoldville, and that I should probably see them as they passed up. I had been nearly five months without seeing an Englishman or hearing news from Europe, and knew nothing whatever of the Emin Relief Expedition. Not a whisper of it had reached us; and Stanley himself was the first to announce, by his appearance on the scene, that he had returned to the Congo.

After this, the *A.I.A.* was kept pretty busy, in the immediate neighbourhood of Bangala, till the end of the month; but in July the steamers *Stanley*, *Peace*, and *Henry Reed* returned from the Aruhwimi. Among other items of news, Captain Shagerstrom (of the *Stanley*) reported that Mr Stanley's boy, Baruti (whom he had freed from slavery on one of his former expeditions, taken to Europe, and educated), had, on getting back to his own country, decamped, taking with him Stanley's revolver and rifle. I afterwards heard that he had been killed and eaten by his own countrymen.

The *Stanley* and *Peace*, having taken in sufficient supplies of firewood, left next day for Léopoldville,—the former to fetch up the rear-guard of the Stanley Expedition, and the latter to return to her missionary duties; but the *Henry Reed* was seized upon by the officers of the State to take an expedition up the Loika or Itimbiri river. This steamer had been first asked for, then demanded, and finally seized, by Stanley, on his arrival at Léopoldville, when the State authorities, upon being appealed to by the missionaries, interfered, and hired the steamer from the Mission at the rate of £100 a month—the sum that had previously been offered by Mr Stanley. A great many letters were written to the newspapers about this affair at the time, and a great many people, doubtless, formed their ideas about it from a legal point of view, as they would have done had the event occurred in England. To those on the spot things look very different. Here was Stanley, with 600 men and several tons of stores and ammunition, passing through some 250 miles of disturbed country, and expecting to find, on his arrival at Stanley Pool, several steamers in readiness to transport his expedition to regions where it could obtain more food than in the much-traversed district of the Livingstone Cataracts. Hardly had he left Matadi, when he heard that one steamer (the *En Avant*) was out of water for repairs, and her engines unfit for use, owing to the absence of some portions which were worn out and required replacing. Another boat was away at Bangala, some 500 miles up-river. He wrote several times to the missionaries asking for the use of the *Henry Reed*, and was refused. He arrived at Léopoldville, where a scarcity of food had already prevailed for some time—the sudden influx of 600 additional mouths was naturally more than such a country could stand, and the food-supplies threatened to give out. Stanley, fully realising the state of affairs, resorted to demands; and as the missionaries—who acknowledged that they did not want to use the steamer for a month to come, and could perfectly understand the position in which he was placed—still refused, he sent down men and seized her. The missionaries then appealed to the State, whereupon down marched a troop of soldiers belonging to the Government, to displace Stanley's men, and take possession of the steamer while negotiations were carried on. These ended in the State hiring the steamer for £100 per month, and handing her over to Stanley.

From a legal point of view the missionaries were, no doubt, perfectly justified in refusing the use of their steamer. It was their property, and every one has a right to do as he likes with his own; but, knowing the circumstances in which Stanley was placed, and not having any use for the steamer for the next month, it was, to say the least of it, very unwise in them to do so, and thus force him to seize the boat, because (which one or two of them acknowledged to me was the reason of their refusal) they did not quite approve of the use to which she was to be put.

Stanley, though perhaps legally in the wrong, was, under the circumstances, quite right in seizing the steamer, having already offered the exorbitant price of £100 per month for her. Had he not acted as he did, we should probably have heard of fights between his men and the natives round Léopoldville, as it would have been impossible to keep 600 hungry savages from stealing food in the neighbouring villages. The *Peace*, belonging to the Baptist Mission, was handed over to Stanley when he asked for her, and duly handed back on her return from the Aruhwimi, as the *Henry Reed* would have been, had she been, in like manner, willingly lent. Having, however, been chartered by the State, she was, on her way down-stream, stopped by some State officials at Bangala; and, in July 1887, I was sent on board her, and we started off, in company with the *A.I.A.*, to explore the Loika, a tributary running into the Congo between Yambunga and Yalulima. I am not sure of the precise object of this exploration; but I believe the intention was to found a station on the upper river, and so gain access to the north-eastern portion of the Congo Free State. However, the country proved altogether unsuitable for the purpose, and we had a most miserable time of it, as we could get very little except bananas to eat—goats and fowls being very scarce, and the country entirely uncultivated. I came away with a very poor impression of the Loika, and have no desire ever to visit it again.

We did not entirely lose our labour, as, on the way up, we stopped at Upoto, and the natives—whether impressed by the lesson they had received when they tried to fight us, or overawed by the sight of the steamers and men of the Emin Pasha Relief Expedition—were this time more peaceably inclined. We ransomed one more Houssa and three women; and the chief of Upoto, coming on board the *A.I.A.* to beg for a present from his blood-brother, Mr Van Kerckhoven (whom he had tried to kill only a month ago), was seized and held as security for the rest. It was then believed that there were only three more women in the hands of the Langa-Langa; and as these three were not forthcoming within a given time, the chief accompanied us up the Itimbiri, to be restored to his people on our return, on condition of their surrendering the women. But on our return, when only two days from Upoto, the chief escaped through the carelessness of the Houssas, who had him in charge. I was at this time on board the *Henry Reed*; and as she returned to Bangala along the south bank, I knew nothing of what took place at Upoto when the *A.I.A.* passed it, beyond the fact that there was some shooting.

About the 1st of August we once more reached Bangala. I had a bad fever, and as soon as the fires were out and I could leave the engine, I went and lay down in the cabin of the *Henry Reed*. I was too enervated and feverish to take much notice of outside sounds, and was but dimly conscious of the arrival of the *Stanley*, which came up from Léopoldville about two hours after we were made fast, till Troup and Ward came to look for me, and helped me up to my room.

The *Stanley* was several days behind the time when we had expected her. She had left Léopoldville with Messrs Troup, Ward, and Bonny on board, in charge of the men and stores of the Emin Relief Expedition rear-guard. Soon after passing Lukolela, she had struck a snag and knocked a hole in her bows, which had delayed her for some days. She left next day for the Aruhwimi; and both the *A.I.A.* and the *Henry Reed*, being in need of repairs, started for Léopoldville, after remaining only two days at Bangala. On her way up with Stanley's expedition the *Henry Reed* had carried Tippoo Tip and his suite up to Stanley Falls, where Tippoo was established as governor of the district for the Congo Free State. In passing through Léopoldville, Tippoo had made the acquaintance of Ngalyema, and on the departure of the *Henry Reed* from Stanley Falls, had sent a fine cow as a present to his new friend.

This cow had been put ashore at Bangala, while the *Henry Reed* explored the Loika, and we now took her on board the hull of the *En Avant* (which had been used by Stanley as a lighter), to be towed down to her destination. When we arrived at Equator, we found Mr Glave, who had returned to Africa for the Sanford Exploring Expedition, in charge of the station; and he (in common with all the Europeans) cast envious glances on the cow —the first beef we had seen for many days—which we thought a great deal too good for Ngalyema.

On August 10th I again reached Léopoldville, after an absence of nine months. Ngalyema was sent for, and came down, with his wives and slaves, to receive his cow. This cow was the mildest of all mild animals, but, like others of her species, did not like being pulled about, and being a little obstinate, refused to cross the planks put for her to walk ashore by. The captain of the steamer then got together as many Zanzibaris as could be crowded into the *En Avant*, and they lifted the cow bodily out on the beach, which she resented with a loud " moo." Hereupon Ngalyema and his mighty warriors, who had, during these proceedings, kept at a respectful distance, turned tail and fled along the shore— the cow following at a trot, and mooing at intervals.

Léopoldville itself had changed little since I last saw it, a new store or two being all the additions to the buildings of the station; but the lower end of

Stanley Pool—or rather the six miles of the Congo between the Pool and "Léo"—presented quite a lively appearance, with the English, American, Dutch, and French flags flying from the different missions and trading factories now established. The *coup d'œil* was somewhat spoilt, a month later, by an edict from Boma, which enacted that no flag but that of the State was to be displayed on any of the flag-staffs on the Upper Congo. The French tricolour still continued to enliven the scene on the north bank; but on the south side all flags disappeared, with the exception of that on Léopold Hill and of the Dutch factory flag, which was removed to a pole on one of the houses. As the *Henry Reed* steamed towards Nshassa, a large sternwheeler, shining with new paint, and carrying the stars and stripes, approached us. She turned out to be the *Florida*, the newly launched steamer of the Sanford Exploring Expedition, now established in the old State station at Nshassa. On the beach before the Dutch factory, and also before that of Daumas, Beraud et C[ie.], on the north bank, were the nearly finished hulls of two more steamers; while at Léopoldville, the frames and plates of the *Roi des Belges*, another stern-wheeler, belonging to the "Compagnie du Congo pour le Commerce et l'Industrie," were only awaiting the arrival of the engineers to be put together; and the beams and planks of the *Ville de Bruxelles*, a wooden stern-wheeler for

the State, were daily arriving *viâ* Lukungu and
Manyanga. The *Henry Reed* having been handed
back to the Livingstone Inland Mission, I rejoined
the *A.I.A.*, and having thoroughly overhauled her,
left for Bangala, August 23d, with Mr Van Kerckhoven on board, besides a Belgian soldier for Bangala, and an Englishman in the service of the Sanford Company, going to Equator. Being heavily
loaded, and travelling slowly, we only arrived September 11th. On the 29th, the Houssas at Bangala
had completed their three years' term of service,
which obliged me to take another trip to the Pool.
Accordingly, the men having been packed on board
almost as tightly as figs in a box, we started; and
though I had not been three weeks at Bangala, it
was no small relief to escape once more from the
forested plain that extends almost uninterruptedly
from Lukolela to the Aruhwimi, and emerge into the
broad channels above Bolobo, with their park-like
banks and grass-covered uplands. Here "hippos"
may be seen by the hundred—sometimes in ones
and twos, more often in herds of from ten to thirty
—standing in the shallow water, or swimming about
just under the lee of a sand-bank, diving, and returning to the surface with a loud snort. Now and
then one may be observed lifting his head out of
the water, and slowly opening his jaws preparatory
to relieving the tedium of hippo life with a yawn.
Slowly and smoothly, as if worked by hydraulic

machinery, his jaws expand, as he raises his head clear of the water—wider and wider becomes his mouth, till his tusks gleam white in the sunlight, and you wonder if it would not be possible, were one near enough, to look down and survey his last meal in process of digestion. But he has not done! Another stretch opens his jaws some six inches wider, and just as you are expecting to see him turn inside out, he closes with a loud snap, and with a splash disappears from view. I have seen a hippo seize a canoe of nearly two feet beam in his mouth, which will give some idea of the extent to which he is capable of opening that feature in an ordinary way ; but even that is nothing to one of his yawns. Flocks of ducks may be seen on the sand-banks of this part of the river, and form a welcome change of " chop " when one can get near enough to shoot one or two ; here also is the beautiful white heron, in company with pelicans and flamingoes, and an occasional adjutant-bird,[1] gravely stalking up and down a stretch of sand ; while flocks of jacos or

[1] Talking of adjutant-birds, I heard a good story from Mr Richards of the Baptist Mission at Lukolela. It seems that Mr Comber, of the same mission, used to keep a tame adjutant at Lutété (or Wathen) Station, which roamed about the station-yard, with clipped wings, in company with monkeys, parrots, and other pets—among them a kitten belonging to Mr Comber. One day this kitten was heard mewing piteously, though it was nowhere to be seen. At last, noticing that the sounds appeared to proceed from the adjutant, who was standing with his beak wide open, as though engaged in swallowing something with an effort, Mr Comber walked up to him, and looking

grey parrots, easily distinguished by the short, quick, agitated motion of their wings, fly screaming overhead. As the steamer rushes past the low banks—the grasses, reeds, and papyrus swaying about in the wash of the screw—a sudden rush and loud splash announce the hasty retreat of a crocodile, disturbed in the middle of his afternoon nap by a rushing fiery monster, which is come and gone almost before he knows what has happened. On a low sand-spit, projecting beyond the grasses, may sometimes be seen a monster crocodile, perhaps upwards of fifty feet long; at any rate, I have seen several considerably longer than the little *A.I.A.*, and she measures forty-two feet. On one occasion I had landed on a large sand-bank to shoot ducks. Having bagged one, and seeing that the rest had alighted beyond a low ridge of sand, I stooped down and crawled along behind the ridge till I thought I was within range, when I raised my head and looked over. Sure enough there were the

down his throat, saw the end of the kitten's tail about to disappear. Thereupon, he grasped the tail and hauled the kitten out, still alive. Mr Richards told me that the truth of this story had been doubted in England; for my part I see no reason to disbelieve it, and would recommend those who do to pay a visit to the Zoo and inspect the adjutants there. Those I have seen on the Congo held their heads as high as a tall man, and had beaks and throats of enormous capacity, adapted—like those of pelicans and other birds which lead a similar life—to the catching and swallowing whole of large fish. The Lutété adjutant, I am told, on another occasion, swallowed a small dead monkey entire. As for the kitten—it is a well-known fact that cats have nine lives.

ducks, not fifty yards from me, while half-way between me and them lay the biggest crocodile I had yet seen. Comparing him with the *A.I.A.*, which lay in deep water some 300 yards off, I reckoned him to be quite fifty feet long; while the centre of the saw-like ridge on the top of his back must have been about four feet above the sand on which his belly rested. Having only a shotgun with me, I had, on first seeing him, sent a native boy who was with me for my rifle, and made the foregoing observations while waiting for his return. The crocodile, meantime, took no notice of me—either because he was asleep, or because I was out of his sight, being, to use a nautical term, on his starboard quarter—while taking care to keep well out of range of his huge tail. As the boy was a long time coming, I considered it advisable to get a little further off, and in so doing alarmed the ducks, which flew away to another bank. As we were quite out of meat on board, this sight so wrought upon my feelings that, forgetting all about the crocodile, I took a snap shot after the ducks, which I missed, but so frightened the huge saurian that he made off for the water, scattering the sand far and wide with a sweep of his tail.

Some miles back, across the grassy plains (which abound in herds of tawny and black buffalo), may be seen the hill-ranges, which, gradually coming nearer, form the high banks of the river about Bolobo. Here, where the islands are fewer and more scattered, the full breadth of the lordly river (between four and five miles) comes into view; while on a clear sunny day the hills on the north bank form a splendid panorama, especially when the sun, setting behind them, bathes the scene in purple and gold. On the south side, the high rocky banks, crowned with villages nestling in groves of palms and bananas, form a welcome change from the monotonous flatness of the plain behind us.

From Bolobo to the Kwa the river is fairly straight, narrowing down to some two miles, with the hills rising in height on either side; and a run down on the strong current, when the evening breeze has tempered the heat of the day, amply repays one for the toilsome ascent. From the mouth of the Kwa its course is nearly due south for about ten miles, when, being suddenly deflected to the east by the rocky point of Ganchu, it scoops a large bay out of the left bank; and finding another rocky barrier opposed to its course in that direction, rushes back to the west, just below the point; and then, both banks being rocky, again takes a southward course, the water below the point whirling and seething as if angry at being forced to turn aside. Below this, on the left bank, is Gobila's (a portrait of this chief may be seen in 'The Congo,' vol. i.

p. 508), near the spot where Mswata station once stood. Here we stopped to buy a fowl or two; and having already been plentifully supplied with fresh vegetables by the French missionaries of St Paul du Kassai, we considered ourselves very well off in the matter of victuals.

Below Gobila's the river winds between towering hills—those on the right bank, which are the highest, being covered with thick forests, alternating with patches of long grass. The forest mostly occupies the valleys and lower slopes of the hills, their tops being clothed with grass; but now and then one sees a hill, the top of which is covered with forest, while the sides are bare or grass-grown; while hills entirely forested or grass-covered occasionally form a pleasing contrast. Those on the left bank are mostly covered with grass—a low scrubby forest lining the river; while fan-palms (*Hyphæne guineensis*), singly or in groves, are seen at intervals. As we descend, the river narrows, till, just below Pururu Island, it is not much more than one mile and a quarter wide, though of tremendous depth, after which the width again increases as we near the Pool. Pururu Island is quite a picture in itself—the upper half being covered with a splendid grove of fan-palms, while the lower is clothed with thick forest, where elephants may sometimes be seen tearing down branches from the trees to get at the young leaves.

A little below this is Dualla Island, smaller in extent and entirely covered with forest; and then we come into view of a brown rocky cliff on the right bank, from the top of which the forest stretches away up the slope of the hills. On the opposite side, a little lower down, is One Palm Point—a rocky ridge projecting into the river, and marked by a splendid *Hyphæne* palm standing conspicuously out above the low scrub.

But amid all this wealth of scenic grandeur and glory, I could not help feeling that " I love better the crags of Arthur's Seat, and the sea coming in ayont them." These words of Sir Walter Scott's had been forcibly brought back to my memory a short time before this date, by reading Mrs Oliphant's 'Joyce,' which one of my kind friends in Scotland had sent out to me among a lot of other literature. One stifling evening, after a hard day's work, I was vainly trying to get to sleep. Under a mosquito-curtain it was too hot and close, and outside the vicious insects gave me no peace. I picked up the first book I found in my box, and, getting a light, began wearily to turn over the leaves. A graphic description of a steamboat-pier on a dark night arrested my attention and brought back refreshing memories of former days spent on the Firth of Clyde, revelling in the beauties of bonnie Scotland. As I read on, the lovely view of the Thames valley from Richmond Hill, so ably described, with all its

THE *EN AVANT* PASSING ONE PALM POINT.

FROM A SKETCH BY THE AUTHOR.

To face page 188.

pleasant associations, rose up vividly before me; and presently I went to sleep, spite of mosquitoes and heat—to awake refreshed at dawn next day. Should the authoress of that book ever read these lines, I hope she will accept my sincere thanks. It brought to my mind's eye the long, parallel straight lines of shining metal in dear old England which some people think so ugly — the memory of which speaks to me of being whirled over the ground in comfortable carriages, at the rate of forty to sixty miles per hour — of palatial hotels, and well-cooked meals on snowy table-cloths, and kind friends waiting to welcome the wanderer home. It is on visions like these that travellers live through the hours of utter misery which they are sure to experience in countries like Africa. When tired and enervated, perhaps hungry and thirsty, the remembrance of lordly London and her imperial pleasures rises up and nerves them to make one more effort to overcome their present difficulties, in hopes of the reward to come. Stanley himself has been heard to say that he preferred a lump of *kwanga* in an African swamp to all the banquets in creation—and why ? Because it is only under such circumstances that one can properly appreciate the luxuries of civilisation. A man who is always eating sugar soon ceases to find any pleasure in the taste. In the same way, a man who always lives a civilised life, though he may be fairly happy, can never experience such intense enjoyment of its blessings as one who knows and has tried the toils, dangers, and hardships of savage countries.

Rounding One Palm Point on a strong current, we came in view of Lissa Market, and the *En Avant* lying among the long grass that fringed the shore. This brave little steamer, which had first borne Stanley up the Congo, was now on her way to mount the Oubangi, whence she did not return till she had solved the vexed question of that river's identity with the Wellé-Makua. As it was about 5 P.M., we steamed in and camped alongside her; and Captain Van Gèle having given me my mails (which he was taking up to Equator), I retired to the *A.I.A.*, where, my boy having made up my bed, I pushed aside the mosquito-net and lay down to digest some home news before going to dine on board the *En Avant*.

The sun was just setting, and some Houssas ashore cutting wood were singing to the tune of "Sailing, sailing — over the bounding main!" "Sailing, sailing!"—how it carried my thoughts back to an almost forgotten August evening, when I stood on the pier at Dunoon, with a bonnie Scotch lassie by my side, waiting for the *Lord of the Isles* to convey me to Greenock. The broad Clyde rolled in front, and beyond, the Cloch lighthouse, bathed in the glow of the setting sun, stood forth, white and gleaming, from the background of woods and hills that stretched away behind Gourock. A little one-eyed newsboy was singing "Sailing, sailing," to a circle of gentlemen who had started him off by the gift of a few coppers. It was my last day in Scotland, and the steamer that was to take me away was lying at the Tail of the Bank, in all her glory of new paint and polished brass, fresh from the builder's yard. I had run over from Greenock to say good-bye to some friends at Dunoon before leaving the country for an indefinite time, and the young lady who had come to see me off was very much distressed at my going to sea, and wanted me, even at the eleventh hour, to give up my ship and stop in England. Poor girl! she had cause to dread the great ocean, which she had only viewed along the western shore of her native land; for a cousin of hers had but a short time previously gone to sea in a Glasgow steamer—his first voyage, I believe—and before the vessel was well clear of the Irish seas, had been washed overboard during a gale and drowned. I had never seen her from that day to this; and now, in the calm of an African evening, the whole scene came back to me as clear as noonday. What had become of the little one-eyed newsboy?—what——? "*Sacré nom de guerre! qu'est-ce que c'est là?*" burst from the officer in charge of the boat, and both he and I began sneezing, and sneezed till the tears ran down our faces. I had, while basking in the "light of other days," opened the first of my letters, and a cloud of pepper falling out, had caused the sensation. The first few words of the letter explained everything. I had, on a former occasion, told my correspondent that, as letters took about six months to reach me, they had better be salted in order to keep the news fresh ; and he had accordingly not only salted his, but peppered it as well,—and to such an extent that I wonder some of the post-office officials did not sneeze their heads off.

Next morning (October 6th) we were off with daylight, and passing the spot where the Wampomo discharges its inky waters into the main stream, and Palmyra Bay—near which a reef of rocks lurks in mid-stream, just below the water, to catch unwary steamers—we entered the Pool about ten o'clock, and before three in the afternoon were once more made fast alongside the *Stanley* on " Léo " beach— within two or three days of a year from the time I had arrived from Stanley Falls with Captain Coquilhat and Mr Deane. The *A.I.A.* had been pretty nearly run to pieces by this time, having had—besides being herself heavily laden—to tow a whaleboat of nearly her own size ; and the repairs which I had to undertake, as well as a slight attack of fever, delayed our departure for Bangala till October 27th.

Having cleared Nshassa, we were steaming across the Pool when my eye was caught by a tent erected

on Long Island on a spot well known to me a year
before as a favourite hunting-camp of Captain
Bayley. I knew that he had lately returned to the
Congo along with Mr Deane (now restored to health)
for the sole purpose of hunting, and had, indeed,
quitted Nshassa for Long Island only two days before. As we turned towards the shore, a second tent
came into view, from which emerged Mr Deane,
shouting to us an invitation to come ashore. We
did so, and found that they had that morning shot
two antelopes and a buffalo. Long Island abounds
in the latter, which is perhaps the most dangerous
animal to the hunter to be met with on the Congo,
as he is extremely hard to kill, unless hit in a vital
part, and very fierce when wounded—charging down
on his enemy, and goring him with his sharp and
powerful horns, should he not be quick enough in
getting out of the way. The antelopes were very
fine animals, of a dark-grey colour, with faint white
stripes down the flanks, with very graceful heads
and horns. I had several times seen both dark-grey and red antelopes marked with white in this
way, and at first thought them different species,
but afterwards discovered that one was the male
and the other the female. I have also bought from
the natives at Mpeza several light-grey skins and
one or two small pairs of horns, which, I believe,
belong to a very pretty little gazelle; but I have
never seen this animal, either dead or alive, though,

judging from the number of skins the Langa-Langa offer for sale, it must be plentiful in their country. Having been regaled by Mr Deane — in the absence of Captain Bayley, who was out hunting — with antelope-steaks, and presented with a hindquarter of the same animal, we started again and camped for the night at the upper end of the Pool. It was a fine, clear, moonlight night, and the view across to Dover Cliffs was like a scene from fairyland.

Next morning we started early, and had a fine long day's run up to Dualla Island. We observed several flocks of guinea-fowl on shore; the bronze ibis, with its long beak and splendid plumage, was occasionally seen flying about in twos and threes, and the spur-winged plover wheeled round and round over the sand-banks; while from the bush came the soft cry of the wood-pigeon. Everything this run seemed to be in our favour. We found plenty of fuel every night, and had no head-winds or storms to delay us.

On November 3d we reached Lukolela, and camped some three miles below the place where the new Baptist Mission Station was slowly but surely approaching completion. Between our camp and this station lay two or three villages, and the chief of one of these was at this time on very bad terms with the missionaries, because they had decided against him in some dispute with his neighbours, which had been referred to the *mundélé*. Being unaware of this, and in haste to reach Bangala, I decided to walk up to the Mission that night with the letters, and so avoid the delay of stopping there by daylight. As soon as I had finished dinner, I gave my boy my Winchester rifle to carry, took the mail and my revolver, lit a bull's-eye lantern, and started. We passed through the first village all right, escorted by a crowd of curious natives, who left us when we came to the belt of dense forest which divides their town from the next. Walking in front of my boy, and carrying the lantern waist-high, I plunged down the dense gloom of the forest-path, stumbling along over roots and stones. At length we reached the cleared ground round the second village, and I was greatly surprised at the noise and commotion our approach seemed to create. As I entered it, men, women, children, goats, and dogs, fled before me as if I had been a pestilence, and I walked right through, greatly puzzled as to the cause of this scare. Another belt of forest, and another village, the inhabitants of which fled in the same mysterious manner, and I at last reached the Mission Station, where all was soon explained. The two last villages through which I had passed were the two that had quarrelled, the first of the two being governed by the chief above mentioned, against whom the missionaries had decided the case. As I approached through the intense darkness, holding the lantern in front of me, they had taken the round, glaring eye, which was all they could see (I and my boy being invisible in the darkness behind), for a bad fetish sent by the missionaries to kill them, and had fled. In the same way the second village had taken it to be an evil spirit sent against them by their enemy, the chief of the first; and I had marched, like a conquering hero, clean through the two hostile towns, without even being aware that anything was wrong. After spending an hour or two with the missionaries, I started on my way back, and, taking care to keep well behind my lantern, once more passed the villages, like an avenging spirit, and reached the steamer about midnight. On the 6th, we stopped an hour or two at Equator to get wood, and continuing our journey, arrived at Bangala before noon on the 9th, having been only a little over thirteen days from Léopoldville—the quickest run yet made.

MR. HERBERT WARD.

*From a photograph, taken at St. Paul de Loanda.
By permission of Mr Rowland Ward.*

CHAPTER IX.

NEWS FROM YAMBUYA.

IMPROVEMENTS AT BANGALA—STATE CAPTIVES NOT YET LIBERATED —WE START FOR UPOTO—FIREWORKS *AU NATUREL*—BURNING OF UPOTO — PURCHASE OF SLAVES AT MPEZA — DOWN - RIVER AGAIN—DEATH ON BOARD THE *A.I.A.*—FUNERAL AT LUKOLELA —SHAGERSTROM'S COCKTAIL—THE *A.I.A.* STRIKES A CROCODILE —THE SON OF MIYONGO — DEATH OF VAN DE VELDE — WARD ARRIVES WITH NEWS FROM THE ARUHWIMI.

AT Bangala the station was fast improving, and a new red-brick house, intended for a mess-room and provision-store, was nearly finished. Owing to the damp climate, wood quickly rots, unless painted or preserved in some other way ; and paint not being procurable in sufficient quantities, Mr Van Kerck- hoven had decided to use as little wood as possible, and therefore made the doors arched, and the windows with a square brick column down the centre, and a double arch at the top in alternate red and white bricks, which gave the building a somewhat ecclesiastical appearance. The front door opened right into a large and lofty room, the walls of which, washed with white clay, set off the window-curtains (composed of blue *savelist* and Paisley shawls, out of the trading stock of the station) to great advantage. This house, besides being strong and durable, was a great improvement in point of appearance on the older clay buildings; and when others are completed in the same style, Bangala will be no undesirable residence, except for the great disadvantage of its isolated position. During my absence some of the Ba-Ngala had been on a trading expedition to Upoto, and had fallen out with the natives of Langa-Langa. The affair ended in the Ba-Ngala seizing several of the up-river people, and paddling off home, arriving with their prizes a few days before the *A.I.A.* came up from Ntamo. Mr Van Kerckhoven, on hearing of this, immediately bought all the prisoners from their captors; and a few days later he started, with Mr Dhanis and myself, for Upoto, to try and bring the unreasonable Langa-Langa to their senses. By November 18th we were again abreast of Bokélé, to which place our prisoners belonged; and as the people of Bokélé had to send for those we wanted from Upoto, we made fast to an island, with a 500 yards' channel between us and the village. Towards evening on the 20th, some canoes came down, with the three women belonging to the State; and having exchanged some of the prisoners for them, we were beginning to think the troublesome business at an end, when one of the women informed us that there were five more still in the hands of the chief of Upoto. Having sent a message to the chief to bring these five, we waited till next morning for an answer, when he sent an insolent demand for five slaves as a ransom for each woman. Mr Van Kerckhoven sent back word that he was going away, and that if the women were not at once given up, on his return he would burn Upoto. On the 22d we arrived at Mobeka, at the mouth of the Ngala river. This town now occupies the same site as it did some years ago; but when I first arrived in the country it was situated some fifteen miles up the Ngala. The reason of its removal was a war with the Ba-Ngala, who completely sacked and burned the town, forcing the inhabitants to seek a more distant spot—till Lusengi, their chief, became the blood-brother of the *mundélé* at Bangala, and having made peace with his old enemies, returned to the former site, where he is fast growing rich by trading in ivory. On our return to Bangala on the 23d, the *A.I.A.* was taken out of the water to be scraped and painted; and on December 2d, the *Stanley* arrived from Ntamo, bringing the longed-for mails, and also Captain Thys, who had come out on a tour of inspection for the company formed to construct the Congo railway, which, for some inscrutable reason, entitles itself *La Compagnie du Congo pour le Commerce et l'Industrie*. Mr Hodister, of the Sanford Exploring Expedition, had also come up to found a station, and thus establish the first trading factory among a people who, six or seven years ago, were nothing but river-pirates, levying blackmail on their neighbours, and hiring themselves out as armed escorts to the trading canoes going up-river to purchase ivory. The *Stanley* left us in a few days, and during the next few weeks I was kept so busy with repairs to the whale-boat, that we could not start for Upoto till after the New Year. On the 9th of January 1888 we got under way again, this time accompanied by Mr Hodister and Mr Verhees. As it had been decided to burn Upoto unless the captives were surrendered, we had on board, besides the usual crew of nine men, over forty Ba-Ngala, and towed the whale-boat and three large canoes, so that the little engine was strained to the utmost.

Two or three days after starting, we moored for the night off a low marshy forest, consisting mostly of rosewood-trees, with groves of palm lining the river-bank. The men having found a large dead rosewood-tree, whose trunk was some two feet six inches in diameter, began cutting it up for fuel, and to obtain light for their work, set fire to the dead stalks and leaves which always surround the trunk of this species of palm. This is a sight which equals, if it does not surpass, the magnificent set pieces let off at an exhibition of fireworks at the Crystal Palace. At first the fire smoulders among the short dead stalks round the foot of the trunk, but gradually gaining power, at length rushes up the tree in one huge column of roaring flame, devouring all the dead foliage, and giving an indescribable beauty to the feathery palm-leaves, which stand out distinct and black against the background of flame and smoke. The end of the show is perhaps the most striking of all, when, the dead leaves being consumed, the fire dies down, leaving the bunch of palm-nuts burning away among the blackened fronds. The ball of fire, flaring away on the tree-top, is a weird spectacle seen from the river in a dark night—further set off by the smoke curling up to the stars, the utter blackness of the surrounding forest, and the reflection of the whole in the water. Two or three palms growing close together sometimes blaze up all at once—sometimes one catches fire from another just dying out. Where there are plenty of palms, the Ba-Ngala always contrive to have one burning when they have any work to do at night. The fire does not kill the trees, only burning up the dead stalks and leaves, and then dying out. This palm has, properly speaking, no trunk—the huge leaves rise right from the ground to a height of thirty or forty feet.

On January 16th we once more steamed round Upoto Point, and found the village up in arms to receive us. Samba and the Ba-Ngala (who had been relegated to the canoes) had paddled ahead of us, as we steamed slowly past the line of villages below Upoto, and on finding the village in regular fighting order, had drawn off and begun a raid among the islands in genuine Ba-Ngala style, capturing a number of women and children hidden there, and drinking all the palm-wine they could find. When we arrived abreast of the chief's house, Mr Van Kerckhoven demanded the surrender of the captives; to which the chief, having first executed a *pas seul*, replied that, if we wanted the women, we must come and fetch them, and then resumed his war-dance — while the group of hideously painted and befeathered warriors behind him joined in, like a chorus, waving their shields and spears about, as they twisted their bodies into all sorts of queer contortions. Some were smeared over from head to foot with grey clay, others were bright red with camwood powder; others, again, painted over with red, white, and yellow streaks. In the midst of this performance, the order was given to our men to fire, and the chief ended his performance with a leap into the air, as a rifle-bullet "let daylight" through him. A few volleys cleared the village, and then we moved off to await the return of the Ba-Ngala, as we were too weak to burn the place without them. They appeared shortly after, having captured some thirty-five prisoners and several canoes. The prisoners were mostly women and children, the few men among them being either old or severely wounded. It is seldom that warriors of this tribe allow themselves to be taken alive. I saw a Ba-Ngala in one of the canoes, on coming alongside the *A.I.A.*, stoop down and lift up a head dripping with blood, which he had just cut off. The sight nearly made me sick, and of course I instantly made him throw it into the river, where it sank like a lump of lead. Another had a small child's hand which he proudly exhibited, as if he had achieved a great feat in cutting it off. What I saw of the Ba-Ngala on this occasion completely disgusted me with the notion of using such savage troops as these, even against savages like themselves. They carefully avoided the village where the Langa-Langa warriors were awaiting them, and went off to the islands where the old men, women, and children were hidden. These they murdered or captured wholesale; and it was only after the village had been cleared by a fusilade from the steamer, that they would land and burn it. It is the custom of the Ba-Ngala and other warlike tribes of the Upper Congo to cut off and carry home the heads of their enemies slain in battle; and I have, in several villages, seen a large tree in front of the chief's hut on whose branches are impaled numerous human skulls. In one village, not only was the tree decorated with some forty of these ghastly trophies, but a heap of them was piled round the trunk; and round this, at a radius of about thirty feet, was a circular seat formed of clay, kept in its place by pieces of old canoes, and adorned here and there with a grinning skull. Several more were lying about, roughly shaped into drinking-cups; for this was the place where the village patriarchs held their evening *symposium*, drinking their *malafu*, like King Alboin, the Lombard, out of the skulls of their enemies.

As the Ba-Ngala — having come across liberal quantities of palm-wine — were all more or less drunk, there was some difficulty in making them hand over their prisoners; but when these were at last all secured on board the *A.I.A.*, we steamed in close to the village, where the natives were awaiting us with flint-lock muskets and spears, while several war-canoes were visible in a creek about half a mile off. Having cleared the village with a volley or two from our rifles, and dispersed the canoes in the same way, we took the steamer in as close as the rocks would allow us; and then the Ba-Ngala, having landed in the canoes, were soon scooting about, cutting down banana-trees, and applying firebrands to the palm-leaf thatch of the huts, which, being dry as tinder, were soon in a blaze. It was a really grand sight, when the flames, with a dull roar, spread up the hillside, lapping round and blackening the green banana-leaves, till it had dried them up, when they shared the fate of the huts. The smoke and flames, rushing in one dense cloud up the hill, made the trees behind, when they were visible at all, look black as ink; and the bright sunshine pouring down from above, gave a very strange effect to the scene. Presently a spreading tree in the centre of the village — under which was the usual heap of skulls — was enveloped in flames; and the heat, which was by this time intense, as the whole hillside was now one mass of fire, soon shrivelled up the foliage, and left the tree as bare as if it had been dead. Above the roar of the flames we heard the bang of the Langa-Langa muskets—they could not have taken good aim, as they hit no one—and the sharper crack of the rifles wielded by the Ba-Ngala, whose black forms were seen rushing about in the fierce heat like so many salamanders. How they endured it I am at loss to imagine, for the heat was so intense where the $A.I.A.$ lay—nearly 100 yards off shore to windward—that I was several times glad to turn away my face. In half an hour all was over, nothing being left on the blackened hillside but smouldering posts and heaps of ashes;

and we steamed away for Bangala—stopping a few minutes at Bokélé to tell the people that we would restore the thirty-five prisoners to Upoto when the State captives were given up. We had, besides the whale-boat, five large canoes in tow, and in all 130 people on board, including Europeans, Ba-Ngala, prisoners, our own crew, and some thirty-five slaves, whose liberty had been purchased by Mr Van Kerckhoven from the natives of Mpeza. Most of them were boys and girls between the ages of ten and fifteen, with a few older men and women.

Knowing how the people of Mpeza treat their slaves, one would be tempted to buy as many as possible; and at first I thought the measure a very good one, but further reflection convinced me that, as the demand creates the supply, the natives would continue to procure slaves by raids on other tribes, and sell them to the State, as long as the latter was willing to buy them—so that, though the condition of those bought would be considerably improved, their place would soon be supplied by others, and perhaps dozens of men killed in some raid undertaken for the sole purpose of capturing a few boys and girls.

As the country was very much disturbed, Mr Hodister, who had come up with us to see what sort of place it was for trade, did not get much ivory. The people of Upoto and the neighbouring villages, however, must have plenty, as all the traders between Bangala and Irebu go up there to purchase the ivory, which they sell to the Bayanzi of Bolobo, who, in their turn, pass it on to the Pool. With the crowd we had on board, it was a great relief to arrive at Bangala on the 19th of January, but there was no rest to be had just yet. Thirty Zanzibaris had finished their three years' term of service, and were to be sent down to Léopoldville; and two Belgians, who had been ill, had grown so much worse during my absence, that, as we had no medical officer at the station, the chief decided to send them down too. This time the whale-boat was required for use at Bangala, and a canoe towed alongside was our only additional accommodation. I leave my readers to imagine the discomfort of this run, especially for the two sick men, whose pain, in spite of all we could do for them, must have been considerably increased by the throbbing and shaking of the little steamer, which, owing to her heavy-laden condition, was more violent than usual. Next day we arrived at Equator, where Mr Banks, of the Livingstone Inland Mission, was kind enough to prescribe for our invalids, who, by his timely assistance, were enabled to pass a quiet night on shore in the Sanford Company's station. Next morning, one of them, who was down with dysentery, and whose sufferings had been so much intensified by the shaking of the steamer that we thought he could never reach Equator alive, seemed to have rallied so far that we again hoped to bring him safely to Léopoldville; all the more so, as he told us that the agonising pain of the day before had nearly ceased. We started as early as possible in order to reach the Baptist Mission Station at Lukolela before night; but our patient soon began to sink rapidly, and at 10 A.M. Mr Dhanis came to me to ask if I could not go any faster, as he did not think the sick man could live many hours. But the little *A.I.A.* was doing all she knew; and there was nothing for it but to await the end, which came a little after mid-day, when, slowly and silently, death entered the boat, and we could do no more. The Zanzibaris, who had been attending on him since we left Bangala, washed the corpse, and covering it with blankets, laid it out on a kind of hurdle astern—as we had decided to try and reach Lukolela sooner than dig a nameless grave in the forest. Owing to a tremendous tornado, we had to stop some three hours, and therefore camped on a sand-bank that night, and did not reach Lukolela till next day. Mr Richards [1] and Mr Darby, of the Baptist Mission, on learning the state of the case, rendered us every assistance in their power—even setting their carpenters to make a coffin, while our men dug a grave at the top of a high bank, behind the old State station,

[1] Since dead, August 1888.

TWO PALM POINT.

FROM A SKETCH BY THE AUTHOR.

To face page 208.

overlooking the river. One grave already marked the spot—being that of Mr Keys, a State official, who had been killed by a buffalo three years before. And there, in the silence of the deep jungle—disturbed only by a prowling bush-cat or jackal, or by the chattering of the monkeys and screaming of the parrots in the lofty trees overhead—we raised a cairn of stones to mark where his mortal remains had been laid to rest. Having still another sick man to consider, we left the Mission the same evening, and having taken in fuel at the lower end of the village, where there was plenty of dry wood, started off once more. The river was very low, and we had much trouble from sand-banks,— especially at Two Palm Point, a few miles above Bolobo—so called from two tall *Hyphæne* palms growing close together, which form a well-known landmark. Having vainly tried to find a channel among the sand-banks at the end of this point, where there were barely three feet of water, we let out a long chain, and all the Zanzibaris, jumping overboard, seized it and dragged the *A.I.A.* bodily over—probably at the expense of the paint on her keel. A tame elephant would have been very useful under the circumstances.

We reached Léopoldville on the 30th of January, without any further incident, except a two hours' halt in the hospitable tents of the two Nimrods of the Congo, Messrs Deane and Bayley, whom we found encamped in a picturesque situation opposite Pururu Island. From them we heard that Baron Rothkirch, who had for some time been ill with abscess of the liver, had died at Nshassa on December 6th, 1887. The invalid having been handed over to the doctor, and the *A.I.A.* made fast alongside the *Stanley*, I was free to discuss the news and a cocktail with the captain and engineers of the latter. The cocktail, however, turned out to be a snare and a delusion; for Captain Shagerstrom, having no spice, surreptitiously introduced into the mixture a few grains of quinine, with the result that we all vowed never to intrust that perfidious Scandinavian with the compounding of another, and that notwithstanding his assurances that he had done it to keep off the fever.

I found that part of the expedition for Stanley Falls was still at Léopoldville, consisting of some officers sent up by the State to assist Tippoo Tip, who had come round from Zanzibar with Stanley and the Emin Pasha Expedition, and gone straight on to his post as governor at the Falls, where he had now been some six months. Captain Van de Velde, in charge of the expedition, was down with fever; and some of his loads not having arrived from Matadi, the *Stanley* was awaiting their arrival and the chief's recovery, to take them all up to Kinsi Katini.

We left again, with stores for Bangala, on Feb-

THE *A.I.A.* AGROUND ON A CROCODILE.
FROM A SKETCH BY THE AUTHOR.

To face page 210.

ruary 3d. Passing Pururu Island three days later, we found Messrs Deane and Bayley still in the same camp, and made fast there for the night. The *Florida* coming up before dark, we all dined together "under the twinkling starlight," which was almost rivalled in brilliancy by the fire-flies among the grass at our feet.

Two or three days after this we suddenly brought up on a sand-bank, with only three feet of water. The engines were at once stopped, but the steamer's bow was embedded in the sand, which seemed to heave up and down under us, and the water was strangely disturbed. I was looking for the cause of this unusual commotion (which I should have set down as being caused by our running into a hippo, had the river been deeper at that spot, but there was not enough water to cover one), when I saw an enormous crocodile—*longer*, I am certain, than the *A.I.A.*, and therefore over forty feet—rush across the bank and tumble into the deep water beyond. I never before saw a large crocodile move so quickly, and I had no time to get a shot at him. He must have heard us coming, and been trying to make for the deep water on our side of the bank, when we ran into him and jammed him into the sand. We struck him while moving at the rate of four miles an hour, but during the short time he was in view, I could not see that he bore any marks of the collision.

On the evening of the 12th we camped at Lukolela, and on the 14th arrived opposite Usindi, where we landed the son of Miyongo, who had come up from Nshassa with us, having been for some time previously employed by the Sanford Exploring Expedition. His father, Miyongo, one of the chiefs of Usindi, was the man rescued by Stanley from the wreck of his canoe below Lukolela, and restored to his village. Next morning, before we left, he came on board with a present of a sheep, eggs, and fowls, and then demanded about twenty times their value in cloth and other goods as a return present—such is the nature of these "blameless Ethiopians." Having at length, if not satisfied, at least convinced him that we were not to be bled any further, he took to his canoe, and with many handshakings allowed us to pursue our way.

We found that during our absence the people of Upoto had, through the medium of some other tribes, made overtures of peace; so we hoped that, on the arrival of the *Stanley*, the expedition would not only establish the State's authority at the Falls, but also settle this troublesome business of ours, which had now been going on for nearly eighteen months. Owing to Captain Van de Velde's death, however, the *Stanley* did not arrive at Bangala till the beginning of April—and then without the expedition, which remained at Léopoldville waiting for Van de Velde's successor. It was expected that, by the time the *Stanley* returned to Léopoldville, all would be in readiness, and the long-delayed expedition to Stanley Falls would at last get under way. But even should there be no more delays, Tippoo Tip would, by the time it arrived at Stanley Falls, have been there nearly a year, during which time not a word of communication has passed between the Falls and Ntamo, so that the state of affairs at the former place was at this time utterly unknown to the outside world.

On the evening of Sunday, April 8th, 1888, the Europeans at Bangala Station were seated at dinner, when one of the Houssas doing sentry by the river came in and reported that he had heard some people in canoes talking Kiswahili; but, as it was too dark to see anything, he could not tell whether there was one canoe or fifty. As no news had come from Stanley Falls for nearly a year, and the force which was to have been sent up to Tippoo Tip had been delayed by various circumstances, we conjectured that the latter had despatched the canoes to make inquiries about it. Following the chief of the station down to the beach, I saw, looming through the darkness, two huge canoes lashed together, slowly approaching the bank. The first man to step ashore was Mr Herbert Ward, who had passed up-river a year ago in the *Stanley* with the last detachment of the Emin Pasha Relief Expedition, and whom I then supposed to be either at Wadelai or on his way thence to the east coast. In answer to my hurried inquiries, I learned that no news had been received from Stanley, except the vague reports of deserters from his caravan; that Major Barttelot and his company were still at the camp on the Aruhwimi Rapids, where Stanley had left them, and where they were living principally on manioc and beans; and that Tippoo Tip, after making various excuses for the non-arrival of the promised 600 carriers, had gone to Kassongo in November 1887. As he had not returned by the following January, Major Barttelot had sent Mr Jameson to hurry his movements, and the latter was still absent when Mr Ward left the Aruhwimi.

The *Stanley* had left Bangala on the morning of the 8th, and Mr Ward started early on the following morning, in order if possible to overtake her at Equator, where she was to stop and take in wood. He had come from the Arab settlement at the mouth of the Lomami (with thirty-five Zanzibaris, in two canoes lashed together) in five and a half days; and pursuing his journey in a smaller canoe, manned by Samba and twenty Ba-Ngala, reached Equator in less than twenty-two hours, arriving an hour or two before the departure of the *Stanley*. He thus performed the entire journey between the Lomami and Equator (a distance of over 500 miles) in six and a half days. The journey could not have been made in a shorter time by any of the steamers at that time on the Upper Congo, which were forced to stop every night to cut wood; whereas Mr Ward took no rest, but travelled day and night, with the exception of a stay of less than ten hours at Bangala—so that the tidings which had left the Aruhwimi on April 2d were known in England by the 1st of May.

CHAPTER X.

MAJOR BARTTELOT'S CAMP.

START FOR YAMBUYA—A ROYAL STOWAWAY—WAR-DRUMS—THE BASOKO—SCENERY OF THE ARUHWIMI—DEPREDATIONS OF THE ARABS—FINE TIMBER—DESCRIPTION OF MAJOR BARTTELOT'S CAMP—SALIM BIN MAHOMED—MANYEMAS—SALIM SENDS HIS IVORY TO THE FALLS—NATIVES LIVING IN CANOES—BLACK "MASHERS"—ARABS AT THE LOMAMI—LARGE CANOES—RASCHID'S HOUSE—HIS ACCOUNT OF THE LOSS OF STANLEY FALLS STATION—YAPORO ONCE MORE—YANGAMBI.

THE thirty-five Zanzibaris mentioned in the last chapter as having come down with Ward, remained for the present at Bangala—the Commissaire de District promising to take them back in the *A.I.A.* Owing to a trip I had to take to Equator on business connected with the station, and the preparations necessary for the run to Stanley Falls, our departure was delayed till April 24th, when the *A.I.A.* left Bangala, with Mr Van Kerckhoven and myself, the thirty-five Zanzibaris, and her own crew of fifteen men, on board. The poor little steamer, having a whale-boat lashed on one side of

MAJOR E. M. BARTTELOT.

From a photograph, by kind permission of Dr Walter E. Barttelot, M.I

her, and a large canoe on the other, and carrying some fifty loads (50 to 65 lb. each) of stores, had hard work to make headway against the current, which, as the river was at the height of its spring rise, was very strong. That evening we stopped at a village called Mutembo, ruled over by a chief named Mablasia, who was said to be one of those who turned out their war-canoes on Stanley, when the latter descended the river in 1879. This chief now came on board with a present of a goat and some fowls, and hearing where we were going, asked permission to accompany us. As we were already pretty crowded, this was refused; and I conducted him and his retinue ashore—of course with a handsome present to console him for his disappointment. The moon being full, and the night clear, we only stopped long enough to get a fair supply of firewood, and left about 10 P.M., so as to gain a little time by a night run. As soon as we had got under way, all the men not engaged in the work of the steamer began to stow themselves away in the whale-boat, the canoe, and the forward section of the steamer, to sleep as best they could. Only four or five were allowed to remain on board, as the forward part of the steamer was full of firewood (the after part, where the loads were stored, being reserved for the Europeans), and it was necessary to keep a clear view for the man at the wheel. About six more went into the canoe; and this—allowing for those on duty—left about thirty, who proceeded to pack themselves into the whale-boat. After witnessing the amount of suffocation an African native will endure before giving up the ghost, I can understand how it was that the old slaving captains contrived to get to America without losing their whole cargo every voyage. Next morning, at daylight, while watching a huge heap of blankets and mats in the whale-boat gradually resolve itself into human arms and legs, I was greatly astonished by seeing Mablasia extricate himself from the bottom of the pile, and go up to Mr Van Kerckhoven, calmly demanding a gun, as he had left his village without his spear. It turned out that, on our refusal to take him on board, he and two of his men, profiting by the confusion of our night start, had stowed themselves away. As it is the native custom to reckon every man as a foe who enters another's house with a weapon in his hand, he had left all his arms behind to prove that his intentions were friendly, and now asked for a gun to defend himself, in case we were attacked by tribes up the river. It says a great deal for the prestige of the Europeans on the Congo that a native chief like Mablasia should trust himself, unarmed, and with only two followers, on board a steamer away from his home. Had the *A.I.A.* been a native trading-canoe, the custom of the country would have sanctioned her owners' seizing him as a slave, and demanding an enormous ransom for his release. Natives, as a rule, are very much afraid of being seized in this way by Europeans, and will never approach a steamer unless in sufficient numbers to resist an attack. As we were now some thirty miles from his village, Mr Van Kerckhoven decided to allow him to come with us. I did not at first relish the notion of having him on board, as my previous experience of chiefs under similar circumstances was anything but pleasant, for they no sooner set foot on deck than they began to order every one and everything about, and could not be persuaded that the steamer did not belong to them. However, during the three months he was with us, Mablasia never gave any trouble, and was altogether the best-behaved native chief it has ever been my lot to meet.

Beyond two or three brushes with warlike natives, nothing worth mentioning occurred during the next few days. As we approached the country of the Basoko, we occasionally heard their huge war-drums, which carried my thoughts back over the intervening two years, to the time when Captain Coquilhat and I were on our way through this region to Stanley Falls, and the war-drums boomed in our ears day and night. Once more I seemed to hear the roar of the cataract of Kiusi Katini and the crack of the Arab rifles, and wondered what the place would be like now. Once more was the little *A.I.A.* on her way to relieve a distant outpost of white men, but this time under happier circumstances; and the memory of those other days now seemed like a bad dream of long ago.

On May 6th we reached the mouth of the Aruhwimi, and turned up that stream, in order to reach Yambuya, where Major Barttelot was encamped. Just inside the mouth of this river are two large native towns; but the crowds who lined the banks, ferociously brandishing spears and knives, deterred us from trying to enter into friendly relations there. These people (called by Stanley Basoko) are great fighters, and their enormous spears, knives, and other weapons are not only more substantial in make than those of other tribes, but the workmanship gives evidence of superior artistic ability; and they are as brightly polished as Sheffield cutlery. A curious weapon manufactured by them is a throwing-knife with several blades, which, owing to an almost imperceptible twist in the metal, revolves in the air, when thrown by a practised hand, with the action of a boomerang. The sight of these crowds, dancing along the banks, and flashing the polished surfaces of their weapons in the sunlight, reminded me of 'King Solomon's Mines'; and had Rider Haggard ever been on the Congo, I should certainly have thought he was describing the Basoko. I am sorry to say that the resemblance ceases when one comes to look for the Roman or Spartan discipline depicted by that writer; but this, I suppose, is in some degree to be found among the Zulus and other South African tribes, or in such a kingdom as that of Uganda under Mtesa, as described by Speke and Grant.

The scenery of the Aruhwimi is finer than that of any of the tributaries of the Congo I have seen. As we steamed up it, the banks gradually increased in height, and the red and yellow sandstone, and patches of white quartz sand showing here and there between the foliage which covered the steep bluffs, gave a variety to the prospect which is wanting to the country between this and Bangala. This river has a very tortuous course, and in several places makes huge bends, with high bluffs on the outer or concave bank, and a lower forest-covered bank on the other side. The numerous islands constitute another beautiful feature. They are mostly long and narrow, with a grove of *Raphia vinifera* palms, usually sheltering a small native settlement, at each end—the centre being thickly covered with forest, above which rise, here and there, the graceful crowns of the same palm, which has a very slender stem, and grows to a greater height than the oil-palm (*Elais guineensis*). On the top of the high banks—some 40 or 50 feet above the river—I noticed large clearings with young banana-plants growing plentifully all about, which led me to conclude that villages had once stood there. A little higher up we came to the site of a village recently destroyed by fire, and learnt that marauding parties of Manyemas, sent out by the Arabs, had been down the river.

Next day, approaching the bend of the river, where we expected to find the town of Yambumba —described by Stanley as truly metropolitan— I noticed that the bluff where he saw it in 1883 was completely bare of huts, only a few banana-plants remaining. The Arabs had burned the whole place, and the natives had removed to the low bank opposite, where they were dragging out a wretched existence, having for houses only a sort of palm-leaf awning, supported on four sticks; while a detachment of Manyemas, left by the Arabs to keep them in subjection, kept them also in constant fear of their lives. After leaving this place, we found that the river had a straighter course, though fairly choked with sand-banks, which gave us much trouble. It was not long before we passed the last island, and arrived, about 5 P.M., at a settlement of Manyemas, with two or three Arabs living among them.

These Arabs are called by the natives "Tamba-Tamba"—a word whose meaning I have been unable to ascertain; while a white man is called

"Tooc-a-Tooc-a," in imitation of the noise made by the waste steam escaping up the funnels of the steam-launches.

As Tippoo Tip had been made governor of Stanley Falls, we stopped about half an hour with these Arabs, and heard from them that Major Barttelot and his companions were all right, and that we should reach the camp at noon the next day. Steaming on for about an hour, we then made our camp—as fuel was running short—opposite a bank formed by the base of a line of hills which sloped down nearly to the water's edge, covered with magnificent trees. It was not the height or foliage of these trees which struck me, so much as their beautifully straight and even trunks—nearly every one running up without a branch to a height of forty or fifty feet, with a diameter of from three to four. The taper was so slight, that the diameter just below the branches was nearly the same as that near the ground; and their smoothness and regularity reminded one of the stately temple-columns of Luxor or Karnak.

Having made the steamer fast, and wishing to refresh myself with a bath before dinner, I undressed, and plunged into the Aruhwimi, but soon wished myself out again, for the water seemed to me as cold as ice. The temperature of the Congo averages about 80° F., and I had never bathed in any other water for over two years. I had unfortunately no thermometer with me, and so am unable to give the exact temperature of the Aruhwimi, but should put it, roughly speaking, as low as 50° F.

Next morning (May 8th), at about 9 A.M., coming in sight of what looked like a brown patch among the bush, on the top of a height four or five miles away, we were informed by some of the Zanzibaris that it was Major Barttelot's camp; and, a few minutes later, the sight of the rapids beyond it convinced us that we had reached our goal. As we approached, the brown patch resolved itself into a strong palisade on the top of a nearly perpendicular bluff some fifty feet high. A few natives, hugging the bank in little dug-outs, were the only living beings visible, and I could see no means of scaling the cliff, unless we went up monkey-fashion. We were now within 300 yards, and could make out a hut or two behind the palisade; so I seized the steam-whistle, and gave a long blast, which had the effect of bringing out a crowd of dark figures through some invisible opening, and presently two Europeans were discerned coming down a zigzag path to the water's edge. These proved to be Major Barttelot and Mr Bonny, both of whom appeared in very good health, considering the food they had been living on for the last few months. Not seeing Mr Troup, I concluded that he was still at Stanley Falls, whither Mr Ward had told me he was gone. Lieutenant Van Kerckhoven having

landed, walked up to the camp with the Major,
while I remained behind to see that everything
was right. When, some half-hour later, I had
climbed the hill and found my way into the camp,
I saw the Major just inside the door of one of the
huts; and going in, found Mr Troup lying on a
camp-bed, looking as if he had not a week to live.
In walking from Yangambi, on his return from
Stanley Falls, he had somehow strained his leg,
and a large tumour had formed, which had not
only lamed him, but affected his health to a serious extent.

As Stanley's expedition has attracted a great
deal of attention in Europe, I will, before proceeding with this account, describe the place where five
British heroes had, for nearly a year, defied all the
dangers of African life. The fort, or stronghold,
containing all the stores, as well as the huts of the
Europeans, was an enclosure some sixty paces (say
twenty-five to thirty yards) square, enclosed by a
strong palisade of sticks, from two to three inches
in diameter, and twelve to fifteen feet in length.
These were planted as close together as possible,
just leaving room to insert the muzzle of a gun
between them. On the side facing the river, the
palisade was planted on the very edge of an almost
vertical descent of fifty feet. This side, being
perfectly unassailable by natives or Arabs, needed
no further defence; but, on the other three sides, a

stage was erected about six feet from the ground, so that two rows of men could bring their guns into use at the same time, the sticks being high enough to afford cover for the upper row. Against natives, who fight with spears and arrows, this stage would have been very useful; but in an engagement with the Arabs, who have rifles and double-barrelled shot-guns (they load the latter with heavy iron slugs, some of them half an inch in diameter), the men on it would have been too much exposed. To provide against this emergency, an embankment, about five feet high, had been thrown up against the outside of the palisade—composed of the clay taken from a trench which surrounded the whole, and had been filled with water, though this was drained off when I saw it. There is no regular rainy season in this part of Africa; but heavy showers fall at uncertain intervals—usually every few days—which not only soon filled the trench, but would have enabled the garrison to obtain water in plenty, had they been cut off from the river. On the land side of the enclosure—which was also that nearest to the Arab camp, were two semicircular redoubts, from which the defenders could have opened a flank fire at any party attempting to approach the trench. Inside the enclosure were five huts of sticks, grass, and planks — the latter obtained by splitting up old canoes. Three of these, which served as the habitations of three

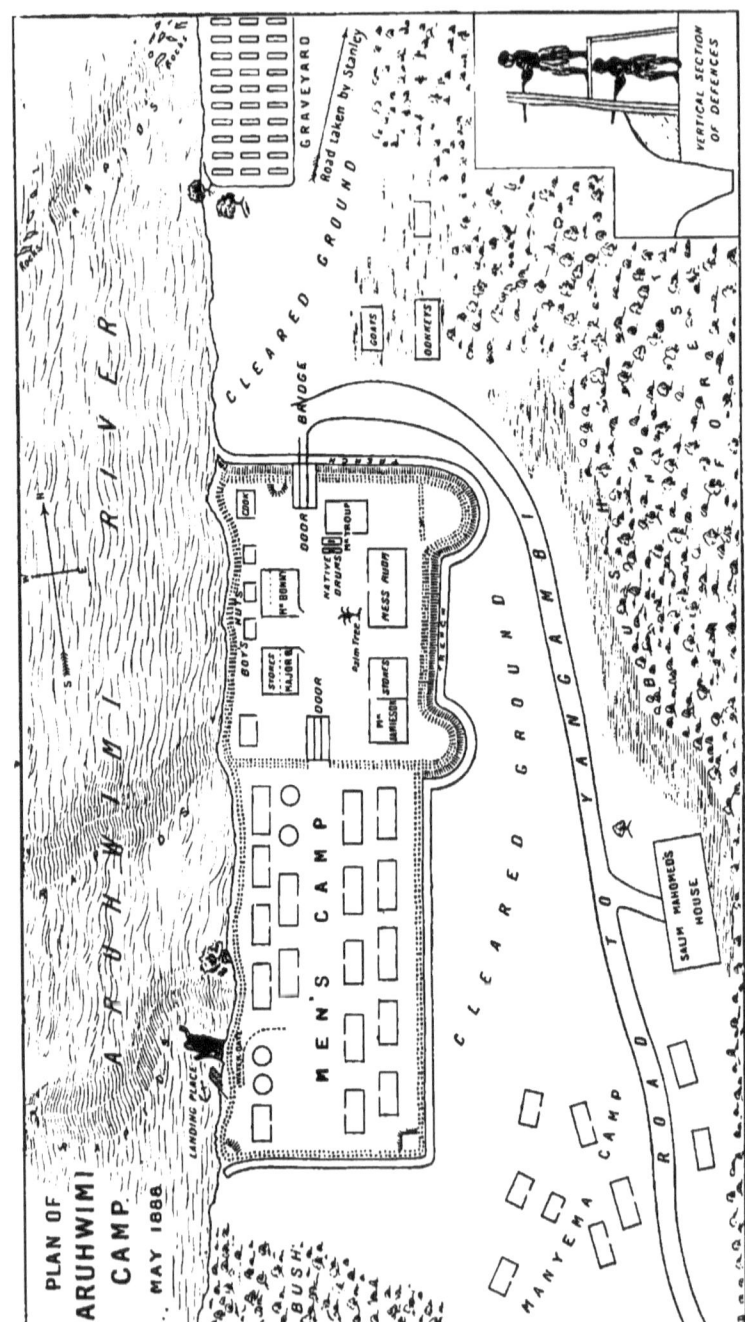

of the Europeans, were half filled up with stores; the fourth was used as a mess-room, and also contained the donkeys' saddles, and various miscellanea, such as spades, hoes, &c. These four were much of a size; the fifth, not being required to hold stores, was only about half as large, and was occupied by Mr Troup. Besides these there was a galley, and four small huts (each about five feet square) for the table-boys.

The two entrances to this enclosure were about three feet wide, and defended by a door formed of planks made from the thick bottoms of large canoes. These doors were hinged at the top, and, during the day, kept open by having their lower ends supported on stout poles: their weight was such as to require four or five men to raise them. They were closed every night, and two men set to guard them. The trench was crossed by means of some light planks, which could have been pulled up in less than half a minute.

The south side of the enclosure was defended only by a palisade,—being covered by the men's camp, a second enclosure, longer than the first, round which the palisade and trench were continued. This outer enclosure contained the numerous small grass huts occupied by the men; and its southern end was just in a line with the foot of the lowest rapid in the river. Among the huts I noticed four with conical roofs, which were all that remained of the village burnt by the Arabs. These conical structures are only five or six feet in diameter, and are built in the following manner : a circle of sticks, two feet high, is first planted in the ground, and this is filled in with clay, which is beaten down hard. On this foundation a very sharp cone of light sticks is erected, and the leaves that form the covering tied to it. These leaves are very large and heart-shaped, and seem, from the quantities used in building, to be plentiful about here, though I have never seen the tree they grow on. The door of these huts is just large enough for a man to crawl through.

Round the whole place the bush had been cleared away, so as to leave no cover for any enemies approaching from the land side. On the north, the clearing had been extended for some distance up the river, and formed a sort of esplanade, where Major Barttelot and his companions took their constitutionals. At the far end of this clearing began the road down which Stanley had led his men a year before ; and just at this spot was the cemetery, where the graves of nearly eighty of Major Barttelot's men (who had succumbed to the hardships of the past year) made one pause, and reflect on the uncertainty of human life. Such was the place in which the Major and his company had lived for nearly a year. On his first arrival, Stanley had, as he wrote to the newspapers, captured the place by means of steam-whistles;[1] after which, having awaited the return of the steamer which he had sent to Stanley Falls with Tippoo Tip, and made all arrangements in his power to facilitate the advance of Major Barttelot on the arrival of the promised carriers, he left Yambuya, June 28th, 1887, hoping to return some time in November of the same year. Tippoo Tip had, as before mentioned, promised to send for 600 men from Kassongo, a place near Nyangwé. Should these men arrive before Stanley's return, Major Barttelot had ample instructions as to the route he was to take in following on his track. Every possible contingency was provided against; and had it not been for the dilatoriness—*in my opinion the treachery*—of Tippoo Tip, and the other Arab chiefs, Stanley would long ere this have achieved his object. After his departure, the Europeans left behind were, for a time, subjected to great privations, as the natives had not yet returned to their homes, and food was difficult to obtain. Beans, which they had brought up the river with them, and manioc from the fields round the camp, were all that could be had for some time. Gradually, however, the people ventured back, and, gaining confidence, were beginning to bring meat and fish to sell to the strangers, when, suddenly, Salim bin Mahomed, one of Tippoo Tip's head-men, appeared on the scene, with 150

[1] See letter published in the daily papers for Aug. 19th, 1887.

Manyemas, and began to raid the country for ivory and slaves. Mr Troup described to me many of the horrible scenes he had been obliged to witness,— among other things, he told me of some women who tried to escape in a canoe, and when it was upset, were shot down in the water by the Arabs while trying to swim to the other side.

I subsequently saw a letter to the *Times*, which referred to this affair in the following terms: "Englishmen have stood and watched while their Manyema *allies* (!) fired at the heads of unhappy women and children who had leaped into the river and were trying to swim across, and have gathered round the Manyema camp-fires at night, to hear them relate their prowess." Now, Major Barttelot and his companions were no more to blame than the Emperor of China for this state of affairs. They had Stanley's orders to keep on good terms with the Arabs and the natives. Had they interfered on behalf of the latter, it would manifestly have been impossible to keep on good terms with the Arabs, as Salim bin Mahomed, who was supposed to be present as the representative of Tippoo Tip, Governor of Stanley Falls (who had agreed with the Congo Free State to do all in his power to prevent the tribes on the Congo, as well as Arabs and others, from engaging in the slave-trade), was raiding the country right and left, unrestrained. Even had the Europeans been free to act according to their own opinion of what was right, what could they have done, with only two hundred men, the greater part of whom were Zanzibaris, and would probably have deserted at once, had there been a fight with the Arabs? As it was, the Major had great difficulty in keeping clear of hostilities; for Salim bin Mahomed became so eager to possess the guns, powder, and other stores left by Stanley, that he did all he could to pick a quarrel with the Europeans, in order to have an excuse for bringing up two or three thousand men, exterminating them (the Europeans), and seizing the stores. The duty of the members of the expedition was to do all in their power to hasten after Stanley with the stores; and a rupture with the Arabs, who were to provide the carriers for these stores, would certainly not have furthered this object. The writer of the letter above quoted seems to have been under the impression that the expedition was sent out to suppress the raids of the Arabs: to have done this effectually would have required a whole army, instead of 200 men, the greater part of whom were Mohammedans, and naturally in sympathy with their co-religionists. As for " sitting round the Manyema camp-fires," &c., I can only say I never heard of any of the five white men doing so; and should think it would have been a somewhat dangerous proceeding, considering the strained relations existing between them and the Arabs.

The letter goes on to say: " The 400 Manyemas who have consented to go with Major Barttelot have only done so after expressly stipulating that they are not to be interfered with; so that pillage, murder, and man-eating will no doubt lay waste the country along the line of march, as they have already the country round the camp. The column will thus throw open still more virgin country to the Manyemas, who will be able to supply the Stanley Falls trading factory with marvellously cheap ivory."

When Mr Jameson arrived at Yambuya, with Tippoo Tip and these 400 men, I heard him mention to Major Barttelot that the Manyemas had made this stipulation; and the Major replied that he would see the State officials about it, and do all in his power to prevent the granting of such a condition. The *Stanley* had by this time arrived at Yambuya, with three or four Belgian officials of the Free State, destined for Stanley Falls Station.

Of these, two, if not three, were, as responsible representatives of the State, in a position to insist on knowing the terms of the agreement between Major Barttelot and the Manyemas; and *one* of them, at least, was aware of the above condition, for I heard Mr Jameson mention it in conversation with him and Major Barttelot.

Major Barttelot's duty was to take the men from Tippoo Tip, and set out immediately to follow

Stanley — who was supposed to have made all necessary arrangements with Tippoo before leaving. The palaver which followed the arrival of the men at Yambuya was caused by extra demands on the part of Tippoo Tip, who — as Governor of Stanley Falls — had, or was supposed to have, undertaken to suppress all raiding for slaves and ivory; while all those officials of the Free State who were in a position to do so, were, on their part, bound to prevent the engagement of the men on such conditions as those named above. Tippoo Tip's demands appeared to me to be made simply with a view to extorting gunpowder; for he demanded and was paid in ammunition which should have gone to relieve Emin Pasha. Indeed there is some ground for the suspicion that he purposely brought only 400 men, instead of the promised 600, so that the Major, being unable to take all his loads, might be the more ready to pay him (Tippoo) in gunpowder, which is here very valuable, and difficult to obtain in any quantity. Here again the State officials might have delayed, if not averted, the evil day for some poor natives; for they knew to what uses the powder would be put, and had they insisted on Tippoo Tip's being paid by cheque instead, he would have had to wait at least a year before that cheque could have been exchanged for ammunition.

As for the " virgin country " to be " thrown

open" by the expedition column, Salim bin Mahomed's men had not only raided the country behind Stanley's back, and in his line of march, to a distance of some fifteen days' journey from Yambuya, but had crossed the Aruhwimi, and laid waste the country to the north and north-west, as well as the right bank of the Aruhwimi, nearly down to its junction with the Congo. With these men raiding in front of them, therefore, very little would have been left for the 400 Manyemas to do.

After Salim bin Mahomed had been for some months raiding round Yambuya, he came into collision with Major Barttelot, and the latter, as the only means of avoiding a fight, walked to Stanley Falls, and, finding Tippoo Tip away, called on Nzigé, his deputy, and so managed matters that Salim either was recalled to the Falls, or went on a long expedition; at any rate he disappeared from Yambuya, and for a time the aspect of affairs improved.

A few days before the arrival of the *A.I.A.* at Yambuya, Salim reappeared with 2000 men, who were quartered in the country round about—Salim himself forming a camp close behind Major Barttelot's. He then forbade the natives to sell food to the white men, demanded for his own use the stores of the Emin Pasha Expedition, which, of course, were refused him, and also sent men to break up the canoes of the expedition, which were lying in the river, at the foot of the bluff on which the camp stood. He would perhaps have proceeded to even greater lengths, had he not heard that Mr Ward had gone down the Congo to send telegraphic despatches to the committee in England.

Such, apparently, was the state of affairs when I arrived at Yambuya in May 1888. Having waited there some four days, owing to a rumour (which, on Major Barttelot's going to investigate the matter, turned out to be false) that Stanley was within two days' march of us on his return to the camp, I got up steam on the morning of May 11th, and we prepared to start. Mr Troup was slightly better than when we found him, and we promised that either the *A.I.A.* or the *Stanley* should come and take him down-river if he did not soon recover. As Tippoo Tip was now an official of the State, the officer on board offered to take the ivory collected at Yambuya by Salim bin Mahomed round to Stanley Falls in the *A.I.A.* This offer was at once accepted, and Salim's men stowed away about 1500 lb. of ivory in our whaleboat. Some of the tusks were very fine; but at least two-thirds of them, which had been taken from villages burnt by the Manyemas, were considerably reduced in value by the cracks and blisters caused by the heat of the burning huts. These tusks contrast very unfavourably with the fine ivory bought peaceably and cheaply by European traders on the Congo, which is worth about four times as much; and afford a striking proof of the low value set on human life by the Arabs, who, for the sake of a few such, will murder scores of men and women. Having taken on board two or three of Salim's men to look after his ivory, we started; and the steamer, being much lighter than before, and having the current in her favour, shot rapidly past the numerous villages on the banks of the Aruhwimi, and by nine o'clock the next morning had turned the corner, and was ascending the Congo towards Stanley Falls. The Aruhwimi district, as I saw it, was certainly the most densely populated part of the Congo Free State I had visited. Villages, large and small, crowded each other along the banks, four of which—Mokulu, Umaneh, Bondeh, and Yambumba—certainly deserved the term "metropolitan," applied by Stanley to the last of the four. This dense population will soon diminish under the rule of the Arabs, who do not allow the natives to build permanent huts, but encourage them to make raids on other tribes and capture slaves and ivory, which they then buy of them. I have been told by men who have been at Nyangwé, that this system has been so thoroughly carried out there, that the country is now so thinly populated as to render it a matter of difficulty to procure food; and that one tribe, who had been supplied by the Arabs with guns and powder for these raids, had revolted, and kept the weapons to go raiding on their own account.

Above the mouth of the Aruhwimi, the Congo narrows considerably and the islands thin out. The north bank gradually rises, till it ends in a grand, forest-topped bluff over fifty feet in height; and this, again, gives place to a range of hills, whose densely wooded sides slope steeply down to the water's edge.

On May 14th we came to a clearing on the south bank, where a number of temporary native huts were erected, and a number of canoes, with a shelter of sticks and grass rigged up amidships, lay alongside the bank. In these the people — who formerly lived in large villages, till the Manyemas descended the Congo and destroyed them — live and sleep, moving about from place to place. About ten of the smaller canoes, paddled by some very nude natives, put off to bring us yams and fish for sale. Very jolly natives these, and evidently very glad to see us, for they started a song and dance in our honour, paddling hard the whole time, and yet, in spite of the dancing, contriving to keep their small craft upright on the water. The words of the song—of which I was unable to obtain a translation—were, as nearly as I could write them down, as follows :—

"I yon so dokélé,
I yon so dokélé,
Duda, duda."

Some of these men had hideously ugly faces, having covered them with cicatrisation to such an extent that it was hard to tell which of the huge lumps of flesh was originally meant for the nose. Others were better-looking, and had fairly pleasant countenances, but all seemed delighted to see us. There is a fashion here of boring a hole in the upper lip and the lobe of each ear, into which is inserted a conical plug of wood or ivory. This is gradually pressed in, so as to enlarge the hole to the required size, and when the latter is extended to suit the fancy of the victim, a circular highly polished slab of ivory is inserted. With one of these in his lip, and another in each ear, the native puts on a "la-di-da" air, and expects to produce a strong impression on the young-lady portion of his acquaintance. Should the gentleman desire to do the complete "masher," two or three plugs, each larger than the last, are used, one after another, till the lobes of the ears and the lips are stretched into a narrow band like a strip of leather. I saw one man who had his mouth completely hidden by a round piece of ivory nearly two inches in diameter, while two more pieces of the same size hung suspended by the lobes of his ears. This man seemed to have reached the "too utterly utter" stage of masherdom, for he could do nothing but lean on his paddle and gaze contemptuously down on the beads and cowries wherewith I tried to tempt him to take out and sell his decorations.

Farther on we came to a succession of clearings just below the junction of the Lomami with the Congo, where I counted over three hundred canoes of various sizes. About the centre of these clearings were several large trees, among which stood an Arab house conspicuous for its size. It was evidently market-day here, for in front of this house was an enormous crowd of natives—there must have been over three thousand men, women, and children gathered there; for there were many more canoes than the three hundred I counted, and ten persons to a canoe is a very low average, as many of them were 40 feet long, by 3 or 4 feet beam, and would be inhabited by several families, numbering, perhaps, altogether between thirty and forty individuals. One of these great canoes is to the natives of Central Africa what an Atlantic liner is to the British merchant—too large a concern to be built or owned by one man, unless that man is a very big chief indeed. Consequently, when a native finds an enormous cotton-tree with a fairly straight trunk growing conveniently close to the river, he forms a company by getting several of his friends to come and help him to cut it down, and carve out the canoe. This business takes from six to nine months to complete, and the families of the men come and camp near the spot where they are at work, catching fish, or otherwise employing themselves till the canoe is finished, when they move on board, and start on their first fishing or trading venture. Up at Stanley Falls it is more usual for several fishermen to join together, and having caught and dried a huge pile of fish, exchange it for a canoe with one of the tribes up the Chofu river, a little to the north, who are great canoe-builders. Sometimes two families inhabiting one canoe fall out; and I have on several occasions been greatly amused watching the men in a large canoe throwing overboard not only the furniture and household gods, but also the dogs, fowls, and goats, and even the women and children of their rivals, while the canoe drifted helplessly downstream. In one canoe the palaver ended in the grass roof amidships giving a violent heave, and going bodily overboard—revealing a mass of struggling niggers, trying to throw each other into the water till they upset the canoe.

Rounding a point just above this, we came in view of the mouth of the Lomami, and some more Arab houses, which turned out to be the headquarters of Raschid,[1] Tippoo Tip's reputed nephew —the man who, two years before, had directed the attack on Stanley Falls Station, and, by his success there, greatly increased his renown among the Arabs and Manyemas. He was quite a young man,

[1] "The wise man."

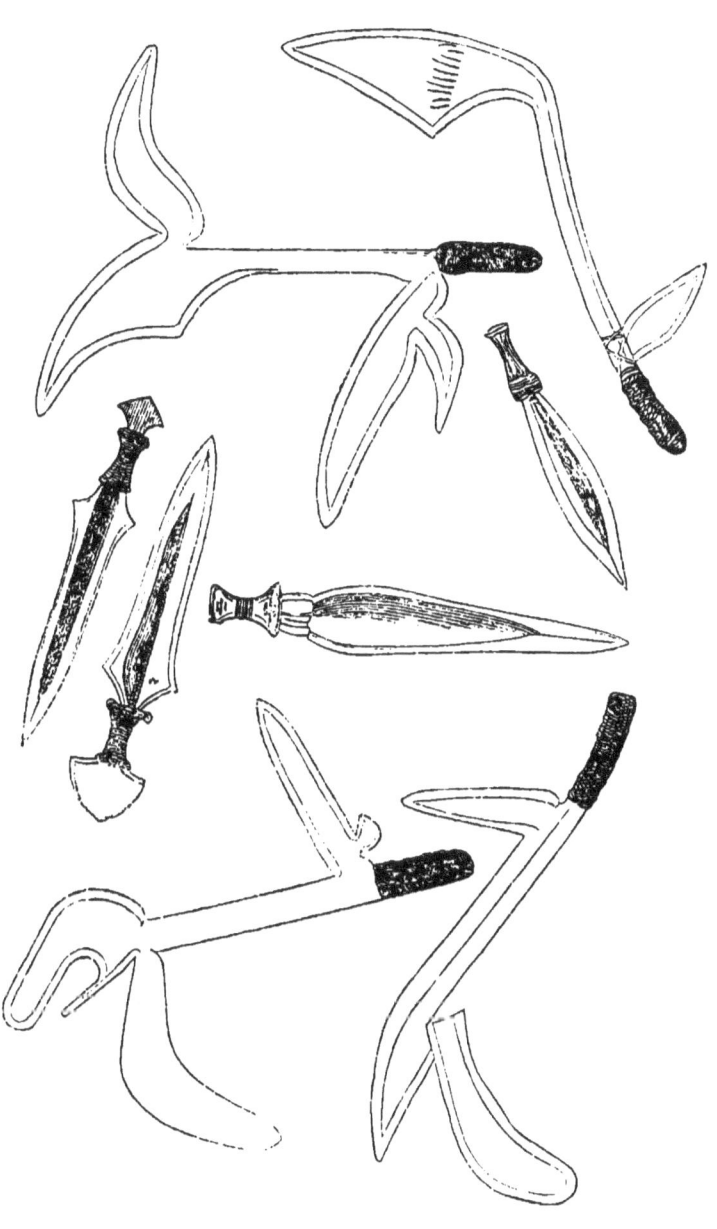

with a light-yellow complexion — suggesting that
of a white man suffering from a bad attack of
yellow jack—bright, restless eyes, and very thin
lips. He was dressed in the usual Mohammedan
style—in long white shirt, and short white embroidered jacket, with a light-yellow turban on his
head. On his invitation we made fast to the shore,
and stopped there for the rest of the day. In the
evening I went up to the top of the high river-
bank, to a house used as a sort of divan, where
I found Raschid and his principal men seated on
mats. On a seat opposite were three or four Kassongo drummers, who performed at intervals, while
the Arabs discussed the topics of the day. A
crowd of Manyemas and natives of the place soon
gathered round, and went through some very in-
tricate dances, in which every one seemed to be
moving in all directions at once. The inhabitants
of the Stanley Falls district certainly excel all
others I have seen in dancing. I have watched
over a hundred of them engaged in a set of most
complicated evolutions for nearly half an hour,
without one man getting out of place. As the
hour of 6 P.M. approached, and the sun neared the
western horizon, prayer-mats began to appear; and
soon all the Arabs were absorbed in their devotions,
bowing down towards the east in a way which
seemed to indicate that they were trying to com-
mit suicide by knocking their foreheads against the

ground. When this performance began, I retired to the steamer, and had my usual evening bath. Soon after I had finished, a Zanzibari came and brought a message, asking me up to "chop" in Raschid's house; so I followed him up the bank into a large enclosure surrounded by a high bamboo fence, and containing several huts, and one house of quite respectable size. The latter was occupied by Raschid, and the huts by his slaves and women. I was conducted into Raschid's bedroom, where I found he had a large double bed furnished with mattress, blankets, sheets, and mosquito-curtain, quite in the European style. Scattered about were various spoils from Stanley Falls, such as Mr Deane's camp-table and chair, a torn copy of Stanley's 'Five Years on the Congo,' in French, a pair of hunting-boots, the station-bell, and a broken revolver. On either side of the door were two or three guns, among which I noticed a Winchester, a Spencer's repeating-rifle, and a self-extracting revolver. All of these, however, as I soon found, were out of repair, and useless for fighting purposes. While we were waiting for dinner, Raschid entertained us with an account of the attack and defence of Stanley Falls Station, two years before, interspersed—he being unaware that I had gone up in the *A.I.A.* to Mr Deane's rescue — with some most atrocious lies as to the number of our men shot down by the Arabs. He also informed me that Deane had been shot through the arm by one of his (Raschid's) men, and was rather taken aback when I told him I knew all about it, having been present when Deane came on board the steamer, and seen him for myself.

Raschid then went on to relate how, when the *A.I.A.* went down-river, he and his compatriots were terribly frightened, not knowing what the resources of the State might be, and expecting that at least twenty large steamers, crammed with men and big guns, would shortly come up and drive them out of the region of the Falls. They had therefore proceeded to strengthen their position to the best of their ability; though, if prompt action had been taken by the State, they would have been obliged to abandon all their posts below Stanley Falls. They had sent express messengers to Kassongo and Zanzibar, and had gradually—as month after month passed, and they still remained unmolested—brought up reinforcements of Arabs and Manyemas; until at last, nearly a year later, when they saw the *Henry Reed* coming up the reach below the mouth of the Lomami, they considered themselves strong enough to defy the State.

Meanwhile, what was the State doing? Month after month I lived in almost daily expectation of seeing an armed force come up the river, fully equipped for re-establishing the lost station, and punishing the Arabs, who had caused the death of one of their officers, and nearly of another. Nearly a year passed, before at length the rumour reached us of a mighty expedition proceeding up-river. It is easier to imagine than to describe my disgust when, on my arrival at Bangala (being absent when the expedition passed), I heard that Tippoo Tip had been appointed Governor of the Stanley Falls District, and that Mr Stanley, who was on his way to relieve Emin Pasha, was going to see him safe to his destination. Nor was this the worst; for, as I now found out, Tippoo had made good use of his five senses on his journey round from Zanzibar. He had been well received at Boma, and shown all there was to see,—had experienced the difficulties of transport past the Livingstone Falls, and discovered what a time it took the State to get goods up to Léopoldville. He knew how many steamers could be mustered on the upper river, and how long they would take to reach Stanley Falls—he had, in short, been shown how weak was the Power which, to him and his chiefs, had probably appeared so formidable. His thoughts on the subject were clearly shown by his answer to a trader who remarked that the Congo Free State was a large country. "Yes," he replied, "it is a large country *on paper*."

One of the Arab women now coming in to say that "chop" was ready, we were shown into the outer room, where was a small table, made from a piece of the bottom of a canoe nailed to two posts planted in the ground. On this were two plates, with knives, forks, and spoons, two glass tumblers, and two large dishes of rice, with one of curried fowl. Raschid, having seen my companion and myself seated, retired to his room, and left one of his women to attend to us. As I was tolerably hungry, and curried fowl a dish I had not seen for a long time, I soon made a considerable hole in the huge pile of rice, and, on getting up from the table, heard my boy—who had been anxiously awaiting the remains—grumble to one of his fellow-servants that, if he did not soon change masters, he would starve, —which, considering that he was as fat as a porpoise, seemed to me an enormous stretch of his juvenile imagination.

As soon as we had finished, Raschid rejoined us, and, after some more talk, we retired to the launch about 10 P.M., and turned in.

Next morning, starting about 6.30 A.M., we crossed the mouth of the Lomami, and in about two hours and a half arrived abreast of Yaporo, where Captain Coquilhat and myself had a brush with the Arabs in 1886, when returning from the Falls with Mr Deane.

There was now a considerable Arab settlement here, with five or six large houses; but the native village had (as usual when the Arabs made their appearance) entirely vanished—numerous covered canoes along the bank showing where the people now lived. Continuing our journey, we crossed to the north bank, and reached Yangambi about 10 A.M. This place is very prettily situated on a piece of flat ground, backed by a semicircle of fine wooded hills, about 400 feet high, across which lies the road to Yambuya. From the top of these hills, I have heard that a splendid view is to be obtained over miles of country, covered as far as the eye can reach with one vast ocean of dark-green forest, through which the lordly Congo ploughs its mighty way.

MR. J. S. JAMESON.

CHAPTER XI.

KINSI KATINI.

ARAB REPORTS OF A LARGE LAKE—MAJOR BARTTELOT COMES ON BOARD AT YALASULA—BWANA NZIGÉ—PRESENT STATE OF WANA RUSARI—WALK ROUND THE ISLAND—POSSIBILITY OF PASSING STANLEY FALLS BY MEANS OF LOCKS—THE BAKUMU AND WENYA —THE CROCODILE AND HIPPO—RETURN OF JAMESON AND TIPPOO TIP—"NUBIAN BLACKING"—TIPPOO KEEPING HIS ACCOUNTS— SALIM BIN SOUDI—HER MAJESTY'S BIRTHDAY—A MANYEMA CHILD WOUNDED—TIPPOO TIP AND HIS FOLLOWERS TAKE PASSAGE FOR YAMBUYA—A *CONTRETEMPS* NEAR CHIOBA ISLAND— A SNAKE ON BOARD—TIPPOO'S METHOD OF SECURING A NIGHT'S LODGING—ARRIVAL OF HIS SECRETARY AND GARRISON—ALTERING THE LOADS—DIFFICULTIES WITH THE MANYEMAS—"GOODBYE"—LEAVE YAMBUYA—TERRIBLE NEWS—THE *HOLLAND*—NEWS OF DEANE'S DEATH—SALIM BIN MAHOMED ARRIVES FROM YAMBUYA—THE LAST OF KINSI KATINI—I AM TAKEN ILL—WARD COMES UP-RIVER.

THE channel in front of Yangambi has very little water, and the *A.I.A.*, drawing three feet, could barely get through. Later on, in the dry season, one can walk right across this channel to the islands in front. There being no news from Yambuya, we left here at 11.30 A.M., and rounded three high, wood-covered, rocky points. There had been a landslip just above one of these, and the exposed soil, with its layers of red sandstone and yellowish-white clay, looked just like the section of a huge side of streaky bacon. About 3 P.M. we arrived at a place called Yalasula (marked Yaruché on Stanley's map), and having no fuel, decided to camp there for the night—the chief Arab promising to get us a supply of wood before morning. After dinner, several of the chief Arabs of the place came down to the steamer, and, over some fragrant cups of coffee, told us about the natives and the country. Among other items, they mentioned that a large lake existed in the region between the lower Lomami and the bend of the Congo. This lake, they say, is connected by a small stream with the Lomami, and can be reached from that river in one day with canoes: steam-launches, they said, were useless, as the connecting stream was not large enough.

Next morning, about half-past five, as I was performing a very elementary toilet, the chief of Yangambi—a man who might have sat for a statue of Hercules—came up in a canoe, and handed me a small piece of folded paper. On opening this, I found that it was a note from Major Barttelot, stating that he had walked over from Yambuya to Yangambi, and would be at Yalasula by 10 A.M., on his way to Stanley Falls. His canoe arrived punctually, and taking him on board, we

proceeded, and about 11 passed Yariembi and
Iuma,—two villages which, on our previous visit
(in 1886), had declined to have any dealings with
us. They were now occupied by Arabs and Manyemas—and the natives, where were they? Above
this, the river is for some distance clear of islands,
and rolls majestically along, in a single stream
over a mile wide. At 3.30 P.M. we arrived at
Yarukombe, the place where, in 1886, Captain
Coquilhat had found Mr Deane lying in a native
hut, more dead than alive. This place was also
subject to the Arabs, and the friendly natives who
had sheltered Mr Deane, and done their best for
him, were now scattered far and wide. I afterwards heard that the chief of this village and
another chief, together with fifty of their followers, had been beheaded by the Arabs for
assisting him. Right opposite, perched on a high
bank in a deep bay, is Yatuka, whither we presently steamed, and made fast for the night on a
long spur of sand. That evening we dined up in
one of the Arab houses, and next morning were
delayed till 7.30 by our hosts coming down with
presents of food for our men as well as for ourselves. We then continued our journey, and,
passing two more Arab settlements — Yatakusu
and Yakusu—arrived about 3 P.M. abreast of the
mouth of the Lukebu or Chofu river. On the
point of the peninsula formed by this river and

the Congo was a small clearing; and here, in 1886, I had made the *A.I.A.* fast, while Samba searched for Deane in the dense bush that covered the point. The current here is very strong; and not getting on so fast as I had expected, we were obliged to camp at a place pointed out to us by Major Barttelot, who had already been up to the Falls in a canoe. Next morning a dense mist detained us till 8 o'clock; but by 10 A.M. we were made fast at the landing-place of the old State station on the island of Wana Rusari. Nothing now remained of this—which had been the first of all the Upper Congo stations—but the gun-shed, and the roads, which the Arabs had, for some reason, kept clear of grass. Before long, we were visited by Tippoo Tip's reputed brother—an old Arab, who appeared to me as if he had just stepped out of one of the pictures of the patriarchs which I used to see in an old family Bible when I was a child. His face was even a lighter yellow than his son Raschid's; and his grey beard, reaching nearly to his waist, gave him quite a venerable appearance. He was dressed in a long, flowing white shirt, and had a white turban on his head. He was called Bwana Nzigé, which means "Master Locust"; and very like a locust he looked, his sharp, thin, yellow face greatly resembling the frontispiece of that insect, in spite of the aforesaid patriarchal characteristics.

I subsequently found out that this patriarch had

an insatiable appetite for chocolate, and would continue eating it as long as the supply was kept up. Some of the Arabs with him were light-complexioned, and others black as negroes; all were dressed in heavily embroidered long white shirts. Having had a good look round, and inquired into the mysteries of the engine and boiler of the *A.I.A.*, the Arabs presently departed, and I was at liberty to go ashore. All the ground where the old State station had formerly stood was now covered with Arab houses and Manyema huts, surrounded by large tracts of cleared ground, planted with rice, maize, manioc, &c. In the gun-shed were the three Krupp guns dismantled by Mr Deane before quitting the station. The breech-pieces, which had been thrown into the river, had been recovered by the Arabs; but the breech-pins, linch-pins, cottas, and all the small pieces were missing. The carriages were so twisted—probably through the explosion of the powder-magazine—that only one gun lay fair in its bearings; and although the hinges of these bearings had been roughly repaired by Zanzibari smiths, so that the guns could have been used as muzzle-loaders, I rather doubt whether the native iron used for these repairs would have stood the recoil of the guns, and suspect that the Arabs would have sustained more damage than they inflicted on their enemies, in attempting to fire them off. Old Nzigé having appointed several empty mud-houses for our use, I removed all my effects into the one occupied by Major Barttelot, but preferred sleeping on board the launch to suffocating in the unventilated, windowless rooms of these huts.

Next day, being Sunday, Major Barttelot (who had previously visited the place) took me round the island to see all the principal Arabs, with whom he seemed to be on very friendly terms. The upper part of the island, I found, consisted of a rocky platform, raised some thirty feet above the lower half, on the edge of which was all that remained of the Wenya village seen by Stanley in 1883. At the upper extremity of the island the cataract tumbles over a reef of rocks twelve or fifteen feet high, after which it pours down in a roaring, foaming rapid, two miles in length, at the foot of which lay the little *A.I.A.*—her white sun-deck gleaming in the mid-day light. A rocky wood-covered islet in the very centre of this cataract formed a peaceful and pleasing contrast to the war of raging waters around; while on the far shore the houses and enclosures belonging to Tippoo Tip and his brother Nzigé, seen against a background of high forest, completed as pretty a picture as any I have seen in Africa.

After spending about an hour in watching the huge Wenya canoes, manned by thirty or forty natives each, poling up the rapids, and then, by desperate efforts, paddling to the very foot of the fall, where, holding on by liana-ropes attached to sticks planted in the clefts of the rock, they set their nets to catch the fish washed over the cataract, we crossed the island, as I wished to inspect the small channel through which Stanley passed his canoes in 1877. The reef of rocks at the upper end of this channel was quite dry—the water only leaking through fissures down below. The channel is about thirty yards wide, and could easily be converted into a canal by which steamers could pass the Seventh Cataract of Stanley Falls, and gain access to the twenty-six miles of navigable water between this and the Sixth Cataract. The latter, Stanley says,[1] might, at certain seasons of the year, be surmounted near the right bank by vigorous rowing. If it could be done by rowing, a powerful steamer would serve the purpose at least equally well, and this would open another twenty-two miles of navigable water.

This channel holds very little water in the dry season, and its lower end is, like the upper, closed by a reef of rocks. If the lower rocks were blasted away, so as to form a deep channel up to the entrance (where a lock with sluice-gates would raise the water in the channel to the level of the river above the cataract), a well-placed charge of gunpowder or nitro-glycerine would soon dispose of the upper reef, and we should have, at a very slight expense, a canal to the upper river. The work

[1] The Congo, vol. ii. p. 155.

could all be done in the dry season, when the stream is low; and as four feet is as deep a draught as any boat can have to be taken up the Congo in safety, six feet would be ample for the channel below the lock. Timber and stone are plentiful enough, but cement and iron gates for the lock would have to be brought from Europe. I say *iron* gates, as wood soon rots in this climate; and once the reef at the head of the channel were blasted away, these gates would have to bear the full pressure of a stream of water thirty yards wide, and about two feet deep. A double set of gates would, of course, be required, so that one set could at any time be removed for painting and repairs.

Judging by what I heard from Jameson (after his return from Kassongo), I believe it would be quite possible to get round the rest of the cataracts of the Stanley Falls series in the same way, and thus open out a continuous road from Nyangwé to Léopoldville. It would certainly be a much more feasible project than the Panama Canal; and when the Congo railway was finished, there would be—with the African Lakes Company's service, *viâ* Zambesi, Shiré, Lake Nyassa, and the Stevenson Road to Tanganika—two well-organised lines of traffic into the very heart of Africa. If the present rage for opening up Africa lasts a few years longer, we shall see Cook and Caygill advertising personally conducted tours across the Dark Continent!

During our walk round the island, Major Barttelot and myself looked in upon several of the chief Arabs in their homes, and were hospitably received by all, and regaled on maize-cakes, honey, and fruit. Passing through the native villages, the men and women crowded round us with loud "Sennené's" and rough handshakings; and more than one sable warrior—when none but his friends were near—asked me if I had come to drive out the Arabs, as his people were quite ready to rise against them. All of these hints I was obliged to pretend I did not understand, for I could not tell what on earth to answer. Had I been free, I would gladly have done all in my power to help them; but I was in the service of the Congo Free State, and this Free State had just appointed Tippoo Tip Governor of Stanley Falls. What could I say to the Bakumu and Wenya who crowded round me? Luckily for myself, I knew not a word of their language, and could easily pretend to misunderstand the interpretation of my Ba-Ngala boy, who knew no English. The Bakumu are certainly the finest-built men I have seen on the Congo, and I never met any natives who seemed more heartily glad to see white men. These people live principally on fish, of which they catch great quantities when the river is flooded; but, unlike the Ba-Ngala, they do not eat crocodiles. The Ba-Ngala give this as a reason why the crocodile does not eat the Bakumu; but I believe that the crocodiles in this part of the Congo must be of a different species, having several times heard the natives, at various places, assert that there are two kinds—one that eats men, and one that does not.

I have often seen, on mud and sand banks, traces of what appeared to me to be a fight between a crocodile and a hippo. One day, when I mentioned this to my Ba-Ngala boy, and asked him which animal was the stronger, he replied, the crocodile; asserting in proof of this, that the latter will never let a hippo eat men, but comes up when the hippo upsets a canoe, drives him away, and eats the men himself. Sometimes a crocodile tries to eat a young hippo, and then the mother fights him, and, according to the Ba-Ngala, always gets beaten, though, for my part, I should think that the hippo, with his huge tusks and wide jaw, would, being able to use his feet, have a great advantage over the crocodile, who is wholly dependent on his teeth, backed up by an occasional lash of his tail.

As Tippoo Tip was still away at Kassongo, and no one seemed to know when he was likely to return, there was nothing to do but wait till he chose to appear. I therefore took the opportunity of getting the launch and whale-boat cleaned out, and put in proper order for whatever work was coming next. On the afternoon of May 22d, a tremendous discharge of muskets on the right bank announced to me that Tippoo Tip, *alias* Tippooru, *alias* Mtipula, *alias* Hamed bin Mahomed, had arrived, and I soon saw Major Barttelot and Lieutenant Van Kerckhoven crossing the rapids in a canoe. Being busy at the time, I was obliged to remain in the *A.I.A.*, in spite of my impatience to find out whether Jameson had come with Tippoo, and whether he had succeeded in getting men. Later in the evening, Major Barttelot returned to the island, and with him was Jameson, dressed in grey trousers, grey flannel shirt, and sun-helmet. After he had washed off the dust of his journey, we all sat down to dinner, and I spent the pleasantest evening I had enjoyed for weeks. Jameson's stock of yarns seemed endless; and during the short time I knew him, he was always the same: no matter how badly things went, he never lost his temper, and always had a song or a joke ready for dull moments. His great regret was the scarcity of game. He had — knowing the Zambesi and Matabele-land — reckoned on finding some sport in a country whither, as yet, few hunters had penetrated, and was much disappointed by the discovery that the country round Stanley Falls was almost useless as a hunting-ground, on account of the impenetrable undergrowth of the forests. As he remarked, he had hardly, as yet, seen anything worth wasting powder on; and when he did catch a glimpse of an animal, it disappeared into the dense jungle before he could get his gun to his shoulder. He further informed me that Tippoo Tip had only been able to get four hundred carriers instead of the promised six hundred, as the men would not go to an unknown country.

A day or two later, on walking in to lunch, I found that Tippoo Tip had come over, and was discussing business with Major Barttelot and Jameson. After the light complexion of the other Arabs, I was somewhat surprised to find Mr Tippoo Tip as black as any negro I had seen; but he had a fine, well-shaped head, bald at the top, and a short black beard, thickly strewn with white hairs. He was dressed in the usual Arab style, but more simply than the rest of the Arab chiefs, and had a broad, well-formed figure. His restless eyes gave him a great resemblance to the negroes' heads with blinking eyes in the electric advertisements of somebody's shoe-polish, which adorned the walls of our London railway-stations some years ago,—and earned him the nickname of "Nubian blacking."

As I was pretty busy getting the launch ready to return to Yambuya, I did not get much chance of observing him further; but a day or two later, I crossed the rapid in a canoe manned by Wenya fishermen—who, knowing every current and whirlpool, manage to ferry over their great canoes with comparatively little exertion—and found Tippoo

Tip engaged in overhauling a large pile of ivory. On seeing me, he cleared a mat by his side, and invited me to sit down; and I spent a couple of hours watching him, as each tusk was brought up and marked by his men, and then entered by him on a piece of paper in Arabic characters. Salim bin Soudi, his interpreter, meanwhile told me how the ivory I saw there—some two tons—had taken about nine months to collect; how some came from the Lomami, and some from the Aruhwimi regions; of the fights they had had with natives, &c., &c., till I could not help wondering how many human lives were represented by each tusk.

This interpreter, Salim bin Soudi, answers so exactly to the description of Mahomed bin Sayid given by Stanley in 'Through the Dark Continent' (vol. ii. p. 119), as to make me suspect him to be the same man under a different name. He was constantly coming to me for such things as oil, cartridges, cloth, &c., telling me Tippoo Tip wanted them; but in so doing he had reckoned without his host, as, in the first place, I was not in command of the State expedition, and could give away nothing without an order from the officer in charge; and in the second, Major Barttelot had found him out, and warned us in time. So one day when he came for some pieces of cloth, ostensibly for Tippoo Tip, he was told they were not at hand, and would be sent over as soon as the bale was opened. No sooner was he out of the way than one of our men was sent to Tippoo Tip with the cloth, and returned in a short time, bringing it back, with the message that Tippoo had never asked for it. After this, Mr Salim never again tried to get cloth out of me under false pretences; but he would freely come up and beg for things on his own account.

The 24th, being the Queen's birthday, was not allowed to pass unnoticed by us; and having obtained permission, I ransacked the "medical comforts" brought up from Bangala, and presented Major Barttelot with one of the two bottles of champagne I found there. Having opened it, he proposed her most gracious Majesty's health, which we drank out of enamelled iron cups, Jameson remarking that it was no use adding Highland honours, as we could not break the cups without the help of a hammer and anvil.

While I was at Stanley Falls, a Manyema woman brought me a boy, about ten years old, who had been cut down in a fight with natives, and left for dead. How he managed to live passes my comprehension, for he had three tremendous wounds, and was so weak from loss of blood that he had to be held up while I dressed them. The first—probably sustained in an endeavour to ward off the knife—was along the right forearm, and was over six inches long, and two and a half wide; the second was a cut on the right shoulder, given from behind,—

the knife had entered as far as the collar-bone and left a mark on the shoulder-blade, but, luckily, did not break it. This blow had knocked him on his face, and then the natives had attempted to finish him with two tremendous cuts across the back, extending from the left shoulder to the lower ribs on the right side, and laying bare the left blade-bone, the spinal column, and several of the ribs. One of these wounds was quite twelve inches long, and two inches across its widest part. It took me nearly two hours every day to clean and dress these injuries, but before I left Stanley Falls they had begun to heal.

On May 26th, Major Barttelot and Jameson left Stanley Falls in canoes for Yangambi, taking with them the 400 men brought by Tippoo Tip from Kassongo, who were to go by land from Yangambi to Yambuya. Tippoo himself was to go round with us in the *A.I.A.* two or three days later. From the 26th to the morning of the 29th I was down with fever, but during the afternoon of the latter day I received a note from the officer in command, saying that Tippoo Tip and twenty of his people would be ready next day, and that a canoe had been sent down-river to tell all the Arabs at the different stations to cut wood for us. A little later two large canoes, containing enough dry wood to keep us in fuel for two days, came alongside. I loaded up with as much as I could carry, and having got everything ready for leaving on the morrow, turned in. Next day Tippoo Tip came off, with all his chiefs and women, in two large canoes. Many of these people, it is true, only came to see him off; but when all were sorted out, I found that, instead of 20 men, he had brought 54 men and 12 women. These, with our own men, brought the total up to 83 souls, all crowded into three small vessels—viz.:

> The *A.I.A.*, 42 feet long by 7 feet 6 inches beam, and 5 feet deep.
> Whale-boat, 30 feet by 7 feet by 3 feet.
> Canoe, 40 feet by 2 feet by 1 foot 6 inches.

There was hardly room to breathe, and the rail of the launch was only some 6 inches above the water. Going to Tippoo Tip, I told him that, if he wanted to take so many people, he must give us a larger canoe; and he accordingly sent for one which, though large enough to hold some sixty people, made me doubt the power of the little steamer to mount the strong current of the Aruhwimi, with the whale-boat on one side and this canoe (60 feet by 4 feet by 3 feet) on the other. However, we were not at the Aruhwimi yet; so I lashed the canoe alongside in place of our smaller one (which was left in charge of the Arabs), and about 8.30 A.M. we started down-river. At eleven we reached Chioba island, and took the right-hand channel. Here, as the officer in command came forward, I

relinquished my place to him, and went aft to
have a look at the engines. Hearing a sudden
shout, I looked up, and saw that we were going
full on to a reef of rocks, over which the water
was dashing itself into foam. I shouted to the
men in the bows to let go the anchor, but they
were too much excited to heed me; so, putting
the engines full astern I rushed forward, but was
too late, for we crashed on to the rocks with tremendous force, bumped over the first reef, and
stranded hard and fast on the second. Tippoo Tip
who had sat still as a statue, was nearly thrown into
the water; and some one having unfastened the
bow-lashing of the canoe, she slewed round, and,
tearing away the stern-ropes, drifted off down-
stream, with the commanding officer and about
forty men on board. Stopping the engine, I tore
off my coat, and going into the water, examined
the propeller, rudder, and as much of the bottom
of the launch as I could reach, to see if any damage
was done. I found that we had escaped with a big
dent in the plates, which, but for the reversing of
the engines, would certainly have been a large hole.
Several canoes full of natives having come up, I
sent every man who could swim into the water;
and Tippoo with his chiefs getting into the whale-
boat (which drew less water, and so had escaped
the rocks), and thus lightening the launch a little,
we contrived, with the assistance of the natives,

to push her over the reef into the deep water beyond. The current was rushing over the reef like a mill-race, but luckily every one held fast to the boat as she drifted clear, and with the exception of a wetting, no one was the worse. By this time the men in the canoes had got out their paddles, and being unable to make headway against the current in the centre of the channel, made for the village of Yatakusu; when, having again lashed the canoe alongside, I got into dry clothes, and at noon we set off once more. We stopped that night at Yariembi, Tippoo and his people sleeping on shore, and next day got off about 6.30 A.M., stopped a few minutes at Yaporo about 10 o'clock, and then went on to the Lomami, where we arrived about 1 P.M. Here we found Raschid, who had come down the day before in a canoe, and had a large pile of firewood waiting for us. We therefore remained for the rest of the day.

In the evening, as I was refreshing myself with a swim in the river, a shout of "*nyoka*" and a general scramble of the Zanzibaris to get out of the *A.I.A.*, made me aware that a snake had contrived to stow away on board. Mounting the stern of the boat, I drew on a pair of boots, and seizing a native spear and a pair of smith's tongs, began the hunt. I soon found that he had visited our chop-box, and sucked nearly all the eggs; then I saw the end of his tail among some spears, and pulling them aside, beheld a long snake of a beautiful dark-green colour, covered with black spots. He reared up his head and tried to bite me; but I pinned him down with the spear, and then, catching his head in the tongs, carried him ashore, where I held him down on the beach while a Zanzibari decapitated him. He measured over 4 feet in length, and 4½ inches in circumference round his thickest part, which was about one-third of his length from the head. Some natives, seeing him dead, came up and asked for him, to eat. As the skin was damaged, I granted their request, and they were soon seated round a fire, roasting small pieces of snake in the hot ashes, and eating them skin and all, much as schoolboys roast and eat chestnuts.

Next morning we left the Lomami at 6.30,— Raschid coming with us,—and at 7.30 A.M., on June 2d, entered the Aruhwimi. As I had anticipated, the *A.I.A.* could not make much headway against the current, with the heavy canoe she was towing, and we mounted but slowly, so that it was late on the evening of June 3d before we arrived at Yambumba, the lowest Arab settlement on this river. Tippoo Tip on hearing that we could reach Yambuya about 4 P.M. next day, if we had not to tow the canoe, gave orders to his people to get out their paddles, and paddle her up. Accordingly, when we started next morning, we left about thirty

Zanzibaris behind, to bring up the canoe. Tippoo Tip, the whole time he was on board, always sat Turkish fashion, in the same place, on some bales of cloth, with his priest on one side, and Raschid on the other. As it was the month of Ramadan, neither he nor his men ate anything during the day. About 4 P.M. we generally stopped at some Arab settlement, where Tippoo and his men, going ashore, spread out their prayer-mats, and occupied themselves in devotion till six, when, the sun having set, they prepared some food, and feasted during the night. As long as we were in the Congo, we always managed to reach an Arab settlement at night; but on returning into the Aruhwimi, we had one night to sleep in a strange country, the Arabs not having yet reached the villages on the lower part of this river. When told that we could not reach Yambumba (the nearest Arab settlement) in time to pass the night there, Tippoo Tip said he would stop at the first island we came to that had a native village on it. A little after 4 P.M. we came to a village on a small island, and approached the shore. As soon as we were near enough, the Arabs and Manyemas jumped ashore, gun in hand, and drove the natives out of the village to the other side of the island, where they took to their canoes, and tried to cross the river, while the Arabs and Manyemas, standing on the bank, poured a perfect hail of iron slugs after the wretched fugitives.

Having cleared the island of natives, the Manyemas started to catch all the fowls, goats, and other live stock they could find; and one of them came out of a hut with a half-boiled, steaming human head—which was, however, speedily thrown into the river by the Arabs. Having seen all right on board the boat, I went ashore, and found Tippoo Tip, Governor of Stanley Falls Station for the Etat Indépendant du Congo, making himself comfortable in the huts whence he had just ejected the rightful owners.

Leaving Yambumba at 6.30 A.M. on June 4th, without the large canoe, we were able to make a good run, and about 11.30 A.M. stopped at a small Manyema settlement to cut up some wood we had on board, which was too large for the furnace of the *A.I.A.* While on shore looking after the wood, I heard a shout from some of my men, and looking up, saw the *Stanley* coming round the far bend of the river. The officer in command of the *A.I.A.* went off with Tippoo Tip in a canoe to meet her; and by the time she was abreast of us, I had enough wood on board, and was ready to follow her up-stream to Yambuya. At 5.30 P.M. I made fast to the bank, just below the spot where Captain Shagerstrom had moored his steamer. This was a full mile from the camp, as the river had fallen during my absence, and there was now not enough water over the rocks to make it safe to approach the rapids. I was very glad to see my old friends

Shagerstrom and De Man, the captain and engineer of the *Stanley*; and as soon as I could get clear of the hundred and one things that had to be attended to, I went on board to pay them a visit. I found that the *Stanley* had brought up the long-expected garrison for the Falls Station, in charge of three Belgian officers, one of whom was to act as Tippoo Tip's secretary; and that, just after passing the mouth of the Aruhwimi, they had heard that we were on our way to Yambuya with Tippoo Tip, and had turned back to follow us. Being a much larger and more powerful steamer than the *A.I.A.*, the *Stanley* had picked up the canoe left by us at Yambumba and brought it up with her. Tippoo Tip, highly elated at the arrival of his long-promised secretary, now departed for Salim bin Mahomed's camp in his canoe, taking with him, to my great relief, all his chiefs, men, women, and household gods. I dined that night on board the *Stanley*, and it was late before I turned in.

Next morning (June 5th) I was up before day light, and at 5.30 A.M. was on my way to the camp, where I found that Major Barttelot and Mr Jameson had arrived all right. Troup was much the same as when I left him, but brightened up when he heard that the *Stanley* had arrived, and that he would shortly be able to start down-river. Bonny had in some manner hurt his right hand, which was swollen to three times its proper size.

When Mr Jameson came back to Stanley Falls, with Tippoo Tip and the 400 carriers, I heard him tell Major Barttelot that he had promised Tippoo that these men should have only half-loads. The Major replied that this would have been all right, had Tippoo supplied eight or nine hundred men, instead of only four hundred, as it would not be possible to take above half the stores by giving them only half-loads. They had a long discussion on this point, and also a palaver with Tippoo, in which the latter stipulated that none of the loads carried by his men were to exceed 40 lb. in weight, and finally got his way. It therefore became necessary to reduce 400 loads from 60 lb. to 40 lb. This meant unscrewing the lid of each case of ammunition, removing a portion of the contents, filling up the empty space with dried grass, and screwing on the lids again. Troup and Bonny being laid up, and the Major busy writing despatches, there was only Jameson to attend to this work. Seeing the state of affairs, I returned to the *A.I.A.*, and having finished the trifling repairs she required, went to the officer in command of the expedition, and telling him my boat was in good order, obtained his leave to take one of my men and go up to the camp to help. As the Manyemas and Arabs had left the *A.I.A.* and whale-boat in a very dirty state, I set the rest of my men to clean them out in my absence, and was just going to start for the camp, when a note arrived from Major Barttelot, asking that two carpenters (natives of Lagos), who had come up on the *Stanley* for the Falls Station, might be sent to assist him. Having obtained these two men, I took a canoe and went up to the camp, where I found Jameson hard at work with a screwdriver, singing all the time. He was very glad to see the three men I had brought, and in a few minutes we were all busy among the ammunition-cases. I was in that camp three days and two nights, and I do not ever remember to have enjoyed a piece of work more than I did the altering of those loads at Yambuya, for Jameson kept up a continuous string of yarns, songs, and jokes, which, in spite of the labour, made me sorry that the day was over, when the watchman came to *piga ngoma* (beat the drum) at 6 P.M. During the evening, and far into the night, we sorted out the lighter loads, and as each was finished, it was stacked in the middle of the camp, under an old tent-cover.

Among these loads were a number containing Stanley's private stores. Finding, when all was done, that the carriers would be insufficient, the Major decided to open such of these as he could, and sort out the contents, only sending on such things as were necessary. As we could get no keys to fit the locks, I cut the hinges of several tin uniform-cases; and the Major and Mr Jameson, having divided the contents into two lots, repacked the cases, and I soldered them up again.

On June 7th we finished the last of the loads; and being by this time fairly tired out, I returned to the *A.I.A.* in the evening, turned in, and had a good sleep. While at the camp I had slept in the mess-room, on an old tent,—the Major and Jameson lending me a couple of blankets. On the morning of the 8th, I went up to see Tippoo Tip muster the caravan. There were 130 surplus loads; and the Major decided that, as he could not get men to carry them, they would be safest at Bangala. Accordingly, Captain Shagerstrom took them down to the *Stanley*, as well as two donkeys—the country through which the expedition had to go being so bad that a donkey would have been no use. About 9 A.M., Tippoo Tip and the Manyemas came for the loads, which were all ready, laid out in rows, just outside the camp-gate. I was talking to Troup inside his hut, when I heard a noise—something between a yell and the howling of hyenas, and rushing out, found that the 400 men brought by Tippoo Tip had refused their loads, because they said some of them were a pound or two over the regulation weight. I do not know whether Tippoo Tip had anything to do with this refusal or not; but he and the rest of the Arabs walked away to Salim bin Mahomed's house, while the Manyemas dispersed to their camp. Major Barttelot, Jameson, and Bonny held a consultation, and the Free State officers having come from the steamers, they all adjourned to Salim bin Mahomed's house, where a big palaver took place. The result of this was very unsatisfactory, Tippoo Tip refusing to force the men to carry the loads as they were. The loads could not be reduced to the required weight without an immense amount of trouble, as the powder and cartridges were in air-tight, soldered tins, weighing about 15 lb. each. Three of these tins, packed in a wooden case, of from 10 to 12 lb. weight, formed a load. Thus, when one tin of powder was taken out, each load, including the case, would weigh 41 or 42 lb. To reduce this, the tins would have to be opened, and, after taking out a pound or two of powder, soldered up again. Except the engineer of the *Stanley* and myself, there was no one at Yambuya who had either the tools or the practice necessary for soldering up the tins; and, as the State officials would not hear of the steamers remaining at Yambuya any longer, things began to look serious.

I had too much to do preparing for departure on the morrow to remain any longer in the camp; so saying good-bye to the Major and his companions, I returned to the launch. Shortly afterwards Troup was brought down in the whale-boat by Captain Shagerstrom; and going on board the *Stanley*, I found him already looking better. In the evening I heard that Tippoo Tip had been persuaded to pass all the loads containing powder and cartridges in air-tight tins, thus leaving only about 120 loads to be reduced. I also received orders to take the whale-boat up to the camp before daylight next morning, and fetch down Raschid and ten other Arabs. At 3 A.M. on June 9th the *Stanley's* fires were lit, and at four I turned out and kindled those of the *A.I.A.* By five I had got my Ba-Ngala into the whale-boat, and was being paddled up the stream by starlight. Just as we passed the *Stanley*, whose open furnace-doors shed a weird light across the dark river, Captain Shagerstrom ascended the bridge and blew a long blast on his whistle, and before I reached the camp she had turned, and was steaming off on her way to the Falls. On arriving at the landing-place, I found Tippoo Tip waiting with a whole crowd of men and women, whom he wanted to send round in the *A.I.A.* He himself intended remaining behind, to see the expedition start, and then crossing to Yangambi, and going up to the Falls in a canoe. Though day was breaking by this time, I determined to have one more look at the members of the expedition; so I dashed up the bluff, through the water-gate into the camp, and into Major Barttelot's hut. The Major was sitting on some boxes, his face buried in his hands, and his elbows on his knees; he seemed more depressed than I

s

had ever seen him before. "Good-bye, Major!" I shouted; "I have only two minutes to spare." On hearing my voice he jumped up like a shot, and seized my outstretched hand, exclaiming, "Don't be in a hurry, old fellow. We may all be dead in another week, you know." Just then, the notes of a bugle sounding the recall, and a long whistle from the *A.I.A.*, came floating up on the still morning air, and one of my men rushed in to tell me she was going to start. I turned to the Major, who continued, "I should like to get home to the old place again. If you get home before news of me arrives, tell my father I was all right when you saw me." "All right," said I, as I rushed out. Jameson and Bonny were in the mess-room, the former in high spirits at the prospect of starting at last. A few hurried words of farewell, and I ran down to the landing-place, when I found that Tippoo Tip had filled up my boat with about fifty men, women, and boys. After much persuasion, he consented to take twenty out; but even then I knew we could not go, as the *Stanley* had left with the large canoe fully loaded, and we had nothing but the small launch and whale-boat. However, I started, and when we reached the *A.I.A.*, Raschid, seeing the overloaded condition of the two boats, disposed of ten more people, and we at length got under way.

Before we had gone very far, the Belgian officer

in command of the *A.I.A.* came and told me that
Tippoo Tip had told the Manyemas that, if the
Major did not treat them well, they were to shoot
him. This was such an astonishing statement that
I could hardly believe it; but it was confirmed by
one of my men (a Zanzibari), and also by several
of Tippoo's own men, then on board, and, some days
later, by Salim bin Soudi, the interpreter. Had it
been in my power, I would have gone back to the
camp and told the Major; but I was not in command, and had to obey orders and go on. From
that time until the day when I received the news
of the Major's death, I realised what the feelings
of Damocles must have been, as, day after day, I
expected to hear that the death which I seemed to
know was coming, yet was powerless to avert, had
overtaken him. Yet when, weeks afterwards, the
sad tidings reached me, I hardly seemed to realise
it. As long as I live, I hope never to be in the
same position again. It seemed like one long, long
nightmare: the everlasting falling down a precipice
which has no bottom is the only thing to which
I can compare the state of suspense I was in for
the next ten weeks. But how different was the
awakening!

Being well supplied with fuel, we soon passed the
Stanley—which, though a much faster boat than
the *A.I.A.*, could only steam six or seven hours
per day, being forced to stop about 2.30 P.M.

every day to cut the immense quantity of wood required by the two locomotive boilers with which she was fitted; and, on the evening of June 11th, we reached the Lomami, where the Arabs had a quantity of dry wood ready for us. The *Stanley* arrived next day, but, as they had provided no wood for her, left after a short stay, in order to search for dried trees higher up river. In the evening we were treated to a water-dance by the natives. About ten canoes, so close together that they looked like a raft, came up the river, paddled by some sixty men, who danced, sang, shook their brass and iron bangles, and threw the water about with their paddles. The canoes were rather small, and there was just space enough between them to allow the crews to use their paddles. Each was entirely independent of the others, yet they all kept exactly abreast, and the men in their dance managed to move from one to another without upsetting any. Leaving the Lomami on the morning of June 13th, we arrived at Stanley Falls about midday on the 15th, having passed the *Stanley*, which came up about an hour later. The *A.I.A.* was to remain ten days at the Falls, so that I took the opportunity of cleaning out the boiler and executing sundry repairs required by the engine; but the *Stanley* was to unload as fast as possible, and return at once to Léopoldville. I was by this time heartily sick of the Arabs and Stanley Falls;

besides which, the soles of my last pair of boots were completely worn out, and I should have been very glad to go down-country again. Troup (who, though still very weak, seemed a little better, now that he was away from Yambuya), seeing the state of my foot-gear, kindly presented me with a pair of hunting-boots; and, on the morning of June 18th, the *Stanley* departed, taking him away on the first stage of his long journey home. Little did I think, as I watched her disappearing down-stream, that I had seen the last of her, and should behold the shores of Old England, and meet Troup restored to health, before I again saw the old stern-wheeler ploughing the dark-brown waters of the Congo.

The day after the *Stanley* left, as I was on board the *A.I.A.* writing a letter to Mr Deane, to tell him about the present position of affairs in his old station, a steamer appeared round the bend of the river. Taking a canoe I went down to meet her, and found she was the *Holland*—the new stern-wheeler of the Dutch Trading Company, with Mr Greshoff (manager of their factories on the Upper Congo) on board. Soon after boarding her, I heard the sad news of Mr Deane's death. I could get no particulars, except that, while out shooting, he had been knocked down by an elephant, which had driven his tusk through his neck from behind. I was also told that Captain Bayley had been obliged to go home on account of illness. The *Holland* had picked up Tippoo Tip and his men at Yalasula, to which place they had marched from Yambuya.

The Arabs having departed to their houses, and the *Holland* being made fast, I went up to lunch. On returning to the *A.I.A.*, my unfinished letter to Deane caught my eye. Deane—whom all the hardships he had suffered, when escaping from the Arabs in 1886, had not been sufficient to deter from returning to Africa :—Deane killed,—and by an elephant! I tore up my letter, flung it into the river, and seizing my gun, went off into the bush to shoot something.

In the evening, on going up to the house for dinner, I heard that the old Emperor of Germany was dead, and that he had been succeeded by his son, the Emperor Frederick, who was not expected to live long, on account of the nature of his disease.

The next few days were spent by me in overhauling the engines of the *A.I.A.*, and by Mr Greshoff in buying Tippoo Tip's ivory with gunpowder. The day before I left Stanley Falls, Salim bin Mahomed arrived from Yambuya, bringing a letter from Major Barttelot to Tippoo Tip. From him I learnt that Barttelot, Jameson, and Bonny, were quite well, that they were encamped six days' march east of Yambuya, that the Manyemas had already begun to give trouble, and that this fact formed the subject of the Major's letter to Tippoo Tip.

On the morning of June 25th we were visited by a tremendous tornado; but by 8.30 A.M. both the *A.I.A.* and the *Holland* had steam up, and were ready to start, which we did shortly after, leaving behind us the three Belgian officers who had come up in the *Stanley* to rebuild the station. As soon as we were clear of the rocky part of the river, which extends some twenty miles below the Falls, the *A.I.A.* was made fast alongside the *Holland*, and together we steamed down to Bangala, where we arrived on the afternoon of July 3d. On July 6th the *Holland* left for Stanley Pool; and on the 7th I was suddenly seized with violent pains in the stomach, and before night was down with acute dysentery. I tried a large dose (60 grains) of ipecacuanha, which seemed to arrest the disease for some hours, but only to break out again in a chronic form. Of all that happened during the next four weeks I have no very clear recollection. I got little if any sleep, until the *En Avant* arrived from the Pool with Mr Herbert Ward, who was returning to Yambuya, after having sent off his despatches to the Emin Relief Committee, from Loanda. As Major Barttelot had left Yambuya, Ward was to remain at Bangala till he received further orders from the Committee ; and on learning what was the matter with me, he set to work to make me as comfortable as he could, so that I soon began to improve a little. The *A.I.A.* having meanwhile left for the Pool, I applied to the chief for a canoe to take me down to the missionary station at Equator.

CHAPTER XII.

MY RETURN HOME.

A WET JOURNEY TO EQUATOR—KINDNESS OF MR AND MRS BANKS—NEWS OF MAJOR BARTTELOT'S DEATH—DOWN-COUNTRY IN A HAMMOCK—OVERTAKEN BY WARD—JAMESON DEAD!—BACK AT MATADI—THE "DEVIL'S CALDRON"—WARD CATCHES THE MAIL—DOWN-RIVER IN A SCHOONER—CONGO STATE COINAGE—IMPROVEMENTS AT BOMA—TWO IN A PORT-HOLE—WAITING FOR THE *AFRICA*—TO LOANDA—HOMEWARD BOUND—KOTONOU—ON BOARD THE *BIAFRA*—THE ADDAH SHIPPING-CLERK'S LETTER—SIERRA LEONE—THE CANARIES—QUARANTINE AT MADEIRA—CHARACTERISTICS OF ENGLISH SCENERY—HOME ONCE MORE!

ON the morning of July 19th, I received notice that the canoe and twenty-two Ba-Ngala were ready for me. I crawled down to the landing-place, and lay down on the top of my boxes, under a kind of awning of mats put up by my boy, and saying good-bye to Ward, I was paddled away. In the evening a heavy rain came on, which continued for the greater part of the next thirty-six hours. I managed to keep dry, by crouching in a heap under the only two blankets I had, and at last arrived at

Equator on the evening of the third day, more dead than alive. Here I was very kindly received by Mr Banks, who took me into his house, and—together with his wife, who made me beef-tea, and anything else that I could take, and was untiring in her efforts for my comfort—did all in his power to restore me to health. In about a fortnight I was able to walk about a little, and began to think I should soon be all right, when eczema broke out all over my lower limbs, and speedily spread, till I was one huge sore from my neck downwards. What saved my face I do not know, but was glad to find that my head was not attacked; while from my neck to the soles of my feet I could hardly find a single square inch of healthy skin.

I found that Mr Glave, of the Sanford Company, had handed over the charge of Equator Station to Mr Boulanger, and was gone up the Oubangi on an ivory-buying expedition, in the *New York*, a new steamer belonging to the company. He did not return before my departure, although I was nearly a month at Equator, and, to my great regret, I had to leave without seeing him. At last—after what seemed to me ages—the *En Avant* arrived from Stanley Falls, bringing the sad news of Major Barttelot's death on July 19th. I left in her the same day, arriving at Lukolela August 19th. It was here that Mr Deane had been killed by an elephant, on May 15th, 1888, and buried close

MY START FOR HOME.
FROM A SKETCH BY THE AUTHOR.

beside the spot where, six months before, I had seen another grave dug for poor Spinnoch—the Belgian who died on my last run down the river.

On August 22d I arrived at Léopoldville. Here I had a slight relapse, and learning from the doctor at the station that I should not recover if I remained in Africa, I applied for a hammock and carriers to take me to the coast, and on August 29th, was carried out of Léopoldville on my way to Matadi. I will pass over the miseries of the first stage of my journey, which I duly survived, arriving at Lukungu, September 5th. Here, through the kindness of Mr Hoste (of the A.B.M.U.), who gave me some oxide of zinc ointment, I obtained some relief from the unremitting pain of the eczema; and here, too, I found a friend of mine, Mr Hens, the artist, who had come out with me nearly three years before, and whom I had not seen since I left him at Boma, when going up-country. Since that time he had been to Europe, and returned to the Congo, and was now on his way home for the second time, only waiting for the arrival of the mail before starting for the coast. On September 7th I was greatly surprised by the appearance of Ward, who was carried into Lukungu in a hammock, being unable to walk, on account of ulcers on his feet. I was greatly shocked by the sad news he told me of Jameson's death from fever at Bangala, on August

17th. While deploring the sad event, I could not but admire the devoted and untiring courage with which Jameson had stuck to his duty till the last; and I hope that when Ward comes home, we shall have full particulars of the events which brought about his death. It seems that after Major Barttelot was shot, Jameson, leaving Bonny to look after the caravan, returned to Stanley Falls with the assassin, and handed him over to the officials of the Free State, who, after trial, sentenced him to death. He then, having made arrangements with Tippoo Tip for supplying men to take the remaining loads to Wadelai, started down-river in a canoe to bring up Ward and the loads lying at Bangala. Two or three days after leaving the Falls with a crew of Manyemas, not feeling very well, he was lying down in the canoe under a mat, when some natives, seeing a canoe full of Manyemas, and fearing that the Arabs were descending the river on a raid, prepared to attack them. On perceiving this, the men came to Jameson, and hearing what was the matter, he stood up in the blazing sun, waving his hat to the natives. The latter, seeing a white man, desisted from the attack; but the exposure brought on fever, and for eight days and nights — until his arrival at Bangala—Jameson lay in the bottom of the canoe, soaked to the skin by the water which had accumulated there, and without a drop of tea or anything but Congo water to quench his burning thirst. With almost superhuman courage he attempted to throw off the fever, and at last reached Bangala alive, but that was all. He lived only two days, but, in spite of his weakness, succeeded in telling Ward the state of affairs at Stanley Falls; and then, having done all that it was possible for him to do, he died, almost his last words being, "Hang this fever! if I could only face it, I could beat it!" showing how, to the very last, he fought against the sinking stupor. As Ward said, it was nothing but sheer pluck that kept him alive till his work was done. He had simply lived for some days on his determination to reach Bangala, where he expected to find Ward, who would be able to relieve him. His object gained, his strong will gave way under the fearful strain, and one more name was added to the long roll of those who have given their lives for Africa.

As soon as he was buried, Ward left Bangala in a canoe for Léopoldville, and was now on his way to Loanda to get instructions from the Committee. He only rested one night at Lukungu, and next morning (September 6th), at 6 A.M., he was off for Matadi. To show the speed with which he travelled, I may mention that, a few hours later, when my carriers appeared, the chief of the station handed me a letter to Mr Ingham, a missionary at Banza Manteka. This letter, as I subsequently found, Ward had sent off by special messenger two days before his departure from Léopoldville; and Mr Ingham, after opening it, turned to me, and asked why Ward had taken the trouble to write to him, and then come on ahead of his letter, to tell him all the news in person—a question I could not answer. At noon I was carried out of Lukungu, and next day was nearly mad with the pain of the eczema, which was rendered worse than ever by the friction caused by the motion of the hammock. On arriving at Banza Manteka, I was again indebted to a missionary—Mr Ingham—for a temporary respite, and spent a very pleasant evening with him and Mr and Mrs Richards. On the morning of September 14th, I passed through Mpallaballa, another station of the A.B.M.U., where I stopped an hour or two with Mr and Mrs Clark. Leaving here at 2 P.M., I crossed the Mpozo about four o'clock. As I was carried over the top of the last ridge, I raised myself in my hammock; and my men, giving a shout, broke into a run, and carried me suddenly into view of the waters of the Lower Congo. There, almost under my feet, rolled the grand old river, her waters looking like a flood of liquid gold in the light of the sinking sun, as they foamed and curled away down their rocky channel towards the ocean. Between me and the river lay a rocky ridge, over which I could just see the tops of a grove of trees, marking the site of Matadi.

Three or four miles down the river I could descry the roofs of the Baptist Mission-station at Underhill, perched on a high rocky point, behind which the river disappeared from view. Opposite this was the "Devil's Caldron"—a large bay surrounded by cliffs from 600 to 800 feet high. The mighty river, in attempting to reach the sea, has scooped out this huge indentation before taking a turn which is nearly at right angles to its former course, and now foams round and round in great whirlpools, which seem to flash streaks of light across the dark shadows thrown by the cliffs—the deep indigo of the mountains on the north bank forming a splendid background to the whole picture.

The prospect of speedily finishing their task seemed to animate my men, and they tore down the steep hill at such a pace that I suffered agonies from the excessive friction of the shaking hammock on my sore skin. However, I did not stop them, as I knew that in half an hour it would all be over. Just at sunset I was carried up to the door of the chief's house at Matadi, and was soon made as comfortable as possible in a room, while my carriers were dismissed to the camp. In the evening I heard that Ward had arrived the day before, but too late to catch the steamer, and had, although dead tired, gone to a great deal of trouble to procure a canoe to take him down to Boma by night, rather than lose the Portuguese mail-boat, by which he intended to send his despatches to the Island of S. Thomé.[1]

This was the second time Ward had come down to the coast with telegrams and despatches, and on both occasions he had made remarkably quick journeys. He certainly had every facility for this—being supplied with fresh relays of men by the commanders of the different stations through which he passed; but no one seems to have been aware that he himself was not relieved as well as his men, but travelled almost day and night—never halting by the way, or sparing himself till his duty was done, and the steamboat and telegraph were carrying his news to England. On his last march to the coast he blistered his feet: the blisters developed into ulcers, and he was forced to take to a hammock; but he went on, and caught the mail, writing some of his letters during his halts at night. Though he twice performed the journey down the river to the coast in a remarkably short time, he got no thanks from the people he was gratuitously serving; and all the notice taken of him in Europe —when the news arrived that he had again started up-country after Stanley—was the remark in one of the newspapers that Ward had for the last year been rushing up and down the Congo like a shuttle on a loom.

[1] There is no telegraph station on the Congo, the cable going right past the mouth to S. Paul de Loanda. S. Thomé is the next nearest station after Loanda.

Having had but little sleep during the last few nights, I obtained some opium-pills from the chief of Matadi, and one of them soon sent me into a kind of doze, from which I did not awake till nearly 8 A.M. the next day, when I heard that a schooner was to leave for Boma at eleven. As it was not likely that another steamer would come up that week, I decided to go in the schooner; and accordingly, having had all my loads stowed on board, I was carried down to the beach, and placed in the stern of the vessel, which was an open boat of ten tons, manned by Cabindas. The wind was up-river, and we had to tack, which so delayed us, that by the time the wind dropped, after sunset, we were still fifteen miles from Boma, and I was obliged to spend the night on the schooner's deck, covered with a blanket. Next morning we were off again at daylight, and reached Boma at 9 A.M., where I was glad to turn into bed, in a room given me by the chief of the station. As I was able to get more nourishing food here than up the river, I soon became stronger, and was able to get about a little. For this improvement in health I was chiefly indebted to Mr Ainsworth, of Messrs Hatton and Cookson's factory, Boma, who sent me eggs and other dainties not to be had in the crowded State station, and even offered to accommodate me in his house until the arrival of the English mail-steamer.

When I arrived at Boma, I found that the Congo State authorities had instituted a new coinage for circulation in their territories. The gold and silver coins were very prettily designed; but the copper ones were made with a hole in the centre, like the Chinese cash. This hole was put in specially for the convenience of the natives, in order that—having no pockets or purses—they might be able to string the coins and hang them round their necks. But a nigger is not to be fooled; he knows what money is, and seeing the holes in the new coins, concluded that a piece had been cut out, and refused to acknowledge them as legal tender. In this way I found I could not get rid of some of the new money I had, before leaving, except by taking it to the post-office at Banana, where I had it changed. Even the silver coins were accounted bad—the natives refusing everything but English money. This reminds me of an incident which occurred on a part of the West Coast, near Lagos, which has recently been annexed by France. The French at once tried to substitute their own coinage for the English, which had long been current there; and it is said that a native, on being offered some ten-centime coppers, remarked in nigger English, as he looked dubiously at the French eagle stamped on one side of the coin, "Me sabey Queen's head; me no sabey them fowl!"

Boma had greatly increased and multiplied since

I passed through it on my way up to Bangala, more than two years before. A broad, well-kept road now led up from the pier to the Sanatorium, and numerous houses had sprung up, both round that place and on the beach. A new three-storeyed iron villa had been erected for the Governor-General; but, as M. Janssens was now in Europe, this was shut up—his deputy, M. Ledeganck, living in a house close by. A row of smaller houses stretched along one side of the road to the Sanatorium; and one of these was ambitiously styled *Palais de Justice*, though *Palais de l'Injustice* would have been a better title. The place was, on the whole, becoming fairly civilised, and the "palm-oil ruffians"[1] no longer had it all their own way; though now and then they would break loose—generally on the arrival of a mail-steamer, when, for two or three days, the "Lord of Misrule" reigned supreme. But law and order were gradually asserting themselves, and the days were fast coming to an end when the officers of the mail-steamers had to extricate the rowdies of Boma from the port-holes of the saloon, where they had stuck in their attempts to go ashore by a short cut.

[1] "Palm-oil ruffian" is a term used on the west coast of Africa in the same sense as the word "larrikin" is in Australia. Palm-oil being one of the principal articles of trade down this coast, the term came to be applied to those traders who made themselves conspicuous for their cantankerousness. It is now used to designate roughs in general, all down the west and south-west coasts of Africa.

Some years ago—in the days when the palm-oil ruffians were fairly rampant — one of the new vessels of the African Steam Navigation Company, which had very large port-holes, arrived at Boma. The saloon was, as usual, well filled with these thirsty gentlemen, almost before she had dropped her anchor, and business was pretty brisk till late at night, or rather early in the morning, when the crowd began slowly to disperse. Two, rather farther gone than the rest, took a fancy to go ashore through the port-holes, and, for some reason best known to themselves, both made for the same scuttle. Somehow—goodness only knows how— they both got their heads and shoulders through, but could get no farther, and there they remained, fighting like two cats hung over a clothes-line with their tails tied together, till the chief officer and three or four of his men managed to extricate them after a great waste of time and trouble.

I did not improve much in health at Boma. I had, it is true, fairly got over the dysentery, but the eczema became much worse, and the doctor either could not cure it or did not take the trouble. The pain and irritation were fearful, and I could not remain still a minute without scratching, which only made matters worse; so I developed a restlessness worthy of the Flying Dutchman of old, and went wandering all over Boma, visiting the different trading establishments, or spending uneasy hours in lolling about Mr Ainsworth's rooms at the English factory, trying to read some of the books he had lying about.

On September 21st, the African Steamship Company's steamer *Africa* arrived from Antwerp. As she had to go to Loanda before starting on her homeward voyage, and it would thus be over ten days before she left Banana for Antwerp, I applied to the Vice-Governor-General (who had come up from Banana on board the mail-steamer) for a passage to Loanda and back. He absolutely refused to do anything for me. I was getting no better,—all I could get from the doctor was his opinion that I should improve when I got out of the country,—and I began to wonder whether I was ever to reach home alive. At last I obtained permission to go to Loanda at my own expense. Accordingly, I embarked, September 24th, and by noon the *Africa* was steaming down the Congo on her way to St Paul de Loanda. Under the care of an English doctor I soon began to improve, and by October 9th (when, at 10 A.M., we reached Banana, on our return from that dirty Portuguese settlement) my health had greatly benefited by the voyage, and I was nearly cured of eczema, though still very weak.

On arriving at Banana, I went ashore to draw the money for my passage; but owing to some order of the Vice-Governor's (who, at the same time, though my half-pay for over two years was still in the hands of the State authorities, kindly wrote to the captain of the *Africa*, telling him that the State would not be responsible for the expense of my passage to Loanda and back, and would not cash any order for money drawn by me on them), I could not get more than £8. This sum was barely sufficient to pay my expenses on board the *Africa*, when I left that boat for the *Biafra* some two weeks later; and had it not been for the kindness of Mr Lemarinel (who was returning home at the same time), and that of Captain Bales of the *Biafra*, I should have landed in Liverpool without a shilling.

Mr Hens, who had been awaiting the return of the *Africa* from Loanda, now came on board, and on October 11th we steamed out of Banana Creek, homeward bound. I now congratulated myself that my troubles were ended, but soon discovered that I had been shouting too soon, for I had not yet "emerged from the forest primeval." A day or two later I had another relapse of dysentery, and on reaching Lagos, my disgust with things in general was further increased by the announcement that the *Africa* had been chartered to proceed to Kotonou, and load palm-kernels for Marseilles.

Where in Africa was Kotonou? We soon found out, for five or six hours' steaming westward from

Lagos brought us to a miserably small French station, situated on a spit of sand behind which was a large lagoon. There was a terrible surf here, and the place swarmed with sharks. We soon found that, owing to the surf, it would take some thirty-five days for the ship to load up; but were saved from utter despair by hearing that the s.s. *Biafra*, belonging to the same company as the *Africa*, would come up in a few days, and take us to Liverpool.

Till she arrived, we had nothing to do but watch the surf-boats bring off the casks of palm-kernels. Now and then a boat would be upset in the surf; and on one of these occasions a man had both his legs bitten off by a shark, and was pulled out of the water dead. Late at night, on October 26th, the *Biafra* made her welcome appearance, and next morning Captain Bales came to fetch all the passengers, and away we steamed — Westward ho! Next day we stopped at Addah, where a black clerk, in charge of some store, sent off to say he had twenty bags of rubber to ship, and wished the steamer to wait for them. The captain replied that he was going on in two hours, and that, if the rubber was not sent off by that time, it would be left behind. Three or four bags arrived during the next hour and a half; then the signal-gun was fired, and preparations made for departure. This brought off a catamaran, with a letter for the captain, which he brought to the poop and read to the passengers, as follows:—

"CAPTAIN BALES, R.N.

"DEAR SIR,—Know thou that, to-morrow being Sunday, they will not work at Accra; therefore be patient, and take my cargo.—Yrs. affectionately,

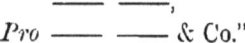
Pro ―― ―― & Co."

Needless to say, the captain was not patient, and we were soon on our way to Accra.

After leaving Accra, we called at numerous small ports all along the coast, picking up instalments of cargo, with here and there a passenger. On November 4th we steamed into Sierra Leone, and were boarded by numerous gaudily dressed black women, with huge bags of kola-nuts, which they take to Gambia, where there is a great demand for them. These women and their property crowded up the decks and were a regular nuisance, and I was very glad to see them go ashore at Bathurst, on the Gambia, where we received several fresh passengers. Among these was a gentleman who had been in the service of one of the telegraph companies, and who was so far gone with fever that he did not live twenty-four hours. His death put us in quarantine at Goree. Next day, soon after leaving this place, he was buried at sea, just as the lighthouse on Cape Verde was vanishing in the distance astern. This was my last glimpse of Africa, and I began anxiously to look out for the Canary Islands as a welcome change. At Grand Canary we only stopped a few hours and then proceeded. I was still feeling very sick and weak; and it was not until we reached Santa Cruz that I began—lying in a comfortable deck-chair lent me by the captain, and watching the sun sink behind the towering peak of Teneriffe—to think life worth living after all, and to find that there were times when one could, in the enjoyment of the present, forget the hardships of the past.

Here three more passengers, a gentleman and two ladies, came on board for Madeira. The cold winds, which we met after leaving Teneriffe, were delightfully refreshing to me, after nearly three years of hot weather, and the long Atlantic rollers seemed like old friends. Two days brought us to Madeira, where we arrived at night, and anchored in Funchal Bay, to wait for dawn. Here we were again quarantined, on account of a rumour of yellow fever at Teneriffe; and the three passengers from the latter place—who had left England only six weeks before with the intention of spending the winter between the Canary Islands and Madeira—were told that they could only land in the lazaretto, where they would have to remain seven days, and be charged an exorbitant sum for expenses—the authorities reserving the right to send them off to England, if they saw fit, at the end of that time, without allowing them to enter the town at all. Under these circumstances, they preferred remaining on board the *Biafra* and going to England. After leaving Madeira, we were let in for a regular north-west gale, and the *Biafra*, being an old boat, built before the days of flat bottoms and great beam, rolled tremendously.

On the morning of November 22d we entered the Mersey. It was rather misty, and I could not see the shore very plainly, and was straining my eyes to make out the outlines of New Brighton, when a very characteristic feature of English scenery came suddenly and conspicuously into view. Standing out in the water, supported on piles evidently driven into a sand-bank, were two huge ugly boards, from the face of which glared the words, "Eat Germ Bread," and "Try Sunlight Soap," in letters very nearly large enough to be read across the Irish Channel. Inwardly confounding mural advertisers and advertisements in general, I made a vow never, if I could possibly help it, either to eat Germ Bread or use Sunlight Soap.

Having landed at the Prince's Landing-Place and cleared the customs, I went off in search of Messrs Hutton & Co., the Liverpool agents of the Congo Free State. Here I saw Mr Wise, who was a great deal more obliging than the Vice-Governor at Boma had been. By the help of the telegraph, he soon obtained me a remittance from Brussels; and his kindness did not end here, for, knowing I wished to leave Liverpool as soon as possible, he went out of his way to come up to my hotel in the evening and bring me the money directly he got an answer to his telegram, and did not leave me till he had done all in his power to assist me.

I experienced a novel sensation when, on landing at Liverpool, I found none but white faces around me, and met fair ladies in every street by the score, of whom, during the past three years, I had perhaps seen a dozen. Before evening I was comfortably established in the North-Western Hotel, and dined there with Mr Herford, a fellow-passenger, who had spent three years on the West Coast. The fresh food, snowy table-cloths, and good cooking, were especially enjoyable after the tinned chop and tough goat of Africa, and the scarcely less leathery beef of the Canaries. We both agreed, as we drank to the girls of Old England in a foaming pint of bitter ale, that no one could properly enjoy a good dinner till he had been to a country where good dinners were unattainable.

300

CHAPTER XIII.

THE BISMARCK OF CENTRAL AFRICA.

TIPPOO TIP—HIS FIRST MEETING WITH LIVINGSTONE—CAMERON VISITS HIS CAMP ON THE LOMAMI—TRAVELS WITH STANLEY IN 1876—HIS DRESS AND APPEARANCE—DESERTS STANLEY AT VINYA NJARA—HIS OWN ACCOUNT OF THIS TRANSACTION—RAIDS OF KAREMA AND OTHERS NEAR STANLEY FALLS—TIPPOO ARRIVES AT THE FALLS IN NOVEMBER 1884—PALAVER WITH VAN GÈLE—GOES TO ZANZIBAR—DEANE ATTACKED—LOSS OF THE STATION—THE ARABS LEFT TO THEIR OWN DEVICES FOR A WHOLE YEAR—TIPPOO RETURNS AS GOVERNOR—HIS FEELINGS TOWARDS THE GERMANS—TERMS OF HIS AGREEMENT WITH STANLEY—HE SEES THE WEAKNESS OF THE CONGO STATE—ADVANTAGES OF THE ARABS—DISTRUST OF EUROPEANS—TIPPOO SETS TO WORK TO STRENGTHEN HIS POSITION AND SUBDUE THE BAKUMU—THE ORIGINAL OBJECT OF THE STATE DEFEATED—ARABS ON LAKE NYASSA—THE AFRICAN LAKES COMPANY—FUTILITY OF ATTEMPTING TO CONTROL AFRICAN OPERATIONS FROM EUROPE—THE SORT OF MEN REQUIRED FOR CENTRAL AFRICA—WHAT THE BAKUMU THINK OF DEANE.

HAMED BIN MAHOMED BIN JUMA BORAJIB—for such is the real name of the man who rejoices in the various *aliases* of Tippooru, Mtipula, and Tipo-Tipo, but is best known by the appellation of Tippoo Tip—is the son of a Zanzibar Arab by a Mrima woman.

He is first mentioned by Livingstone, who notes, in his 'Last Journals,' that he met him at the village of Ponda, near the south end of Lake Tanganika, on July 29th, 1867. Livingstone speaks of him as Tipo-Tipo, which he explains to mean "the gatherer together of wealth,"—a name adopted by Tippoo himself, after taking a great deal of spoil in a fight with Nsama.

Livingstone travelled with Tippoo Tip, and two or three other Arabs, to Kabwakwa in Kabwiré, where he left them in order to go to Lake Moero with some of Tippoo's men, who were on their way to Cazembe's to buy ivory. Later on, Livingstone heard that Tippoo was setting up as a potentate in Itawa, and demanding that all ivory should be brought to him as his tribute. When Livingstone again returned to the country south of Tanganika, he found he could get no food, for Tippoo had been raiding through the land, and had left the abomination of desolation in his rear.

Tippoo then evidently went west, for the next news of him comes from Commander Cameron, who met him at Nyangwé on the Lualaba, where Tippoo arrived from a camp on the Lomami. Wishing to reach a Lake Sankorra, of which he had heard, and which has since turned out to be the Sankuru river, Cameron left Nyangwé with Tippoo—at that time one of the richest and most powerful of the Arabs who roam this part of Africa—and accompanied him to his camp on the Lomami. Cameron says that he met with great kindness from Tippoo, and that the only drawback to his enjoyment of the comforts of the Arab camp was the "number of slaves in chains who met his eyes at every turn." As a chief named Kassongo would not allow Cameron to pass through his country, he was obliged to give up the idea of reaching Lake Sankorra, and started off to complete his memorable journey across Africa.

Tippoo is next heard of at Nyangwé, where Stanley met him in October 1876, and described him as having the appearance of an Arab gentleman in very comfortable circumstances, with a fine, intelligent face, and a black beard. His account of Tippoo's dress also bears out Cameron's statement that the latter was the greatest dandy among the Arab traders. But when I met Tippoo at Stanley Falls in 1888, I was struck with the simplicity of his dress, compared with that of the other Arabs —a long white shirt, and the usual *doti* or waistcloth, being all he usually wore; and I have heard from Mr Jameson that, when on the march, he would discard the long shirt, and, with only the *doti*, stride on through the jungle at a pace which Jameson—no mean walker—found it hard to keep up. His beard was at this time thickly sprinkled with grey hairs, and I should have put his age down as about 50. His twitching, restless eyes, and his dark complexion seem to have been noticed by every one who has come in contact with him—also his politeness and good-breeding. Jameson, in describing his conduct to me, termed him a perfect gentleman: this may be true enough, as far as manners go, but hardly so when his actions are viewed in other lights.

Stanley having made arrangements with Tippoo to accompany him, with 400 men, a distance of sixty camps, for a consideration of 5000 dollars, they started, in November 1876, on a march through the forest of Uregga. Every step of the way had to be cut through the dense undergrowth, and the men were decimated by smallpox. Tippoo several times tried to persuade Stanley to return, but in vain; and at length, on reaching Vinya Njara, refused to accompany him any farther, though the sixty camps had not been completed.

Stanley, in 'Through the Dark Continent,' says that, feeling the courage of his escort was exhausted, he consented to release Tippoo from his engagement (on condition the latter used his influence to induce the men belonging to the expedition to follow their leader into the unknown country), and gave him the following present in payment for his escort so far: a draft for 2600 dollars, one riding-ass, one trunk, 30 *doti* cloth, 150 lb. beads, 16,300 shells, one revolver, 200 rounds ammunition, 50 lb. brass wire, besides numerous presents to his chiefs and men. This done, Stanley sailed off down the Lualaba—December 25th, 1876—on his way to the Western Ocean.

Tippoo's own version of this parting—as told by him to Mr Jameson, from whom I had it—is very different. According to him, when they reached the forest of Uregga, and travelling became difficult, the men belonging to Stanley's expedition refused to proceed, and it was only through Tippoo's influence and persuasions that they went on to Vinya Njara. Here (to continue Tippoo's account) the men mutinied, and insisted on turning back; whereupon Stanley came to Tippoo, and cursed him up hill and down dale, till he went to the men, and after some time, and with great difficulty, succeeded in persuading them to follow Stanley to the sea. The latter then again came to Tippoo, and told him that if he reached the sea by going down that river, and got safe to Europe, he would be a great man, and would send him not only a large sum of money, but also a double-barrelled rifle and ammunition, besides various other presents. Having made these promises, Stanley departed; and from that day to this, Tippoo avers he has never received his dues. He also repeated to Jameson what he had previously told Lieutenant Becker (as narrated by the latter in his book, '*La Vie en Afrique*'), viz., that Stanley only made himself obeyed by getting his men into dangerous situations, whence they did not know how to escape—entirely ignoring the fact that Stanley himself went into danger as well as his men, and it was he, and he alone, who extricated them.

In 1881, Becker ('*La Vie en Afrique*') mentions him as having lived for ten years in Manyema, where, though nominally subject to the Sultan of Zanzibar, he enjoyed—as he still does—absolute power.

Having seen Stanley disappear down the Lualaba, Tippoo, after subjugating the country round Vinya Njara, also began to descend the river, raiding as he went, for ivory and slaves. Whether he himself reached Stanley Falls on this occasion is not known, but when Stanley returned, in 1883, to establish a station at the Seventh Cataract, he found the Arab Karema near the mouth of the Lomami, and Tippoo's men in full power at the Falls. Here was a dilemma: Stanley had been sent out by the King of the Belgians to found stations and make treaties with the natives in the name of the International African Association, in order to establish a Free State from which slavery should be rigidly excluded; and here he found himself forestalled by the slavers themselves. Hoping to impress them with the advantages of free trade and an easy route to the coast, he took several of their confidential slaves down the Congo with him; but the innate treachery of the Arab character balked all his good intentions. These slaves, having disposed of the ivory they had brought down with them, were sent back to Stanley Falls, and thence to Tippoo Tip, and described to him—probably with a great deal of exaggeration—the stores of ivory possessed by the natives on the banks of the Congo. This (combined with the reports of the Zanzibaris in the service of the State, as to the extent of its resources in arms and men) excited the avarice of Tippoo Tip, who was fully alive to the danger of his position, should civilisation get the upper hand in Central Africa. Having obtained forces from Said Barghash, and also, as he alleges, power to act in the Sultan's name, he set out from Zanzibar, and on arriving at Stanley Falls (November 14th, 1884), began to play the potentate over Lieutenant Wester, who, knowing himself to be powerless, quietly waited his opportunity. Captain Van Gèle, arriving at the cataracts shortly after, held a long palaver, after which matters assumed a more favourable aspect—but this did not last long. Tippoo went away to Zanzibar, and left his brother Bwana Nzigé as his deputy—Mr Deane having by this time taken command of Falls Station. The story of Mr Deane's heroic attempt to put down slaving in this territory has already been told. Had he been provided with a few more rounds of ammunition, or had his men shown a little more pluck, he would probably have succeeded; for I afterwards heard Raschid (the man who commanded the Arabs in their attack on the station) assert that he had not the least notion of Deane's resources, and that, had the latter held out only two days longer, the Arabs—who were becoming disheartened—would have given up the attack and gone east. This statement of Raschid's looks very strange when compared with another statement of his—viz., that the Arabs came off very well in the fight, only losing six men in all; while, judging from the reports of the Wenya and Bakumu to whom I spoke on my visit to the Falls in 1888, I should have put down the number at sixty or seventy.

What were Tippoo's orders to his deputy, when he left the Falls for Zanzibar, will probably never be known; but I should not be surprised to learn that he left no definite orders at all, and went away in the hope that some complication might arise which would enable the white men to be disposed of during his absence.

After Deane had been rescued by Captain Coquilhat, and taken away to Europe, the Arabs were for the best part of a year left to themselves. Having no definite information as to the actual power of the Free State, they were naturally at first in a state of terror lest a large force of armed steamers should ascend the river and annihilate them. But as time went on, and the authorities at Boma and Brussels neglected to strike while the iron was hot, they gained confidence; and when at last Tippoo appeared on the scene, coming up the Congo in a steamer under the flag of the Free State, they were so strongly intrenched that they considered themselves ready to meet any force, and actually (not knowing he was in it) fired at the canoe which was conveying Tippoo to the shore.

Meantime a special messenger had informed Tippoo at Zanzibar of all that had happened at Kinsi Katini. I have been told that, on hearing hostilities had broken out, Tippoo went to the Sultan and asked his advice; but that the Sultan told him in reply to settle the business himself: to fight, if he wished to fight; if not, to negotiate with the Powers in Europe. He was shut in on the east coast by the Germans, of whom I afterwards heard him complain that they had entered the Sultan's territory, made secret treaties with the native chiefs subject to him, and then claimed the country as annexed by Germany, and forced the Sultan to sign it away,—Great Britain looking apathetically on while the Germans undermined her interests.[1] On the west his way was barred by the Congo Free State, which, he thought, was not as yet strong enough to hold its own against him.

[1] Tippoo said something to this effect. I cannot give his exact words, as he spoke in Kiswahili, and the man who interpreted for me could not speak very good English.

His chief grievance against the Germans was the heavy tax they had put on his ivory, and he had probably determined to try and get a new route to the sea by going back with a large number of men and plenty of ammunition to force his way down the Congo, when Stanley arrived at Zanzibar on his way to relieve Emin Pasha, and affairs took an entirely different course. I have heard a report —whether true or not, I do not know—that when Stanley first spoke to Tippoo at Zanzibar about the settlement of the dispute at Stanley Falls, the latter flew into a tremendous rage, and swore that not a single man of the Emin Relief Expedition should ever pass through his territory. Stanley's usual diplomacy, however, overcame all difficulties, and Tippoo finally signed a treaty by which he became Governor of the district of Stanley Falls at a salary of £30 per month. One of the first clauses in this treaty is intended to prevent the tribes of the Aruhwimi and Upper Congo, as well as the Arabs, from engaging in the slave-trade.[1]

[1] This treaty is published in the Parliamentary Correspondence for 1888 (Africa, No. 8), and the text of it is as follows :—

"*Agreement.*

"Mr Henry Morton Stanley, on behalf of his Majesty the King of the Belgians and Sovereign of the Congo State, appoints Hamed-bin-Mohammed al Marjebi, Tippu Tip, to be Wali of the independent State of the Congo, at Stanley Falls district, at a salary of £30 per month, payable to his agent at Zanzibar, on the following conditions :—

"1. Tippu Tip is to hoist the flag of the Congo State at its sta-

This clause he was certainly not carrying out when I was at Stanley Falls in 1888, for I saw him one day engaged in organising an expedition to attack some tribe or tribes west of the Lomami, in order to obtain their ivory.

Stanley, having completed his arrangements at Zanzibar, went round the Cape to the mouth of the Congo, taking with him Tippoo and his retinue, among whom, by the by, was the priest mentioned on a former occasion—for Tippoo is a devout Mohammedan, and carries the sword in one hand and the Koran in the other. Being entertained at

tion near Stanley Falls, and to maintain the authority of the State on the Congo and all its affluents at the said station downwards to the Biyerré or Aruhwimi river, and to prevent the tribes thereon, as well as Arabs and others, from engaging in the slave-trade.

"2. Tippu Tip is to receive a resident officer of the Congo State, who will act as his secretary in all his communications with the Administrator-General.

"3. Tippu Tip is to be at full liberty to carry on his legitimate private trade in any direction, and to send his caravans to and from any place he may desire.

"4. Tippu Tip shall nominate a *locum tenens*, to whom, in case of his temporary absence, his powers shall be delegated, and who, in the event of his death, shall become his successor in the Waliship; but his Majesty the King of the Belgians shall have the power of veto, should there be any serious objection to Tippu Tip's nominee.

"5. This arrangement shall only be binding so long as Tippu Tip or his representative fulfils the conditions embodied in this agreement.

       (Signed) " HENRY M. STANLEY.
           " TIPPU TIP (in Arabic).
 (Signed) " FREDC. HOLMWOOD.
      " KANJI RAJPAR (in Hindi).

" ZANZIBAR, *February* 24, 1887."

Boma, and then taken up past the Livingstone Falls to Léopoldville, he was enabled to judge for himself of the weak points of the Congo State, and confirm with his own eyes the reports he had previously heard. What must he have thought of the disorganised transport-service between Matadi and Léopoldville, compared with the resources at his command for bringing his stores inland from Zanzibar by means of enormous caravans of slaves! How reassured he must have felt, on arriving at Léopoldville, to find that the State had only two steamers there, one of them engineless, and to witness the reluctance of the missionaries to allow Stanley the use of their boats; while he could bring thousands of men down from Kassongo and Nyangwé in canoes, and pour them upon Stanley Falls, at the rate of a hundred for every one the State could bring up in their steamers. True, the State might have better arms and better men than Tippoo's horde of savages; but numbers and power of endurance tell more than anything else in a contest of this sort, and the Stanley Falls garrison could soon have been starved out. But this was an advantage of which the Arabs were probably ignorant until they went up the river from Banana.

Then came the long days on the river, traversing the 500 odd miles that separated Léopoldville from Bangala, the distance to the latter isolated spot seeming all the greater from the fact that the steamers, heavily loaded, and towing two whale-boats each, took nearly three weeks to accomplish the journey in place of the usual fortnight. Then came another stretch of unoccupied country to the Lomami, where the Arabs were found to have strongly intrenched themselves; and then, when Stanley Falls was reached, Tippoo Tip, the most powerful of all the slave-raiding Arabs between the Aruhwimi and Tanganika, was established there as governor, and the country round about left for a whole year to the mercy of men whose only objects in life are—like those of the Spaniards of old—the amassing of wealth for themselves, and the spreading of their religion—a religion of carnage, sensuality, and lust.

Had Stanley been free to remain on the Congo, and govern the district of Stanley Falls *through* Tippoo Tip, as Sir John Kirk for twenty years governed the whole of East Africa through the Sultan of Zanzibar; or had some man with a strong will and much experience of the Arab character been sent with Tippoo as resident officer, at the time of his first arrival at the Falls,—all might have been well.

But left to himself for a whole year, without even a letter to tell him why the European officer had not arrived, Tippoo naturally followed the promptings of his Arab instincts, and raided the country right and left. The state of depopulation, on my arrival in the spring of 1888, showed only too plainly how he had fulfilled the terms of the treaty.

Suspicion and distrust, which are part of every Arab's nature, may also have had something to do with this. As month after month passed, and, though the expedition for the Falls was delayed from various causes, no word was sent to Tippoo to explain this delay, what was more natural than for such a man to suspect that he was being led into a trap, and that a great force was perhaps collecting at Léopoldville, to ascend the Congo, and drive him east of the cataracts? Under these circumstances he would, of course, set to work at once to strengthen his position, and get the upper hand of the Bakumu, who, he knew, would immediately rise against him, should Deane (who was at this time on the Lower Congo) reappear at the head of a large force. That Tippoo did distrust the Europeans was pretty evident from the questions he put about Stanley. He once asked me what Stanley's object was in ascending the Aruhwimi; and on my replying that it was to relieve Emin Pasha, he again asked whether he was going to found stations and take the country, as he had done all the way up the Congo. He seemed to me to have a sort of suspicion that the relief of Emin was only a blind, and that Stanley's real object was to extend the territory of the Congo Free State. This being so, I only wonder that he did not, months before we started to relieve Major Barttelot, descend the Congo with a large force of Manyema cannibals, and sweep Bangala Station off the face of the earth.

By the conditions under which Tippoo was left at Stanley Falls, after his appointment as governor, the flag of the Congo State was made to afford protection to the oppressor, and the Lone Star banner of freedom was dragged in the mire.

Newspapers and telegraphs being scarce on the Upper Congo, I had heard little or nothing of what was taking place on the east coast; but when, on reaching Boma, I heard that the Germans and English were blockading the Swahili coast, and that hostilities had arisen between the African Lakes Company and the Arabs, at the north end of Lake Nyassa, Tippoo Tip's excessive eagerness to be paid (not only by Major Barttelot, but by the traders to whom he sold his ivory) *in gunpowder*, recurred very forcibly to my memory. I had several times heard Tippoo Tip express his dislike to the Germans, who, as he said, were driving him out of his country. What more likely than that he should wish to send this powder over to the Zanzibar Arabs, who are fighting the Germans on the east coast? Of what use is a blockade on that coast, while Tippoo Tip is Governor of Stanley Falls, and has the Congo route open for bringing up arms and ammunition?

To make the blockade effective, the west coast must be closed to the importation of arms as well as the east; and even this would leave an opening for them to reach the interior through the Portuguese colonies—in spite of Portugal's ostensible approbation of the blockade.

Mr Jameson, on his return from Kassongo, mentioned to me, among other matters, that Tippoo Tip had eagerly questioned him about the country round Lake Nyassa and Matabele-land (which latter place Jameson had visited), and asked if it would be possible for him to conquer the country as he had done Manyema. He also inquired with much interest about the position and power of the European settlers in Nyassa-land, and asked what Power claimed that part of Africa.

Affairs at the north end of Lake Nyassa are now much in the same state as they were at Stanley Falls when Deane went to take command. Let those interested take heed that history does not, in this instance, repeat itself, or in two or three years' time we may find that the Arabs have managed to get the upper hand, when they will soon reduce the country to the same state of desolation as now reigns round Stanley Falls. Should the Lakes Company succeed in inflicting a crushing defeat on the Arabs, and in keeping them down, the victory will be gained, as the natives will then see that they are strong enough to hold their own, and will cast in their lot with them, and gradually other tribes will be brought to see who is their best friend. Until the natives see that the whites are strong enough to offer a successful resistance to the Arabs, they will not fight for them, for fear of the vengeance of the latter, who will, when victorious,[1] slay scores of men belonging to the tribes who assisted their enemies, burn their villages, and carry off the women and children into slavery. The Arabs, once having got the upper hand, will know how to keep it; and the entire work of Livingstone, and that of all the missionaries who have so nobly carried it on after his death, will be undone.

In a country like Africa, it is not possible, as it is in England, to control affairs from headquarters. There is no telegraph or railway, and before orders given out in a London office can reach their destination, matters will have completely changed, and all may be over, one way or another. Such was the case at Stanley Falls : the orders, which would have saved thousands of lives, only reached Captain Coquilhat on his return from the rescue of Mr Deane.

All that could be done at the present crisis would be to send out a man thoroughly acquainted with the character of African natives, who should be

[1] As at Stanley Falls, in 1886, when they cut off the heads of two chiefs and fifty other men, for helping Deane.

well supplied with men, arms, and ammunition. But such a man would have to be unhampered by orders from home, unless these were such as to leave a wide margin for the exercise of his discretion. It would be next to impossible for an entire stranger to the country to attempt to raise and discipline regiments among the savage tribes of Central Africa. The natives of Africa are thorough Conservatives, and must be firmly convinced of the good of any change before they can be persuaded to adopt it. They yield to power, but to nothing else; and it is the exhibition of power that enables the Arab to obtain such an ascendancy over them. Show them that one power is good and another bad, and they will desert the power which is seeking their extermination for that which is working for their good. Such men as Emin Pasha and Deane alone can do this. Such men will the poor uneducated natives follow and fight for. To their mind, might is right; and seeing the Arabs everywhere victorious, they, powerless to hold their own, yield doggedly to what they consider their inevitable fate, and are carried off into slavery. But should a white man come among them powerful enough to conquer their oppressors, what follows? Do not the Bakumu and Wenya still swear by the name of Deane, though he was at last driven out of the Falls? What has followed in the case of Emin Pasha? Has he not, through nobly sticking to his post after the fall of Khartoum and the death of General Gordon, saved a province larger than Great Britain from the curse of slavery, and, by the help of his native allies, held at bay the Mahdist hordes who have laid waste the whole of Upper Egypt?

Had Deane,—the only man who has ever struck a blow at the real root of the East Coast slave-trade—who, when all alone in the centre of Africa, more than five hundred miles from the nearest station, calmly stood up for the natives, and told their oppressors that he could not and would not give up the poor wretches who had sought his protection—who, knowing that his only European companion was too ill to remain with him, and that he must be left alone, coolly informed a great Arab chief that he was quite able to take care of his own head—who, when his request for ammunition was ignored, and the promised reinforcements not sent, bravely remained at his post, when he would have been perfectly justified in consulting his own safety (not having been supplied with the means of defence), by evacuating the Falls Station, and going down to Bangala,—had he been properly supported in the first instance, or even sent back—as I am told he asked to be—with a sufficient force to retake Stanley Falls, there is no doubt that the whole of the Wenya and Bakumu would have sided with him, and helped to drive back the

Arabs; and thriving villages would still stand on the banks of the Aruhwimi, where now is utter desolation.

The natives would fight in their own fashion, it is true, but discipline would only be a work of time, and they would soon come to learn of the man who could lead them to victory. The Ba-Ngala pirates, who so fiercely assailed Stanley on his first descent of the Congo, are now being drilled as soldiers by the authorities at Boma; but it was a long time before they could be induced to enter the service of the State, and even now, a man, to manage them properly, must have lived a year or two in their country, and be one whom they know and can trust. If this has been done with the Ba-Ngala, why not with the Bakumu, who are a much finer, more industrious, and more intelligent race of men?

In the deep quiet of the glorious forest of Lukolela are three cairns of stone, one of which covers the remains of as brave a man as ever trod African soil. Unhonoured, almost forgotten, as Deane's name is in Europe, its memory is fresh and green among the warriors of the Wenya and Bakumu To these poor superstitious natives he seemed to bear a charmed life, and to be capable of accomplishing almost anything. Their belief in him and his promises remained firm and unshaken, though for nearly two years they never saw a sign of him or the help he had promised them; and when I was at Stanley Falls, they came to me in crowds to ask whether we had come to drive out the Arabs, and offer their help, inquiring if Deane was coming up-river at the head of a conquering army to re-establish them in the homes whence the Arabs had mercilessly driven them. How could I explain to these poor people why we were on friendly terms with the Arabs? The news of Deane's death was a great shock to me, but I found it easier afterwards to answer the questions of the Bakumu, by telling them that the Great Good Spirit had taken Deane away to fight in Mputu; and it was a great satisfaction to me to be able to keep up his reputation among his sable admirers by explaining that it was not an Arab who had killed him, but an elephant. "Ah!" replied the poor natives—" that *tembo* bad fetish!"

CHAPTER XIV.

CONCLUSION.

INDUCEMENTS TO SLAVE-RAIDS—EXTINCTION OF THE ELEPHANT—IMPROVED TRANSPORT THE ONLY EFFECTUAL MEANS OF PUTTING AN END TO THE SLAVE-TRADE—IVORY BOUGHT BY THE SANFORD COMPANY AND THE CONGO STATE ON THE UPPER CONGO—BLACK AND WHITE TUSKS—DIFFERENT ROUTES TO THE INTERIOR—THE NILE BASIN—EAST COAST ROUTE—THE TANA RIVER—DIFFICULTIES OF THE CONGO ROUTE—RAILWAY PAST THE LIVINGSTONE CATARACTS—PROPOSED BULLOCK-ROAD—AFRICAN LAKES COMPANY—PORTUGUESE CLAIMS—SHALL LIVINGSTONE'S WORK BE IN VAIN?

ONE of the greatest inducements for the slave-raids carried on by the Arabs in Central Africa is ivory, which, on account of its high value, is the only article which will at present pay for its transport from such an inaccessible region. It has been asserted that, when the poor elephant is exterminated, and not before, will slavery come to an end. It is my belief that facility of transport to the coast by means of railways and steamers will do more, by making slave-caravans unprofitable, to put down the curse of Africa, than the extinction

x

of all the elephants on the face of the earth. Slaves are at present a necessity to the Arab, if he is to get his ivory to the coast cheaply enough to enable him to reap the enormous profits dear to the Moslem heart. But when steam has opened up a cheaper means of transport, he will be compelled to use it, as caravans of slaves could never compete with even the roughest of pioneer railways in carrying goods through a country where, at the best of times, food is scarce. Besides this, they would be able to sell their ivory on the spot—no matter how far in the interior—at very nearly as large a profit to themselves as if they took it to the coast, and would thus be without the inducement they now have to raise large caravans, and conduct them over hundreds of miles of forest and mountain. Were the interior of Africa as accessible to the European trader as the interior of India now is, the Arabs would soon be unable to procure any ivory at all, except by fair trade, as the natives would quickly dispose of all they possessed to the white man. The trading companies who, in these days of keen competition, would swarm up any new route, would soon exhaust the present stock of dead ivory; and the natives—instead of, as at present, hiding their ivory round their villages, or burying it under the floors of their huts, to await a fit opportunity for trade—would, when they had killed an elephant, convey his tusks to the nearest trader, and get the highest price obtainable for clean, white ivory; and the Arabs would find—after raiding and burning the villages—that all their expenditure of labour and gunpowder had been in vain. Were Tippoo and his Manyemas even now to descend the Congo, and raid some of the villages below Upoto, I doubt if he would get enough ivory to pay for his powder, as these villages are visited every two or three weeks by the trading steamers of the Sanford Company and the Dutch House, who buy up the ivory as fast as the natives can procure it. I remember that on one occasion, when the steamers were delayed at Stanley Pool, and did not go up-river for some months, the natives of Mobeka and Ikolungu brought their ivory down to the Sanford Station at Bangala, and having exhausted the stock of brass wire and other barter goods at that place, proceeded to the Dutch factory at Lulanga. Finding the *mundélé* in charge at that place also unable to meet the demand, they went on down to Equator, where there was another station of the Sanford Company. The African savage may be a cantankerous individual, but he knows the advantages of fair trade.

While at Bangala, I was for several months running about in a steam-launch with an official of the State, who was buying ivory; and I saw several tons of this beautiful substance purchased from the natives and sent down the country by the State, besides huge quantities on board the trading steamers and in the factory stores. On our first visit to any village, the ivory produced would be black and dirty on the outside, as it had been lying in the bush, or buried under a hut, for two or three years; but as time went on, and we still continued to come and buy, the tusks brought for sale grew lighter in colour, till, before I left the Upper Congo, we were buying, among the rest, a number of perfectly white tusks, some of which still had undecayed gristle and bits of flesh attached to them, showing that they had been brought direct for sale as soon as the elephant was killed, instead of being kept lying in the villages. Had the Arabs tried raiding these places just then, they would have got very little for their trouble.

I shall therefore, by way of conclusion, devote a few words to the consideration of the different lines of communication between the coast and the vast interior plateau of Africa, which are now in course of being opened up.

Let us begin with the oldest, and perhaps the most impracticable, of all these—the basin of the Nile. For years past, the Soudan Arabs have carried on a trade in ivory in the same way as is now done by the Zanzibar Arabs—obtaining it by means of raids, and conveying it to Khartoum, and thence either to Cairo or Suakin, on the shoulders of slaves, or in sailing-boats which they haul through the vast reed-beds of the Upper Nile—an almost insuperable obstacle to the navigation of this river by steamers. Some years ago an attempt was made to lay a railway across the desert from Suakin to Berber; but this turned out a failure, chiefly because the constructors of the line proceeded on the same principles as they would have done in peaceful England, and laid down a line in the ordinary way with wooden sleepers. This line was easily torn up by the hostile Arabs, who no doubt chuckled to themselves as they replenished their camp-fires with the creosoted timber which was to have carried the rails along which their enemies would have poured troops and supplies into the heart of the Mahdi's district. Had this line been laid down on one of the new patent systems, with some such contrivance as Hipkins's stamped steel sleeper—which, when once laid down, forms an almost continuous rail, whose sections cannot easily be taken up by natives or Arabs—we should probably have a very different tale to tell. But even were this railway complete and in working order, the obstacles to navigation on the Upper Nile would throw this route entirely out of competition; and Emin Pasha, foreseeing this, has always maintained that an open trade-route to the east coast, or, as General Gordon suggested years ago, to the Upper Congo, would be necessary to enable him properly to develop the Equatorial province of Egypt.

With regard to the East Coast route, the British East African Association have a fairly good road through their territory to Lake Victoria Nyanza waiting to be developed. The Tana river is, according to Denhardt, navigable for boats drawing about one metre of water to a distance of thirty days' journey from the coast. I do not know at how many miles Denhardt reckons a day's journey, but should think that this river could easily be made navigable for light-draught steamers to within 200 miles of Lake Victoria. Here there is a sudden rise; but when the plateau above is reached, the ground is level enough to lay down a railway as far as the lake. It is true that food is scarce round the head-waters of the Tana, but with good steamers plying on that river, this would be a difficulty easily overcome. Lake Victoria is large enough and deep enough to be navigated by ironclads; but the Nile between that lake and the Albert Nyanza is one series of cataracts and rapids, and another railway of about 150 miles would be required to connect the two. This would pass through the country of Uganda, which is—or was until recent troubles—the best developed and most civilised of all the native states of Central Africa.

This would give Emin Pasha a much shorter road to the coast than that *viâ* the Congo; and Stanley's recent journey has shown that the difficulties in the way of opening up the latter line of communication would be much greater than in the case of the East Coast route. To begin with, the Aruhwimi is impassable for steamers above Yambuya, and this place is distant over 360 miles from Lake Albert Nyanza. It would, moreover, obviously be a more difficult task to lay a railway through the dense forest described by Stanley as covering the greater part of this region, than across the undulating grass-covered uplands of Uganda and Unyoro, and the open plateau between Lake Victoria and the head-waters of the Tana.

On the West Coast, a railway some 235 miles in length has long been in contemplation—to run past the Livingstone Falls on the Congo river, and tap the vast resources of the great plain between Stanley Pool and Stanley Falls. The surveys for this railway have already been completed at a cost of £80,000; and the latest strange news is that, instead of proceeding with the construction of the railway, the authorities are devoting their attention to organising a system of transport by means of bullock-waggons. Now a railway of, say, three feet gauge, heavy enough to carry all the traffic likely to pass between Stanley Pool and the lower river for the next ten or fifteen years, could be laid down at a cost of about £2000 per mile—exclusive of viaducts and bridges. Assuming the correctness of Stanley's estimate of £450,000 for the yearly revenue from the traffic over the line, this railway would begin to pay at once, and, as soon as the traffic exceeded its capacity, could be gradually replaced by one of broader gauge and heavier rail.

Under present circumstances, it would pay far better to lay down a pioneer railway of much narrower gauge than to make the proposed bullock-road, especially as food for the bullocks would be difficult to procure in the cataract regions of the Congo, and domestic animals in that country only keep in good health so long as they are not compelled to work, and sicken and die when put to hard labour for any length of time. Such a narrow-gauge line could (according to calculations from data kindly furnished me by Mr Lord of Birmingham) be laid at the rate of about £600 per mile (exclusive of bridges), and would certainly perform the transport in a much more effective way than the above-mentioned bullock-road.

The Lower Congo is easily navigable for ocean steamers, and the railway past the Livingstone Falls would open up over 1000 miles of water on the main stream alone, besides some 6000 miles of tributaries, navigable at all seasons for light-draught steamers. In Chapter XI. of this work I have, when speaking of Stanley Falls, shown how the seven cataracts could easily be surmounted, thus adding at least 800 miles more of navigable water to the above.

But the greatest advance of all, in the direction of opening up the interior of the continent, has been made by the African Lakes Company, the promoters of which, seeing, some years ago, that the real cure for the slave-trade lay in the introduction of legitimate commerce, formed this company, not so much for profit as to assist the missionary societies, by encouraging a trade which would go a long way towards abolishing the curse of slavery in Nyassaland. This company has launched steamers on the lower Zambesi and Shiré rivers, has constructed a road past the Murchison Falls on the latter, and runs steamers from the upper end of these falls to the northern extremity of Lake Nyassa. Here a road was being constructed to Lake Tanganika, and forty miles of it were already completed when the present troubles with the Arabs began. When railways replace the roads between the lakes and past the Shiré falls, this will be the best route of all to the lake region of Africa; but at present, matters are somewhat at a standstill. The Portuguese, having watched the Company gradually overcoming all difficulties, and opening up the country, have suddenly laid claim to the whole of Nyassaland; and the time has come when the Lakes Company must either turn its attention to organising itself into a commercial syndicate powerful enough to hold its own against Portuguese and Arabs alike, or entirely go to the wall, and see the work on which it has spent thousands of pounds undone. People in this country are not fond of putting their money into anything which offers no prospect of an immediate return; but money, and money alone, can now prevent the door which Livingstone opened from being closed. It was nearly shut for Upper Egypt, when General Gordon died at Khartoum; but Emin Pasha has nobly stood at his post, and kept it open. It *is* nearly shut on the Upper Congo, by the appointment of Tippoo Tip as Governor of Stanley Falls. Is it also to be shut on Lake Nyassa? Have the weary years passed by Livingstone in Africa been spent in vain? Will it have to be said of the richest nation in the world, that she allowed Nyassaland to be lost out of sheer apathy, and that Livingstone and Gordon worked and died in vain? Down the long vista of future years, this work, for which so many noble lives have been sacrificed, will go on, till Africa is ransomed from the curse of slavery, and the natives learn that not only beads and brass wire, but also the blessing of freedom, has come to them from that mysterious far-away *Mputu* which, ten years ago, was nothing more to them than a dim, visionary, unknown " Beyond."

JUSQU'À LA FIN.

INDEX.

A.B.M.U., 31, 70, 77, 283, 286.
Accra, 296.
Addah, 295.
Adjutant-birds, 183.
Administrateur - Général, 28, 34. See also Governor-General.
Africa, s.s., 293.
African Lakes Company, 315, 329.
A.I.A., steamer, 55, 69, 75, 102, 109 *sq.*, 123, 128, 135, 142, 150, 151, 161, 167-171, 174, 179, 182, 184, 192, 199, 209, 211, 216, 235, 247, 261 *sq.*, 269, 273-279.
Ainsworth, 289, 293.
Akoulas, 137.
Alcohol, use and abuse of, 61, 66, 67.
Amelot, 89.
Anæmia, 67.
Anderson, Captain, 56, 118, 130.
Antelopes, 73, 193.
Ants, act as scavengers, 157.
Antwerp, leave, 3.
Arabs, 88-91—Deane comes in collision with, 94—reports of their raids, 106—our first sight of, 107 —attack us, 109—skirmish with, at Yaporo, 114-117—Deane escapes from, 119-122—their camp at the Lomami, 240, 276—at Yaporo, 245—at Yalasula, their reports of a new lake, 248—kill the chief of Yarukombe, 249, 316—at Stanley Falls, 250-260, 305-308 — on board the *A.I.A.*, 261 *sq.*, 273—their treatment of a native village, 266, 267 — superior resources of, 311, 312—character of, 313—their action in Nyassaland, 314-316—their method of carrying on the ivory-trade, 322 —Soudan, destroy Suakin-Berber railway, 325—on Lake Nyassa, 315, 329—compared to Spaniards of sixteenth century, 312.
Aruhwimi, 104, 221, 265—camp on the, 226-228—district, 236.
Association Internationale Africaine, 23.

Baert, Lieut., 100, 132, 135, 140, 141, 147, 149.
Bakumu, tribe near Stanley Falls, 108, 110, 111, 255, 317—song, 236—dancing, 241—their admiration for Deane, 319, 320.
Bamu island, 52, 69, 129, 193.
Banana, 14-18, 293.
Ba-Ngala, 31, 79, 85, 100, 165, 201 —ferocity of, 203—drilled, 319.
Bangala Station, 31, 55, 78-85, 133, 197—leave, 280.
Bangweolo, Lake, 21, 22.
Banks, Mr, missionary, 207, 282.
Banza Manteka, 44, 285, 286.
Barttelot, Major, 214—his camp on the Aruhwimi, 224-228—Stanley's instructions to, 229—not to blame for the conduct of the Manyemas, 230—Salim bin Mahomed

anxious to pick a quarrel with, 231—his objection to the terms demanded by the Manyemas, 232 —goes to Stanley Falls, 234— comes on board the *A.I.A.* at Yalasula, 248—at Kinsi Katini, 252, 255, 257—leaves for Yambuya with 400 carriers, 261—his palaver with Tippoo about the loads, 269—asks for assistance in reducing the loads, 270—prepares to start, 271—further difficulty with the loads, 272—parting with, 273, 274—Tippoo Tip's directions to the Manyemas concerning, 275—news of his death, 282.
Baruti, 174.
Basoko, 137, 220.
Bathurst, 296.
Bats, used for food in S. Thomé, 12, 13.
Baumann, 95.
Bayley, Captain, 129, 193, 209, 211, 277.
Becker, Lieutenant, quoted, 304, 305.
Belgians, King of the, 20, 164.
Belgique, steamer, 16, 17, 39.
Berlin Conference, 28.
Biafra, s.s., 294, 295.
Bihé, 7.
Binnie, 27, 89.
Bissao, 9.
Blood-brotherhood, 159, 178, 199.
Bokélé, 158, 161, 198.
Bokuti, 158, 161.
Bolama, 9.
Bolobo, 73, 186.
Boma, 24, 32, 34-37, 289-291.
Bondeh, village, 236.
Bonny, Mr, 268, 269, 272, 274, 278.
Boola Mbemba Point, 17, 33.
Boulanger, Mr, 282.
Bove, Captain, 47, 69.
Brazza, De, 24.
Brazzaville, 32, 53, 57.
British Congo Company, 38.
Buffalo, 193, 209.
Bullock-road, proposed, 327.
Bwana Nzigé (Tippoo Tip's brother), 96, 97, 108, 234, 250.

Cameron, 22, 301, 302.

Camwood, 79, 154, 202.
Canary Islands, 297.
Cannibalism, 85, 86, 106, 165, 267.
Canoes, 239—people living in, 106, 237, 240.
Caô (or Cam), Diego, 21.
Cape Verd Islands, 8, 9.
Capello and Ivens, 30.
Cartridges, 95, 103, 104.
Casement, 39.
Cataract region, 24, 26 — march through, 41-47—proposed railway through, 52, 200, 327.
Cataracts of Stanley Falls, 252, 253.
Chambezi, 21.
Champagne-bottles, 63.
Charters, Mr, 95, 96.
Chibalé hills, 21.
Cicatrisation, 85, 155, 238.
Chikwanga (or kwanga), 62, 63, 119.
Chills, 61.
Chioba island, 107, 262.
Chitambo's, 22.
Chofu (or Lukebu) river, 107, 111, 240, 249.
Chumbiri, 73.
Cintra, 5.
Clark, Mr, 286.
Climate, 49, 50, 64, 65.
Cocktails, 210.
Coinage, 296.
Congo State, founded (1882), 26— its constitution, 29 — successive governors of, 27, 28—changes in administration, 28.
Congo river, discovery of, 21 — Tuckey's expedition to explore, *ib.*—theories as to the course of, *ib.*—Livingstone discovers sources of, *ib.*—Cameron reaches, 22— explored by Stanley, *ib.*—A.I.A. formed to exploit, 23 — first steamers launched on, 24—course of, 29-32—current of, 54—scenery of, 65—cañon of, 69—winds in, 70—thirst, *ib.*—Compagnie du, 200—railway, 327, 328.
Comité d'Etudes du Haut Congo, 23.
Copal, 153.
Coquilhat, Captain, 38, 55, 66— arrives at Bangala, 78—welcomed by the natives, 79, 80 — Mata Bwyki's affection for, 81—station

INDEX. 333

built by, 84—receives orders to take command at Stanley Falls, 97 — receives news of the loss of Falls Station, 98, 99 — holds a court-martial, 100 — recovers stolen goods from the Ba-Ngala, 101—starts for Stanley Falls, 102 —restores people kidnapped by the Ba-Ngala, 104—his sufferings on the journey, 106, 107, 108, 118 —rescues Deane, 113—wounded at Yaporo, 116—invalided home, 123.
Crocodiles, 68, 143, 184, 185, 211, 256.
Cronstedt, Captain, 5.
Currie, Mr, missionary, 7.
Cyclone, 144, 145.

Dancing, native, 75, 82, 241, 276.
Daumas, Beraud, et Cie, 38, 181.
Deane, Mr Walter, attacked by Arabs, 88—leaves Léopoldville to take command at the Falls, 91—attacked near Monongiri Channel, 92—returns to Léopoldville, *ib.*—goes up again, 93—attacked at Mpeza, *ib.*—takes command of Falls Station, 94—asked for protection by a slave, 95—refuses to give her up, 96—short of cartridges, 97, 103, 118—news of, 105—found at Yarukombe, 113 —his story, 117-122—goes home, 123—camped on Bamu, 193—another meeting with, 209, 211—news of his death, 277—his name a solemn oath among the Bakumu, 317—his conduct at Stanley Falls, 318—attachment of the natives to, 319, 320.
Delatte, Captain, 56, 69, 72, 75, 76.
Demeuse, Mr, 5, 11.
Devil's Caldron, 287.
Dhanis, Lieutenant, 69, 72, 74-76, 100, 168, 208.
Diaz, 11.
Diseases, 156.
Districts of Congo State, 29.
Dover Cliffs, 52, 194.
Drainage, natural, 155, 158.
Drums, 104 (footnote).
Dua (interpreter), 100, 104, 105,

138, 139, 168—(chief of Ikolungu), 151, 152.
Dualla island, 71, 188, 194.
Dubois, Lieutenant, 78, 82, 109, 118, 120.
Ducks, 183.
Dutch House, at Nshassa, 62, 277, 323.

Eczema, 282.
Eddie, Mr, missionary, 77, 96.
Elephants, 187, 321.
Emin Pasha, 173, 317, 318, 330— relief expedition, 171, 172-177, 210, 213, 214, 309-312. See also Aruhwimi, Barttelot, Tippoo Tip, &c.
Empreza Nacional, steamship company, 6.
En Avant, steamer, 24, 55, 56, 180, 190.
Engineers, difficulties of, on the Congo, 58.
Equator Station, 31, 77, 123, 131, 207, 282.
Etat Indépendant du Congo, 28, 29.
Eycken, 93, 95.

Fabrello, 47, 69.
Fan-palms. See Hyphæne.
Fay, Mr, missionary, 7.
Fetish, 45, 196, 320.
Fevers, 43-51, 65, 66, 77, 179, 261.
Florida, steamer, 181, 211.
Flushing, 4.
French claims on Upper Congo, 132 — station, see Brazzaville — mission, see Missions — coinage, 290—factories, see Daumas, Beraud, et Cie.
Funchal, 8, 297.
Funeral customs of Ba-Ngala, 80, 81.

Gambia, 290.
Ganchu, 186.
Gazelle, 194.
Germans, blockade of E. coast by, 314.
Glave, 180, 282.
Gobila, 186.
Goldsmid, Sir F., 26, 27.
Gordon, General, 27, 318, 330.
Gordon-Bennett river, 53.

Goree, 296.
Governor-General of Congo State, 28, 291.
Grenfell, Mr, missionary, 96, 134.
Greshoff, 277, 278.
Gum-copal, 153.
Gun-room, sleeping-quarters in the, 83, 98.

Håkansson, 16.
Hamberg, Mr, 98.
Hamed bin Mahomed—see Tippoo Tip.
Hanssens, Captain, 89.
Harou, 25.
Hatton & Cookson's factory at Boma, 38, 329.
Head-hunting, 203, 204.
Henry Reed, s.s., 55, 122, 141, 174 *sq.*—asked for by Stanley, 175.
Hens, Mr, 5, 283.
Heron, steamer, 17, 33.
Heuse, 5, 8.
Hippopotami, 74, 130, 131, 142, 182, 183, 256.
Hodister, 200, 206.
Holland, steamer, 277, 279.
Hoste, Mr, missionary, 283.
Houssas, 99, 113, 119, 182—missing, 148 *sq.*—ransomed from Upoto, 159, 163, 178.
Hyphæne palm, 71, 187, 209.

Ibanza, chief of Mpeza, 155.
Iboke, village on Ngala, 137.
Iboko, 31, 165, &c. See Bangala Station.
Ikolungu, 103—defences of, 150— Dua, chief of, 151, 152.
India-rubber, 153.
Ingham, Mr, missionary, 285, 286.
International Association of the Congo, 23, 28.
Irebu, 113.
Isangila, 24, 32.
Italian expedition, 47, 78, 82.
Itimbiri, or Loika, 175, 177.
Ivory, 136, 235, 321-324 — ornaments of Bakumu, 238 — trade, 321-324.

Jacos, or grey parrots, 183.
Jameson, Mr J. S., 214, 232, 254, 257, 260, 261, 304, 315—reduces loads of Expedition, 269, 270— his illness and death, 284, 285.
Janssens, Mr, 28, 291.
Jephson, Mr, 173, 174.
'Joyce,' 188.
Junker, Dr, his explorations, 31.

Kajumba, 89.
Kallina Point, 32, 53, 69.
Karema, 89, 305.
Kassai (or Kwa), 25, 31, 69, 186— St Paul du, 187.
Kassongo, 229—drummers, 241.
Katanga, 23, 30.
Katembo, 105.
Keys, 209.
Kimpopo, 32, 52, 69, 118, 130.
Kinsi Katini, 106, 219, 252. See also Stanley Falls.
Kirk, Sir John, 312.
Kissanga, 34.
Kotonou, 294, 295.
Krupp guns at Bangala, 84, 101— at Stanley Falls, 118, 251.
Kwamouth, 31, 72, 130.

Lake between Lomami and Congo, 248.
Landalip, 248.
Langa-Langa, 149, 155, 160, 178, 198.
Lanji, Lake, 30.
Lawson river, 31.
Ledeganck, 28, 291, 293.
Lemarinel, 128, 129, 294.
Léopoldville (Ntamo), 25, 32, 44, 55 *sq.*, 60, 117, 180, 192, 283.
Leopold II., King, 20, 59, 164.
Lisbon, 5, 6, 7.
Lissa market, 71, 190.
Livingstone, 22, 301.
Loanda, 293.
Loika, 175, 177. See Itimbiri.
Lomami, 107, 239, 240, 248, 276.
Long Island. See Bamu.
Lualaba, 21, 22.
Luapula, 21, 29.
Lukebu. See Chofu.
Lukolela, 31, 77, 194-196, 212, 282, 319.
Lukungu, 44, 46, 285.
Lulanga, 124, 323.
Lulangi, 158.
Lusengi, chief of Mobeka, 136, 167, 199.

Lusengo, 164.
Lutété, 47, 60, 66, 183.
Luvwa, 29.

Mabengu, or Mense mountain, 52.
Mablasia, 217-219.
Madeira, 7, 297.
Mahomed Tenné, 99, 100, 102.
Makoko, 24.
Malafu, 79.
Malaria, 50.
Malarial poisoning, 65.
Maloney, Mr, chief of Matadi, 39.
Mankula, 137.
Manyanga, 24, 32.
Manyema child wounded, 260.
Manyemas, 222, 230, 232, 271.
Mark Twain, his Mississippi pilot, 73.
Massanga, 79 — drinking customs, 164-166.
Mata Bwyki, king of Iboko, 79-81, 151.
Matadi, 38, 287.
Matebba island, 33.
McKittrick, Mr, missionary, 123.
Mendongé, 142.
Mense, Dr, 48, 123.
Methodist Mission, 32.
Mfwa, 53.
Missionaries: Mr Fay, 7—Mr Currie, *ib.*—Mr Swan, 8—Mr Scott, *ib.*—Bishop Taylor, 37, 130—Mr Eddie, 77, 96—Mr Grenfell, 96, 134—Mr Charters, 96—Mr McKittrick, 123—Mr Banks, 207, 282—Mr Richards (Lukolela), 208—Mr Darby, *ib.*—Mr Hoste, 283—Mr Ingham, 285, 286—Mr Clark, 286—Mr (and Mrs) Richards (Banza Manteka), *ib.*
Missions, American Baptist (A.B.M.U.), 31, 42, 77, 96, 283, 286—Baptist (English), 31, 32, 47, 183, 195, 208, 287—Livingstone Inland, 42, 123, 207, 282—Methodist, 32, 130—Roman Catholic (French), 31, 38, 72, 187—(Belgian), 72.
Miyongo, 212.
Mobeka, 135, 198—chief of. See Lusengi.
Mocro, 21, 30.
Mohrya, Lake, 137.
Mokulu, 236.
Monongiri Channel, 91.

Mpallaballa Station, 42, 60, 66, 286.
Mpeza, on the Congo, 93, 154, 194 — slaves bought at, 196 — on Ngala, 137.
Mpozo, 286.
Mputu, village on Ngala river, 138 —"the Country Beyond," 330.
Mswata, 25, 71.
Mtipula. See Tippoo Tip.
Mutembo, 217.
Mwafa, native name of Captain Coquilhat, 79.

Ngalyema, 24, 61—his cow, 179, 180.
Ngala river, 132-141.
Ngiri, 134.
Ngombe, 135.
Nimpsch, Baron, 55, 61.
Nozo, 41.
Nshassa, 32, 52, 62, 129, 181.
Ntamo, 24, 25, 32, 56. See Léopoldville. Burning of, 61—cataract, 52, 53.
Nyangwé, 22, 30, 236.
Nyassa, Lake, 315, 329—land claimed by Portuguese, 329.
Nzigé. See Bwana Nzigé.

One Palm Point, 190.
Orchilla-weed, 153.
Orera, 105, 106.
Oubangi, 31, 132-134, 190, 282.
Owls at Upoto, 160.

"Palm-oil ruffians," 36, 37, 292.
Palm-tree cut, 151.
Palms, 71, 187, 201, 209, 221.
Palmyra Bay, 192.
Peace, steamer, 95, 174, 177.
Pechuel-Loesche, Dr, 25, 26.
"Plenty big bird," 15.
Ponta da Lenha, 34.
Porpoises, 33.
Portuguese claims on West Coast, 21—in Nyassaland, 329.
Portuguese settlements in Africa, 9.
Principé (Prince's Island), 10.
Pururu island, 71, 187, 210, 211.

Quarantine, 297, 298.

Railway, company formed to construct, 200, 327, 328 — Suakin-

Berber, 325—proposed, to Lake Victoria, 326.
Raphia. See Palms.
Rapids on Ngala, 139—at Upoto, 154—on Aruhwimi, 224—at Stanley Falls, 252.
Raschid, Tippoo Tip's nephew, 240-245, 264.
Richards, Mr, missionary at Lukolela, 208—at Banza Manteka, 286.
Roget, Mr, 5.
Roi des Belges, steamer, 181.
Rothkirch, Baron, 38, 41, 43, 210.
Royal, steamer, 24, 56, 59.
Rubunga, 154.

S. Antonio, 8.
S. Thomé, island, 11-13.
St Vincent, 8.
Saibis, 141.
Said Barghash, 91, 308.
Salim bin Mahomed, 229-231, 234, 273—bin Soudi, 259, 275.
Samba, 110-112, 124-127, 158, 161, 202.
Sanatorium at Boma, 34.
Sand-crabs, 17, 18.
Sanford Exploring Expedition, 31, 32, 129, 180, 212, 282.
Santiago, 9.
Schwerin, Baron, 78, 82.
Scott, Mr, missionary, 7.
"Sennené," 255.
Shagerstrom, Captain, 5, 9, 38, 41, 43, 44, 109, 174, 210, 267, 271-273.
Shiré river, 329.
Sierra Leone, 296.
Slave-raids, 106, 107, 221, 222, 231-234, 236, 301, 305, &c.
Société d'Alger (French Mission), 31, 72.
Société du St Esprit (French Mission), 31, 72.
Stanley, references to, 19, 22, 27, 49, 124, 153, 172, 175-177, 217, 228, 229—Falls, 27, 30, 103, 252—Pool, 24, 48, 52, 129, 193, 194.
Stanley, steamer, 56, 57-59, 68, 69, 78, 82, 87, 93, 97, 98, 147, 174, 179, 192, 210, 212, 214, 232, 235, 267, 268, 271, 272, 273, 274, 275, 276, 277.

Steamers. See *A.I.A.*, *Stanley*, *Peace*, *Henry Reed*, *En Avant*, &c.
Stein, Baron, 5.
Stella Bank, 15.
Stimulants. See Alcohol.
Strauch, General, 28.
Swan, Mr, missionary, 7.
Swedes. See Anderson, Shagerstrom, Cronstedt, &c.
Swinburne, Mr, 129.

"Tamba-Tamba," 222.
Tana river, 326.
Taylor, Bishop, missionary, 37, 130.
Teetotallers, mistakes of, 66, 67.
Thys, Captain, 199.
Timber, valuable, 154.
Tippoo Tip, 90—palaver with Captain Van Gèle, 91 – leaves for Zanzibar, 95, 306—news of his appointment as Governor of Stanley Falls, 172 — officers sent to assist, 210, 213—fails to procure carriers, 214—treachery of, 229—his extra demands, 233—mistake made in his appointment, 244, 255—arrives at Kinsi Katini, 257 —my first meeting with, 258—keeping his accounts, 259—takes passage in the *A.I.A.*, 261—raids an island in the Aruhwimi, 266, 267—insists on his men having half-loads, 269—musters caravan, 271—sends his people to Kinsi Katini in the *A.I.A.*, 273 — his orders to the Manyemas about Major Barttelot, 275—his origin, 300—notices of, 301, 302—meets Stanley at Nyangwé, 302 — declines to accompany him, 303—his own account of the matter, 304—descends the Congo, 305—obtains forces from the Sultan of Zanzibar, 306—arrives at Stanley Falls, *ib*. — his conference with the Sultan, 308—his feelings towards the Germans, *ib.*, 309—makes a treaty with Stanley, 309 —a devout Mohammedan, 310— sees weakness of Congo State, 311 —suspects motives of white men, 313—asks Jameson about Nyassaland, 315.
"Tooc-a-Tooc-a," 223.

INDEX.

Tornadoes, 143, 144.
Treaty between Stanley and Tippoo Tip, 309, 310.
Troup, Mr J. Rose, 39, 174, 179, 225, 230, 268, 277.
Tuckey's expedition, 21.
Two Palm Point, 73, 209.

Ulf, Mr, 39.
Umaneh, 236.
Underhill, mission station, 287.
Upoto, 103, 149, 158-160, 178, 198-200, 212—burning of, 205.
Usindi, 212.

Van Gèle, Captain, 91, 92, 97, 122, 123, 134, 190.
Van de Velde, Captain, 210, 212.
Van Kerckhoven, Lieutenant, arrives at Bangala, 147—his expedition to the Langa-Langa, 150—negotiations with the natives, 158-160—attacked by the people of Upoto, 161—his reasons for ransoming the Houssas, 163—makes another attempt to come to terms with the Langa-Langa, 198, 199—burns Upoto, 202-205—buys slaves at Mpoza, 206—starts for Yambuya, 216—other references, 167, 169, 170, 178, 182, 197, 224, 257.
Verhees, Mr, 147, 200.
Ville de Bruxelles, steamer, 181.
Vivi, 24, 27, 28, 32, 39, 40.

Wabika, 135.

Walker, Mr, 68.
Wampomo, 192.
Wana Rusari, 27, 89, 109, 250. See also Kinsi Katini and Stanley Falls.
War-drums, 104, 219.
War-paint, 202.
Ward, Mr Herbert, 17, 174, 179 213-215, 279, 283, 285, 288, 289.
Water-dance, 276.
Wéllé-Makua, 31, 132, 190.
Wenya, 111, 252, 255, 317.
Wester, Lieutenant, 89, 91, 92.
Winds, 69, 70.
Winton, Sir F. de, 27, 36.
Wolf, Dr, 47.
Wood-worms, 120.

Yakusu, 249.
Yalasula, 248.
Yambinga, 124.
Yambunga, 104.
Yambuya, 224 *sqq.*, 267-274.
Yambumba, 222, 236, 265, 266.
Yangambi, 246, 248, 261.
Yaporo, 107, 111, 114-116, 245, 264.
Yariembi, 249, 264.
Yarukombe, 107, 112, 113, 121, 249 —chief of, 122, 249, 316.
Yatakusu, 249, 264.
Yatuka, 107, 249.

Zambesi, 329.
Zanzibar, Tippoo Tip at, 90, 95, 308
Zanzibaris, 46, 61, 62, 69, 102, 131, 142, 207, 214, 216, 231

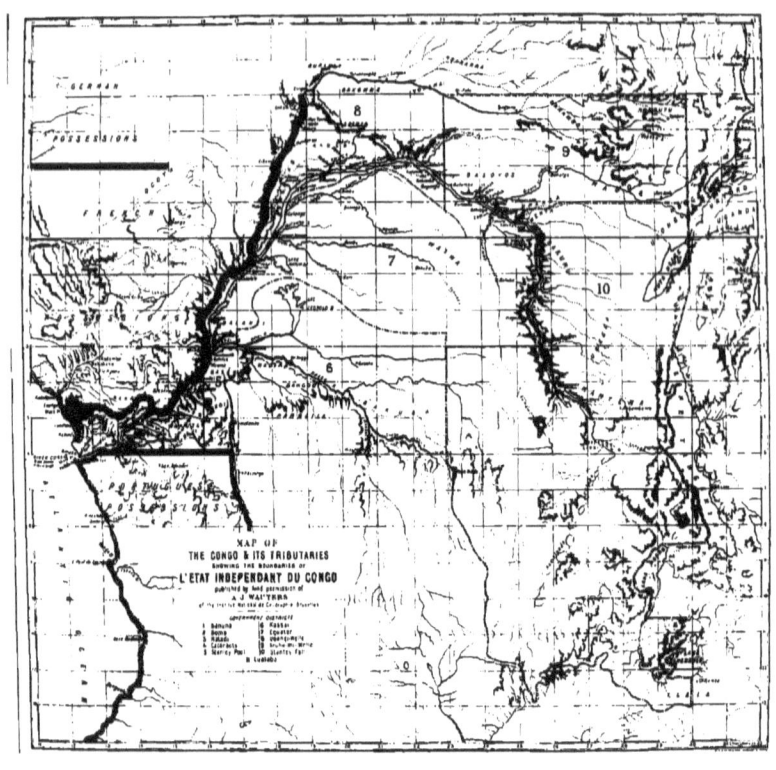

GREAT REDUCTIONS

IN THE PRICES OF MANY OF THE

PUBLICATIONS OF

MESSRS W. H. ALLEN & CO., LONDON,

JUST PURCHASED BY

JOHN GRANT,

WHOLESALE BOOKSELLER,

EDINBURGH.

	PAGE
Miscellaneous Works	2
Scientific Works	29
Natural History.	
Botany.	
Mosses, Fungi, &c.	
Veterinary Works and Agriculture	34
India, China, Japan, and the East	36

The Reduced Prices of these Books can be had on application to any Bookseller at Home and Abroad. The Published Prices are affixed to each book.

The Trade supplied direct, or through
Messrs SIMPKIN, MARSHALL & Co., London.

CATALOGUE.

ARTHUR PENRHYN STANLEY, D.D. (Dean of Westminster).

Scripture Portraits and other Miscellanies collected from his Published Writings. By Arthur Penrhyn Stanley, D.D. Crown 8vo, gilt top, 5s.

Uniform with the above.
VERY REV. FREDERICK W. FARRAR, D.D., F.R.S.
(Archdeacon of Westminster).

Words of Truth and Wisdom. By Very Rev. Frederick W. Farrar, D.D., F.R.S. Crown 8vo, gilt top, 5s.

Uniform with the above.
SAMUEL WILBERFORCE, D.D. (Bishop of Winchester).

Heroes of Hebrew History. Crown 8vo, gilt top, 5s.

Uniform with the above.
CARDINAL NEWMAN.

Miscellanies from the Oxford Sermons of John Henry Newman, D.D. Crown 8vo, gilt top, 5s.

For the Reduced Prices apply to

CAPTAIN JAMES ABBOTT.

Narrative of a Journey from Herat to Khiva, Moscow, and St Petersburgh during the late Russian invasion at Khiva, with Map and Portrait. 2 vols., demy 8vo, 24s.

Throughout the whole of his journey, his readers are led to take the keenest interest in himself, and each individual of his little suite. The most remarkable anecdote of this part of his journey is concerning the prosecution of the Jews, for an alleged insult to Mohammedanism, not unlike the pretext of Christian persecutors in the days of the Crusaders.

From St Petersburgh, Captain Abbott returned to England, where he gives an amusing account of the difficulties, and mental and physical distresses of his Afghan follower. The book concludes with the author's return to India, and with notices of the fate of some of the individuals in whom we have been most interested by his narrative.

"The work will well repay perusal. The most intrinsically valuable portion is perhaps that which relates to the writer's adventures in Khaurism, and at the Court of Khiva; but the present time imparts a peculiar interest to the sketches of Russian character and policy."—*London Economist.*

MRS R. K. VAN ALSTINE.

Charlotte Corday, and her Life during the French Revolution. A Biography. Crown 8vo, 5s.

"It is certainly strange that when history is ransacked for picturesque and interesting subjects, no one has yet told in English—for so Miss van Alstine remarks, and our own recollection supports her negatively—the romantic story of Charlotte Corday. The author has carefully studied her authorities, and taken pains to distinguish fact from fiction, for fiction, it need hardly be said, has mixed itself plentifully with the story of Charlotte Corday. Miss van Alstine has been able to add to this story several genuine details that greatly heighten its effect."—*Spectator.*

EDWARD L. ANDERSON.

How to Ride and School a Horse, with a System of Horse Gymnastics. Fourth Edition, revised and corrected, crown 8vo, 2s. 6d.

"An admirable practical manual of riding."—*Scotsman.*

"The book deserves perusal by all who have dealings with horses."—*Birmingham Gazette.*

"Though practice is of course essential, it is equally necessary that the practice should be guided by some principle, and the aspirant who adopts the methods explained and recommended by Mr Anderson is not likely to regret his choice of an instructor."—*Morning Post.*

D. T. ANSTED and R. G. LATHAM.

The Channel Islands. Revised and Edited by E. Toulmin Nicolle. Third Edition, profusely illustrated, crown 8vo, 7s. 6d.

"A useful and entertaining book. The work is well done, and to those who have not even paid a flying visit to this beautiful group it is calculated to cause a strong desire to explore and enjoy its attractions."—*Daily Chronicle.*

"We are extremely glad to see a new edition of this fascinating work. . . . All who know the Channel Islands should read this admirable book; and many who read the book will certainly not rest until they know the Channel Islands."—*Black and White.*

PROFESSOR D. T. ANSTED.

Water, and Water Supply. Chiefly with reference to the British Islands. With Maps, 8vo, 18s.

Towns and their water-supply is becoming a clamant grievance.

Any Bookseller at Home and Abroad.

MAJOR J. H. LAWRENCE-ARCHER, Bengal H.P.
The Orders of Chivalry, from the Original Statutes of the various Orders of Knighthood and other Sources of Information. With 3 Portraits and 63 Plates, beautifully coloured and heightened with gold, 4to, coloured, £6. 6s., Plain, £3. 3s.

"Major Lawrence-Archer has produced a learned and valuable work in his account of 'The Orders of Chivalry.' He explains that the object of the book is to supply a succinct account of the chivalric orders in a convenient form. The literary form of the work is amply convenient for reference and study. Its material form could be convenient only to some knight of the times when armour was worn in the field, and men were stronger in the arm than they are now. It is a handsome volume. The size of the book is doubtless due to the introduction of a series of engraved plates of the badges and crosses of the various orders described. These plates are executed in a finished style, and give the work an exceptional value for students of heraldic symbolism. The author may be congratulated on the successful issue of a laborious and useful task."—*Scotsman*, 14th May 1888.

SIR EDWIN ARNOLD, M.A., Author of "The Light of Asia," &c.
The Book of Good Counsels, Fables from the Sanscrit of the Hitopadésa. With Illustrations by Gordon Browne. Autograph and Portrait, crown 8vo, antique, gilt top, 5s.

——— The Same. Superior Edition, beautifully bound, 7s. 6d.

"It is so long since Sir Edwin Arnold's Indian fables were in print that they may practically be regarded as a new book. In themselves they are almost the fathers of all fable, for whereas we know of no source whence the 'Hitopadésa' could have been borrowed, there are evidences of its inspiration and to spare in Bidpai, in Æsop, and in most of the later fabulists."—*Pall Mall Gazette*.

"Those curious and fascinating stories from the Sanskrit which Sir Edward Arnold has retold in 'The Book of Good Counsels' give us the key to the heart of modern India, the writer tells us, as well as the splendid record of her ancient gods and glories, quaint narratives, as full of ripe wisdom as the songs of Hiawatha, and with the same curious blending of statecraft and wood-magic in them."—*Daily Telegraph*.

"A new edition comes to hand of this delightful work—a fit companion to 'Æsop's Fables' and the 'Jungle Book.' Sir Edwin has done well to republish this record of Indian stories and poetical maxims from the Sanskrit. And the illustrations, a specimen of which we give here, what shall we say of them? Simply that they are equal to the text. No more pleasant series of 'Good Counsels' is it possible to find, and we are convinced that it is not an ill counsel—far from it—to advise our readers to forthwith get this charming work. They will derive not a little pleasure, and perchance instruction, from a perusal of the story of the jackal, deer, and crow, of the tiger and the traveller, of the lion, the jackals, and the bull, of the black snake and golden chain, of the frogs, and the old serpent, and of all the other veracious chronicles herein set forth."—*Whitehall Review*.

S. BARING-GOULD, M.A., Author of "Mehalah," &c.
In Troubadour Land. A Ramble in Provence and Languedoc, with Illustrations by J. E. Rogers. Medium 8vo, 12s. 6d.

"The title of Mr Baring-Gould's book only indicates one of the many points of interest which will attract the intelligent traveller during a tour in Provence and Languedoc. Besides troubadours, there are reminiscences of Greek colonisation and Roman Empire, of the Middle Ages, and of the Revolution.... The illustrations which adorn the pages of this very readable volume are decidedly above the average. The arm-chair traveller will not easily find a pleasanter *compagnon de voyage*."—*St James's Gazette*.

"A most charming book, brightly written, and profusely illustrated with exquisite engravings."—*Glasgow Herald*.

"A charming book, full of wit and fancy and information, and worthy of its subject."—*Scotsman*.

For the Reduced Prices apply to

SIR E. C. BAYLEY.

The Local Muhammadan Dynasties. Gujarat. Forming a Sequel to Sir H. M. Elliott's "History of the Muhammadan Empire of India," demy 8vo, 21s.

WYKE BAYLISS.

The Enchanted Island, the Venice of Titian, and other studies in Art, with Illustrations. Crown 8vo, 6s.

"Richly imaginative and full of eloquent and frequently highly poetical thought."—*Standard.*

"A charm which would render it difficult for any one to lay the book aside till the last page is reached."—*Art Journal.*

"A clever lecturer might pick more than one chapter as a good bit for evening readings."—*Graphic.*

The Higher Life in Art. Crown 8vo, with Illustrations, 6s.

"The style has the grace which comes by culture, and no small share of the eloquence bred of earnest conviction. Mr Bayliss writes as a man who, having seen much, has also read and thought much on fine art questions. His views are therefore entitled to that respectful attention which the pleasant dress in which he has clothed them renders it all the easier to accord."—*Scotsman.*

"The writing is that of a scholar and a gentleman, and though the critical faculty is often evinced in a subtle and discriminating form, all allusions to individuals are made with so much of the kindliness of true good taste, that we are almost conscious of a reluctance in disagreeing with the author."—*The Spectator.*

"Mr Wyke Bayliss is at the same time a practical artist and a thoughtful writer. The combination is, we regret to say, as rare as it is desirable. . . He deals ably and clearly—notably so in this present book—with questions of the day of practical and immediate importance to artists and to the Art public. . . We prefer to send the reader to the volume itself, where he will find room for much reflection."—*The Academy.*

"One of the most humorous and valuable of the general articles on Art is Mr Wyke Bayliss' 'Story of a Dado.'"—*The Standard.*

MISS SOPHIA BEALE.

The Churches of Paris from Clovis to Charles X., with numerous Illustrations. Crown 8vo, 7s. 6d.

CONTENTS:—Notre Dame; Notre Dame des Champs; Notre Dame de Lorette; Notre Dame des Victoires; Geneviève; Val de Grace; Ste. Chapelle; St Martin; St Martin des Champs; Etienne du Mont; Eustache; Germain l'Auxerrois; Germain des Prés; Gervais; Julien; Jacques; Leu; Laurent; Merci; Nicolas; Paul; Roch; Severin; V. de Paul; Madeleine; Elizabeth; Sorbonne; Invalides.

"An interesting study of the historical, archæological, and legendary associations which belong to the principal churches of Paris."—*Times.*

"A comprehensive work, as readable as it is instructive. The literary treatment is elaborate, and the illustrations are numerous and attractive."—*Globe.*

"For the more serious-minded type of visitor who is capable of concerning himself in the treasures of art and store of traditions they contain, Miss Beale has prepared her book on the *Churches of Paris*. It is more than an ordinary guide-book, for it mingles personal opinion and comment with curious information drawn from the old and new authorities on the history and contents of the more ancient and celebrated of the Paris churches."—*Scotsman.*

"A monument of historical research and judicious compilation is *The Churches of Paris from Clovis to Charles X.*, by Sophia Beale (Allen and Co.). This valuable work, copiously and gracefully illustrated by the author, is destined to serve as a complete vade-mecum to those British visitors to the French capital who take a special interest in ecclesiastical architecture and in the curious mediæval lore connected with several of the venerable Parisian fanes that have survived wars and sieges, revolutions and spasms of urban 'improvement,' throughout from six to eight centuries."—*Daily Telegraph.*

Any Bookseller at Home and Abroad.

MONSEIGNEUR BESSON.

Frederick Francis Xavier de Merode, Minister and Almoner to Pius IX. His Life and Works. Translated by Lady Herbert. Crown 8vo, 7s. 6d.

"The book is most interesting, not only to Catholics, but to all who care for adventurous lives and also to historical inquirers. De Merode's career as an officer of the Belgian army, as a volunteer in Algeria with the French, and afterwards at the Papal Court, is described with much spirit by Monseigneur Besson, and Bishop of Nimes, who is the author of the original work. The book, which is now translated, was written with permission of the present Pope, and is, of course, a work agreeable to the authorities of the Vatican, but at the same time its tone leaves nothing to be desired by those who are members of the communions."—*Athenæum.*

SIR GEORGE BIRDWOOD, M.D., K.C.I.E., &c.

Report on the Old Records of the India Office, with Maps and Illustrations. Royal 8vo, 12s. 6d.

"No one knows better than Sir George Birdwood how to make 'a bare and shorthand' index of documents attractive, instructive and entertaining, by means of the notes and elucidatory comments which he supplies so liberally, and so pleasantly withal, from his own inexhaustible stores of information concerning the early relations of India with Europe."—*Times.*

"The wonderful story (of the rise of the British Indian Empire) has never been better told.... A better piece of work is very rarely met with."—*The Anti-Jacobin.*

"Official publications have not as a rule any general interest; but as there are 'fagots and fagots' so there are reports and reports, and Sir George Birdwood's Report on the Old Records of the India Office is one of the most interesting that could be read."—*Journal des Débats.*

HENRY BLACKBURN, *Editor of "Academy Notes."*

The Art of Illustration. A Popular Treatise on Drawing for the Press. Description of the Processes, &c. Second edition. With 95 Illustrations by Sir John Gilbert, R.A., H. S. Marks, R.A., G. D. Leslie, R.A., Sir John Millais, R.A., Walter Crane, R. W. Macbeth, R.A., G. H. Boughton, A.R.A., H. Railton, Alfred East, Hume Nisbet, and other well-known Artists. 7s. 6d.

A capital handbook for Students.

"We thoroughly commend his book to all whom it may concern, and chiefly to the proprietors of the popular journals and magazines which, for cheapness rather than for art's sake, employ any of the numerous processes which are now in vogue."—*Athenæum.*

"Let us conclude with one of the axioms in a fascinating volume: 'Be an artist *first*, and an illustrator afterwards.'"—*Spectator.*

"'The Art of Illustration' is a brightly written account, by a man who has had large experience of the ways in which books and newspapers are illustrated nowadays. ... As a collection of typical illustrations by artists of the day, Mr Blackburn's book is very attractive."—*The Times.*

"Mr Blackburn explains the processes—line, half-tone, and so forth—exemplifying each by the drawings of artists more or less skilled in the modern work of illustration. They are well chosen as a whole, to show the possibilities of process work in trained hands."—*Saturday Review.*

"Mr Blackburn's volume should be very welcome to artists, editors, and publishers."—*The Artist.*

"A most useful book."—*Studio.*

For the Reduced Prices apply to

of Messrs W. H. Allen & Co.'s Publications. 7

E. BONAVIA, M.D., Brigade-Surgeon, Indian Medical Service.
The Cultivated Oranges and Lemons of India and Ceylon. Demy 8vo, with oblong Atlas volume of Plates, 2 vols., 30s.

"The amount of labour and research that Dr Bonavia must have expended on these volumes would be very difficult to estimate, and it is to be hoped that he will be repaid, to some extent at least, by the recognition of his work by those who are interested in promoting the internal industries of India."—*Home News.*

"Dr Bonavia seems to have so thoroughly exhausted research into the why and wherefore of oranges and lemons, that there can be but little left for the most enthusiastic admirer of this delicious fruit to find out about it. Plunging into Dr Bonavia's pages we are at once astonished at the variety of his subject and the wide field there is for research in an everyday topic. Dr Bonavia has given a very full appendix, in which may be found a few excellent recipes for confitures made from oranges and lemons."—*The Pioneer.*

R. BRAITHWAITE, M.D., F.L.S., &c.
The Sphagnaceæ, or Peat Mosses of Europe and North America. Illustrated with 29 plates, coloured by hand, imp. 8vo, 25s.

"All muscologists will be delighted to hail the appearance of this important work . . . Never before has our native moss-flora been so carefully figured and described, and that by an acknowledged authority on the subject."—*Science Gossip.*

"Mosses, perhaps, receive about as little attention from botanists as any class of plants, and considering how admirably mosses lend themselves to the collector's purposes, this is very remarkable. Something may be due to the minuteness of the size of many of the species, and something perhaps to the difficulties inherent in the systematic treatment of these plants; but we fancy the chief cause of comparative neglect with which they are treated is to be sought in the want of a good illustrated English treatise upon them. In the work which is now before us, Dr Braithwaite aims at placing the British mosses on the same vantage-ground as the more favoured classes of the vegetable kingdom; and judging from the sample lately issued, he will succeed in his endeavours."—*Popular Science Review.*

"*TOM BOWLING.*"
Book of Knots (The). Illustrated by 172 Examples, showing the manner of making every Knot, Tie, and Splice. By "TOM BOWLING." Third Edition. Crown 8vo, 2s. 6d.

Edited by JAMES BURROWS.
Byron Birthday Book. 16mo, cloth, gilt edges, 2s. 6d.
A handsome book.

B. CARRINGTON, M.D., F.R.S.
British Hepaticæ. Containing Descriptions and Figures of the Native Species of Jungermannia, Marchantia, and Anthoceros. **With plates coloured by hand.** Imp. 8vo, Parts 1 to 4, all published per set, 15s.

S. WELLS WILLIAMS, LL.D., Professor of the Chinese Language and Literature at Yale College.
China—The Middle Kingdom. A Survey of the Geography, Government, Literature, Social Life, Arts, and History of the Chinese Empire and its Inhabitants. Revised Edition, with 74 Illustrations and a New Map of the Empire. 2 vols., demy 8vo, 42s.

"The work now before us is second to none in thoroughness, comprehensiveness, and all the tokens of accuracy of which an 'outside barbarian' can take cognisance."
—A. P. PEABODY.

Any Bookseller at Home and Abroad.

SURGEON-MAJOR L. A. WADDELL, M.B.
The Buddhism of Tibet. With its Mystic Cults, Symbolism, and Mythology, and in its relation to Indian Buddhism, with over 200 Illustrations. Demy 8vo, 600 pp., 31s. 6d.

SYNOPSIS OF CONTENTS:—Introductory. *Historical*—Changes in Primitive Buddhism leading to Lamaism—Rise, Development, and Spread of Lamaism—The Sects of Lamaism. *Doctrinal*—Metaphysical Sources of the Doctrine—The Doctrine and its Morality—Scriptures and Literature. *Monastic*—The Order of Lamas—Daily Life and Routine—Hierarchy and Reincarnate Lamas. *Buildings*—Monasteries—Temples and Cathedral—Shrines (and Relics and Pilgrims). *Mythology and Gods*—Pantheon and Images—Sacred Symbols and Charms. *Ritual and Sorcery*—Worship and Ritual—Astrology and Divination—Sorcery and Necromancy. *Festivals and Plays*—Festivals and Holidays—Mystic Plays and Masquerades and Sacred Plays. *Popular Lamaism*—Domestic and Popular Lamaism. *Appendices*—Chronological Table—Bibliography—Index.

"By far the most important mass of original materials contributed to this recondite study."—*The Times.*

"Dr Waddell deals with the whole subject in a most exhaustive manner, and gives a clear insight into the structure, prominent features, and cults of the system ; and to disentangle the early history of Lamaism from the chaotic growth of fable which has invested it, most of the chief internal movements of Lamaism are now for the first time presented in an intelligible and systematic form. The work is a valuable addition to the long series that have preceded it, and is enriched by numerous illustrations, mostly from originals brought from Lhasa, and from photographs by the author, while it is fully indexed, and is provided with a chronological table and bibliography."—*Liverpool Courier.*

"A book of exceptional interest."—*Glasgow Herald.*

"A learned and elaborate work, likely for some time to come to be a source of reference to all who seek information about Lamaism. . . . In the appendix will be found a chronological table of Tibetan events, and a bibliography of the best literature bearing on Lamaism. There is also an excellent index, and the numerous illustrations are certainly one of the distinctive features of the book."—*Morning Post.*

"Cannot fail to arouse the liveliest interest. The author of this excellently produced, handsomely illustrated volume of nearly six hundred pages has evidently spared no pains in prosecuting his studies. . . . The book is one of exceptional value, and will attract all those readers who take an interest in the old religions of the far East."—*Publishers' Circular.*

"The author is one of few Europeans who have entered the territory of the Grand Lama, and spent several years in studying the actualities of Lamaism as explained by Lamas. A Lamaist temple with its fittings was purchased, and the officiating priests explained in full detail the symbolism and the rites as they proceeded. Other temples and monasteries were visited and Lamas employed for copying manuscripts, and searching for texts bearing upon the author's researches. Enjoying special facilities for penetrating the reserve of Tibetan ritual, and obtaining direct from Lhasa and Tashi-lhunpo most of the objects and explanatory material needed, much information has been obtained on Lamaist theory and practice which is altogether new."

"The internal developments and movements of Lamaism are now for the first time presented in an intelligible and systematic form. Details of the principal rites, mystic and other deep-rooted demon worship and dark sorcery, the religious Plays and Festivals, are given fully."

With numerous illustrations from originals brought from Lhasa, and from photographs by the author.

For the Reduced Prices apply to

M. C. COOKE, M.A., LL.D.

*⁎⁎⁎ For fuller notices of Dr Cooke's works see under Scientific, pp. 29, 30.

The British Fungi: A Plain and Easy Account of. With Coloured Plates of 40 Species. Fifth Edition, Revised, crown 8vo, 6s.

Rust, Smut, Mildew, and Mould. An Introduction to the Study of Microscopic Fungi. Illustrated with 269 Coloured Figures by J. E. Sowerby. Fifth Edition, Revised and Enlarged, with Appendix of New Species. Crown 8vo, 6s.

Handbook of British Hepaticæ. Containing Descriptions and Figures of the Indigenous Species of Marchantia, Jungermannia, Riccia, and Anthoceros, illustrated. Crown 8vo, 6s.

Our Reptiles and Batrachians. A Plain and Easy Account of the Lizards, Snakes, Newts, Toads, Frogs, and Tortoises indigenous to Great Britain. New and Revised Edition. With **Original Coloured Pictures of every species, and numerous woodcuts**, crown 8vo, 6s.

F. C. DANVERS.

Report to the Secretary of State for India in Council on the Portuguese Records relating to the East Indies, contained in the Archivo da Torre de Tombo, and the Public Libraries at Lisbon and Evora. Royal 8vo, sewed, 6s. net.

REV. A. J. D. D'ORSEY, B.D., K.C., P.O.C.

Portuguese Discoveries, Dependencies, and Missions in Asia and Africa, with Maps. Crown 8vo, 7s. 6d.

CONTENTS.

Book I.
Introductory.
The Portuguese in Europe and Asia.
Portugal and the Portuguese.
Portuguese Discoveries in the Fifteenth Century.
Portuguese Conquests of India in the Sixteenth Century.
The Portuguese Empire in the Sixteenth Century.

Book II.
The Portuguese Missions in Southern India.
Early History of the Church in India.
First Meeting of the Portuguese with the Syrians.
Pioneers of the Portuguese Missions.
The Rise of the Jesuits.
The Jesuits in Portugal.
St Francis Xavier's Mission in India.
Subsequent Missions in the Sixteenth Century.

Book III.
The Subjugation of the Syrian Church.
Roman Claim of Supremacy.
First Attempt, by the Franciscans.
Second Attempt, by the Jesuits.
The Struggle against Rome.

Book III.—*continued*
The Archbishop of Goa.
The Synod of Diamper.
The Triumph of Rome.

Book IV.
Subsequent Missions in Southern India, with special reference to the Syrians.
Radiation of Mission of Goa.
The Madura Mission.
Portuguese Missions in the Carnatic.
Syrian Christians in the Seventeenth Century.
Syrian Christians in the Eighteenth Century.

Book V.
The Portuguese Missions, with special reference to Modern Missionary efforts in South India.
The First Protestant Mission in South India.
English Missions to the Syrians 1806-16.
English Missions and the Syrian Christians.
The Disruption and its Results.
Present State of the Syrian Christians.
The Revival of the Romish Missions in India.

Any Bookseller at Home and Abroad.

C. L. EASTLAKE.

Notes on the Principal Pictures in the Royal Gallery at Venice. Crown 8vo, 3s. 6d.

VERY REV. FREDERICK W. FARRAR, D.D., F.R.S.
(*Archdeacon of Westminster*).

Words of Truth and Wisdom, by Very Rev. Frederick W. Farrar, D.D., F.R.S. Crown 8vo, gilt top, 5s.

CONTENTS.

Christian Statesmanship.
Legislative Duties.
The Use of Gifts and Opportunities.
The Brotherhood of Man.
Energy of Christian Service.
Christianity and the Human Race.
Christianity and Individual.
The Victories of Christianity.
The Christian Remedy against the Frailties of Life.
Prayer, the Antidote of Sorrow.

The Conquest over Temptation.
Too Late.
The Souls of the Departed.
What Heaven is.
No Discharge in the War against Sin.
The Dead which die in the Lord.
The Resurrection of the Dead.
The Blighted Life.
Wisdom and Knowledge.
The Voice of History.

The Monks.
The Early Franciscans.
The Hermits.
The Missionaries.
The Martyrs.
Seneca.
Seneca and St Paul.
Gallio and St Paul.
Roman Society in the days of St Paul.
Sanskrit.
Greek and Hebrew.
Aryan Migrations.
Words.

"In theological views he might be described as standing between the Evangelical party and the Broad Church; but his knowledge, coloured by a poetic temperament, his superabundant fertility, and eloquent luxuriance of style, have gained for him a unique position in the theological thought of the last twenty years."—*Celebrities of the Century.*

GENERAL GORDON, C.B.

Events in the Taeping Rebellion, being Reprints of MSS. copied by General Gordon, C.B., in his own handwriting; with Monograph, Introduction, and Notes, by A. Egmont Hake, Author of "The Story of Chinese Gordon." With Portrait and Map, demy 8vo, 18s.

"The publication of this volume completes what may be called the personal narrative of General Gordon's eventful life told in his own words."—*Manchester Guardian.*

"There is no doubt that a wide circle of readers will like to read the story in the very words of the gallant leader of the 'Ever Victorious Army.'"—*Daily Graphic.*

A handy book of reference.

Companion to the Writing Desk; or, How to Address, Begin, and End Letters to Titled and Official Personages. Together with a Table of Precedence, copious List of Abbreviations, Rules for Composition and Punctuation, Instructions on Preparing for the Press, &c. 32mo, 1s.

A useful manual which should be in every office.

BARON CUVIER.

The Animal Kingdom, with considerable Additions by W. B. Carpenter, M.D., F.R.S., and J. O. Westwood, F.L.S. New Edition, Illustrated with 500 Engravings on Wood and **36 Coloured Plates**, imp. 8vo, 21s.

For the Reduced Prices apply to

M. GRIFFITH.

India's Princes, short Life Sketches of the Native Rulers of India, with 47 full-page Illustrations. Demy 4to, gilt top, 21s.

The contents are arranged in the following order:—THE PUNJAUB—H.H. The Maharaja of Cashmere, H.H. The Maharaja of Patiala, H.H. The Maharaja of Kapurthalla. RAJPUTANA—The Maharaja of Oudipur, The Maharaja of Jeypore, The Maharaja of Jodhpur, The Maharaja of Uwar, The Maharaja of Bhurtpur. CENTRAL INDIA —H.H. The Maharaja Holkar of Indore, H.H. The Maharaja Scindia of Gwalior, H.H. The Begum of Bhopal. THE BOMBAY PRESIDENCY—H.H. The Gaikwar of Baroda, H.H. The Rao of Cutch, H.H. The Raja of Kolhapur, H.H. The Nawab of Juurrghad, H.H. The Thakore Sahib of Bhavnagar, H.H. The Thakore Sahib of Dhangadra, H.H. The Thakore Sahib of Morvi, H.H. The Thakore Sahib of Gondal. SOUTHERN INDIA—H.H. The Nizam of Hyderabad, H.H. The Maharja of Mysore, H.H. The Maharaja of Travancore, &c.

"A handsome volume, containing a series of photographic portraits and local views with accompanying letterpress, giving biographical and political details, carefully compiled and attractively presented."—*Times.*

GEORGE GRESSWELL.

The Diseases and Disorders of the Ox. Second Edition, demy 8vo, 7s. 6d.

"This is perhaps one of the best of the popular books on the subject which has been published in recent years, and demonstrates in a most unmistakable manner the great advance that has been made in Bovine and Ovine Pathology since the days of Youatt. . . . To medical men who desire to know something of the disorders of such an important animal—speaking hygienically—as the Ox, the work can be recommended."—*The Lancet.*

C. HAMILTON.

Hedaya or Guide, a Commentary on the Mussulman Laws. Second Edition, with Preface and Index by S. G. Grady, 8vo, 35s.

The great Law-Book of India, and one of the most important monuments of Mussulman legislation in existence.

"A work of very high authority in all Moslem countries. It discusses most of the subjects mentioned in the Koran and Sonna."—MILL's Mohammedanism.
"A valuable work."—ALLIBONE.

JOSEPH HAYDN.

Book of Dignities, containing lists of the Official Personages of the British Empire, Civil, Diplomatic, Heraldic, Judicial, Ecclesiastical, Municipal, Naval, and Military, from the Earliest Periods to the Present Time, together with the Sovereigns and Rulers of the World from the Foundation of their respective States; the Orders of Knighthood of the United Kingdom and India, and numerous other lists. Founded on Beatson's "Political Index" (1806). **Remodelled and brought down to 1851 by the late Joseph Haydn. Continued to the Present Time, with numerous additional lists, and an Index to the entire Work, by Horace Ockerby, Solicitor of the Supreme Court.** Demy 8vo, 25s.

"The most complete official directory in existence, containing about 1,300 different lists."—*Times.*
"The value of such a book can hardly be overrated."—*Saturday Review.*
"A perfect monument of patient labour and research, and invaluable for many purposes of reference."—*Truth.*
"This valuable work has cost its editor, Mr Horace Ockerby, a great deal of labour, and does infinite credit to his research and industry."—*World.*

Any Bookseller at Home and Abroad.

Rev. H. R. HAWEIS, M.A., Author of "Music and Morals."

Sir Morell Mackenzie, Physician and Operator, a Memoir, compiled and edited from Private Papers and Personal Reminiscences. New Edition, with Portrait and copy of Autograph Letter from the Queen, crown 8vo, 3s. 6d.

CONTENTS.

Family Tree.	Private Practice.	The Respite.
Surroundings.	Leisure Hours.	The Last Voyage.
Boyhood.	The Emperor.	Last Glimpses.
A Vocation.	The German Doctors.	The End.
The Throat Hospital.	The Book.	

"Mr Haweis writes not only fearlessly, but with remarkable freshness and vigour. He is occasionally eloquent, and even pathetic. In all that he says we perceive a transparent honesty and singleness of purpose."—*Saturday Review.*

"A deeply interesting book, and one which challenges in a most striking and fearless manner the stern verdict which Sir Morell's own profession so generally passed upon his conduct before and after the death of his illustrious patient the Emperor. . . The volume is full of absolutely interesting details, many among them new."—*Daily Telegraph.*

HOWARD HENSMAN, Special Correspondent of the "Pioneer" (Allahabad) and the "Daily News" (London).

The Afghan War, 1879-80. Being a complete Narrative of the Capture of Cabul, the Siege of Sherpur, the Battle of Ahmed Khel, the March to Candahar, and the defeat of Ayub Khan. With Maps, demy 8vo, 21s.

"Sir Frederick Roberts says of the letters here published in a collected form that 'nothing could be more accurate or graphic.' As to accuracy no one can be a more competent judge than Sir Frederick, and his testimony stamps the book before us as constituting especially trustworthy material for history. Of much that he relates Mr Hensman was an eye-witness; of the rest he was informed by eye-witnesses immediately after the occurrence of the events recorded. There could, therefore, be little doubt as to the facts mentioned. Credibility might be concurrent with incorrect deductions, but we are assured by Sir Frederick Roberts that Mr Hensman's accuracy is complete in all respects. Mr Hensman enjoyed singular advantages during the first part of the war, for he was the only special correspondent who accompanied the force which marched out of Ali Kheyl in September 1879. One of the most interesting portions of the book is that which describes the march of Sir Frederick Roberts from Cabul to Candahar. The description of the Maiwand disaster is given with combined clearness, simplicity, and power, and will be read with the utmost interest. Indeed, the book is in every respect interesting and well written, and reflects the greatest credit on the author."—*Athenæum.*

SIR JOHN F. W. HERSCHEL, Bart., K.H., &c., Member of the Institute of France, &c.

Popular Lectures on Scientific Subjects. New Edition, crown 8vo, 6s.

"We are reminded of the rapid progress made by science within the last quarter of a century by the publication of a new edition of Sir John Herschel's *Popular Lectures on Scientific Subjects.* In 1861, spectrum analysis, as applied to the heavenly bodies, was referred to as a possibility; now it is not only an accomplished fact, but the analysis of the gases contained in the sun has led to the discovery of one of them, helium, upon the earth. Some of the lectures, such as that on light, are practically popular treatises on the particular subject to which they refer, and can be read with advantage even by advanced students."—*The Westminster Review.*

For the Reduced Prices apply to

REV. T. P. HUGHES.

Dictionary of Islam. Being a Cyclopædia of the Doctrines, Rites, Ceremonies, and Customs, together with the Technical and Theological Terms of the Muhammadan Religion. With numerous Illustrations, royal 8vo, £2. 2s.

"Such a work as this has long been needed, and it would be hard to find any one better qualified to prepare it than Mr Hughes. His 'Notes on Muhammadanism,' of which two editions have appeared, have proved decidedly useful to students of Islam, especially in India, and his long familiarity with the tenets and customs of Moslems has placed him in the best possible position for deciding what is necessary and what superfluous in a 'Dictionary of Islam.' His usual method is to begin an article with the text in the Koran relating to the subject, then to add the traditions bearing upon it, and to conclude with the comments of the Mohammedan scholiasts and the criticisms of Western scholars. Such a method, while involving an infinity of labour, produces the best results in point of accuracy and comprehensiveness. The difficult task of compiling a dictionary of so vast a subject as Islam, with its many sects, its saints, khalifs, ascetics, and dervishes, its festivals, ritual, and sacred places, the dress, manners, and customs of its professors, its commentators, technical terms, science of tradition and interpretation, its superstitions, magic, and astrology, its theoretical doctrines and actual practices, has been accomplished with singular success; and the dictionary will have its place among the standard works of reference in every library that professes to take account of the religion which governs the lives of forty millions of the Queen's subjects. The articles on 'Marriage,' 'Women,' 'Wives,' 'Slavery,' 'Tradition,' 'Sufi,' 'Muhammad,' 'Da'wah' or Incantation, 'Burial,' and 'God,' are especially admirable. Two articles deserve special notice. One is an elaborate account of Arabic 'Writing' by Dr Steingass, which contains a vast quantity of useful matter, and is well illustrated by woodcuts of the chief varieties of Arabic script. The other article to which we refer with special emphasis is Mr F. Pincott on 'Sikhism.' There is something on nearly every page of the dictionary that will interest and instruct the students of Eastern religion, manners, and customs."—*Athenæum.*

Dictionary of Muhammadan Theology.

Notes on Muhammadanism, by Rev. T. P. Hughes. Third Edition, revised and enlarged. Fcap. 8vo, 6s.

"Altogether an admirable little book. It combines two excellent qualities, abundance of facts and lack of theories. . . . On every one of the numerous heads (over fifty) into which the book is divided, Mr Hughes furnishes a large amount of very valuable information, which it would be exceedingly difficult to collect from even a large library of works on the subject. The book might well be called a 'Dictionary of Muhammadan Theology,' for we know of no English work which combines a methodical arrangement (and consequently facility of reference) with fulness of information in so high a degree as the little volume before us."—*The Academy.*

"It contains *multum in parvo*, and is about the best outlines of the tenets of the Muslim faith which we have seen. It has, moreover, the rare merit of being accurate; and, although it contains a few passages which we would gladly see expunged, it cannot fail to be useful to all Government employés who have to deal with Muhammadans; whilst to missionaries it will be invaluable."—*The Times of India.*

"It is manifest throughout the work that we have before us the opinions of one thoroughly conversant with the subject, and who is uttering no random notions. . . . We strongly recommend 'Notes on Muhammadanism.' Our clergy especially, even though they are not missionaries, and have no intention of labouring amongst Muhammadans, or consorting with them, ought to have at least as much knowledge of the system as can be most readily acquired, with a very little careful study, from this useful treatise."—*The Record.*

SIR W. HUNTER.

Bengal MS. Records. A Selected List of Letters in the Board of Revenue, Calcutta, 1782-1807, with an Historical Dissertation and Analytical Index. 4 vols., demy 8vo, 30s.

A Statistical Account of Bengal. 20 vols., demy 8vo, £6.

Any Bookseller at Home and Abroad.

J. HUNTER, late Hon. Sec. of the British Bee-keepers' Association.
A Manual of Bee-keeping. Containing Practical Information for Rational and Profitable Methods of Bee Management. Full Instructions on Stimulative Feeding, Ligurianising and Queen-raising, with descriptions of the American Comb Foundation, Sectional Supers, and the best Hives and Apiarian Appliances on all Systems. Fourth Edition, with Illustrations, crown 8vo, 3s. 6d.

" We are indebted to Mr J. Hunter, Honorary Secretary of the British Bee-keepers' Association. His Manual of Bee-keeping, just published, is full to the very brim of choice and practical hints fully up to the most advanced stages of Apiarian Science, and its perusal has afforded us so much pleasure that we have drawn somewhat largely from it for the benefit of our readers."—*Bee-keepers' Magazine (New York).*

" It is profusely illustrated with engravings, which are almost always inserted for their utility. . . . There is an old saying that 'easy writing is hard reading,' but we will not say thus much of Mr Hunter's book, which, taken as a whole, is perhaps the most generally useful of any now published in this country."—*The Field.*

MAJOR LEIGH HUNT, Madras Army, and ALEX. S. KENNY, M.R.C.S.E., A.K.C., Senior Demonstrator of Anatomy at King's College, London.
On Duty under a Tropical Sun. Being some Practical Suggestions for the Maintenance of Health and Bodily Comfort, and the Treatment of Simple Diseases; with remarks on Clothing and Equipment. Second Edition, crown 8vo, 4s.

"This little book is devoted to the description and treatment of many tropical diseases and minor emergencies, supplemented by some useful hints on diet, clothing, and equipment for travellers in tropical climates. The issue of a third edition proves that the book has hitherto been successful. On the whole we can commend the hints which have been given for the treatment of various diseases, but in some places much has been left to the knowledge of the reader in the selection and application of a remedy."—*Scottish Geographical Magazine.*

" Is written more especially for the rougher sex, and is only less important than Tropical Trials' because it has had many more predecessors. It is now in a third edition, and contains practical suggestions for the maintenance of health and bodily comfort, as well as the treatment of simple diseases, with useful remarks on clothing and equipment for the guidance of travellers abroad."—*Daily Telegraph.*

Tropical Trials. A Handbook for Women in the Tropics. Crown 8vo, 7s. 6d.

" Is a valuable handbook for women in the East, and, we are glad to see, now in its second edition. It does not treat theoretically of the maladies incidental to Europeans in hot climates, or go deeply into those matters which properly belong to the experienced doctor, but it gives plain, wholesome advice on matters of health. which, were it scrupulously followed, it is not too much to say would add fifty per cent. to the enjoyment of our countrywomen abroad. She could scarcely have a better guide as to what to do and what not to do than this excellent handbook, which deserves to be included in every woman's foreign outfit."—*Daily Telegraph.*

JOHN H. INGRAM.
The Haunted Homes and Family Traditions of Great Britain. Illustrated. Crown 8vo, 7s. 6d.

Epitomised in One Volume by R. O'BYRNE, F.R.G.S., &c.
James' Naval History. A Narrative of the Naval Battles, Single Ship Actions, Notable Sieges, and Dashing Cutting-out Expeditions, fought in the days of Howe, Hood, Duncan, St Vincent, Bridport, Nelson, Camperdown, Exmouth, Duckworth, and Sir Sydney Smith. Crown 8vo, 5s.

For the Reduced Prices apply to

MRS GRACE JOHNSON, Silver Medallist Cookery, Exhibition.
Anglo-Indian and Oriental Cookery. Crown 8vo, 3s. 6d.

"Overflows with all sorts of delicious and economical recipes."—*Pall Mall Budget.*

"Housewives and professors of the gentle art of cookery who deplore the dearth of dainty dishes will find a veritable gold mine in Mrs Johnson's book."—*Pall Mall Gazette.*

Appeals to us from a totally original standpoint. She has thoroughly and completely investigated native and Anglo-Indian cuisines, and brought away the very best specimens of their art. Her pillau and kedgree are perfect, in our opinion; curries are scientifically classed and explained, and some of the daintiest recipes we have ever seen are given, but the puddings particularly struck our fancy. Puddings as a rule are *so* nasty! The pudding that is nourishing is hideously insipid, and of the smart pudding it may truly be said that its warp is dyspepsia, and its woof indigestion. Mrs Johnson's puddings are both good to taste and pretty to look at, and the names of some of her native dishes would brighten any menu.

H. G. KEENE, C.I.E., B.C.S., M.R.A.S., &c.

History of India. From the Earliest Times to the Present Day. For the use of Students and Colleges. 2 vols, with Maps. Crown 8vo, 16s.

"The main merit of Mr Keene's performance lies in the fact that he has assimilated all the authorities, and has been careful to bring his book down to date. He has been careful in research, and has availed himself of the most recent materials. He is well known as the author of other works on Indian history, and his capacity for his self-imposed task will not be questioned. We must content ourselves with this brief testimony to the labour and skill bestowed by him upon a subject of vast interest and importance. Excellent proportion is preserved in dealing with the various episodes, and the style is clear and graphic. The volumes are supplied with many useful maps, and the appendix include notes on Indian law and on recent books about India."—*Globe.*

"Mr Keene has the admirable element of fairness in dealing with the succession of great questions that pass over his pages, and he wisely devotes a full half of his work to the present century. The appearance of such a book, and of every such book, upon India is to be hailed at present. A fair-minded presentment of Indian history like that contained in Mr Keene's two volumes is at this moment peculiarly welcome."—*Times.*

An Oriental Biographical Dictionary. Founded on Materials collected by the late Thomas William Beale. New Edition, revised and enlarged, royal 8vo, 28s.

"A complete biographical dictionary for a country like India, which in its long history has produced a profusion of great men, would be a vast undertaking. The suggestion here made only indicates the line on which the dictionary, at some future time, could be almost indefinitely extended, and rendered still more valuable as a work of reference. Great care has evidently been taken to secure the accuracy of all that has been included in the work, and that is of far more importance than mere bulk. The dictionary can be commended as trustworthy, and reflects much credit on Mr Keene. Several interesting lists of rulers are given under the various founders of dynasties."—*India.*

The Fall of the Moghul Empire. From the Death of Aurungzeb to the Overthrow of the Mahratta Power. A New Edition, with Corrections and Additions, with Map, crown 8vo, 7s. 6d.

This work fills up a blank between the ending of Elphinstone's and the commencement of Thornton's Histories.

Fifty-Seven. Some Account of the Administration of Indian Districts during the Revolt of the Bengal Army. Demy 8vo, 6s.

Any Bookseller at Home and Abroad.

DR TALBOTT, and others.

Keble College Sermons. Second Series, 1877-1888, crown 8vo, 6s.

"To those who desire earnest, practical, and orthodox doctrine in the form of short addresses, these sermons will be most acceptable; and their lofty tone, their eloquent wording, and the thorough manliness of their character, will commend them to a wide circle of readers."—*Morning Post.*

"Dr Talbot has a second time thoughtfully placed on public record some of the lessons which were taught during his Wardenship in *Sermons preached in the Chapel of Keble College, Oxford,* 1877-1888. The sermons are fresh and vigorous in tone, and evidently come from preachers who were thoroughly in touch with their youthful audience, and who generally with much acuteness and skill grappled with the spiritual and intellectual difficulties besetting nowadays the University career."—*Church Times.*

G. H. KINAHAN.

A Handy Book of Rock Names. Fcap. 8vo, 4s.

"This will prove, we do not doubt, a very useful little book to all practical geologists, and also to the reading student of rocks. When a difficulty is incurred as to a species of deposit, it will soon vanish. Mr Kinahan's little book will soon make it all clear. The work is divided into three parts. The first is a classified table of rocks, the second part treats of the *Ingenite* rocks, and the third part deals with those rocks which are styled *Derivate.* Dana's termination of *yte* has been most generally used by the author, but he has also given the *ite* terminations for those that like them. The book will be purchased, for it must be had, by every geologist; and as its size is small, it will form a convenient pocket companion for the man who works over field and quarry."—*Popular Science Review.*

REV. F. G. LEE, D.D. (Vicar of All Saints', Lambeth).

The Church under Queen Elizabeth. An Historical Sketch. By Rev. F. G. Lee, D.D. (Vicar of All Saints', Lambeth). Second Edition. Crown 8vo, 7s. 6d.

"There is the same picturesqueness of detail, the same vigorous denunciation, the same graphic power, which made the earlier book pleasant reading even to many who disagree heartily with its tone and object. . . Dr Lee's strength lies in very graphic description."—*Notes and Queries.*

"This is, in many ways, a remarkably fine book. There it is powerfully written no one acquainted with Dr Lee's vigorous style would for a moment dispute."—*Morning Post.*

"Presenting a painful picture of the degradation into which the Church had sunk in Elizabeth's reign."—*Daily Telegraph.*

Sights and Shadows. Being Examples of the Supernatural. New Edition. With a Preface addressed to the Critics. Crown 8vo, 6s.

"This work will be especially interesting to students of the supernatural, and their name is legion at the present moment. It deals with more than one branch of what is commonly known as spiritualism. The introduction gives a brief resumé of various forms of magic and divination which have obtained credence in all ages, and later on we find well-authenticated accounts of apparitions, supernatural warnings, hypnotic experiments, and miracles of healing. Mr Lee evidently believes that 'there are more things in heaven and earth than are dreamt of in our philosophy,' and few sane people will disagree with him, though they may not be inclined to accept all his opinions and assertions as they stand."—*Lady.*

"Here we have ghostly stories galore, which believers in supernatural visitations will welcome as upholders of the faith that is in them. Dr Lee is a hard hitter and a vigorous controversialist, with a righteous contempt for your Darwins and Stuart Mills, and such like folk, and is not above suggesting that some of them have a decided worship of the god Self. As for 'the pompous jargon and silly cynicism which so many public scribes again and again make use of to throw discredit upon any phase of the supernatural,' I have nothing to say. They can take care of themselves. This much I know, that 'Sights and Shadows' gives one an eerie feeling as midnight approaches and the fire flickers on the hearth."—*Gentlewoman.*

For the Reduced Prices apply to

COL. G. B. MALLESON.

History of the French in India. From the Founding of Pondicherry in 1674, to the Capture of that place in 1761. New and Revised Edition, with Maps. Demy 8vo, 16s.

"Colonel Malleson has produced a volume alike attractive to the general reader and valuable for its new matter to the special student. It is not too much to say that now, for the first time, we are furnished with a faithful narrative of that portion of European enterprise in India which turns upon the contest waged by the East India Company against French influence, and especially against Dupleix."—*Edinburgh Review.*

"It is pleasant to contrast the work now before us with the writer's first bold plunge into historical composition, which splashed every one within his reach. He swims now with a steady stroke, and there is no fear of his sinking. With a keener insight into human character, and a larger understanding of the sources of human action, he combines all the power of unimated recital which invested his earlier narratives with popularity."—*Fortnightly Review.*

"The author has had the advantage of consulting the French archives, and his volume forms a useful supplement to Orme."—*Athenæum.*

Final French Struggles in India and on the Indian Seas. New Edition. Crown 8vo, 6s.

"How India escaped from the government of prefects and sub-prefects to fall under that of commissioners and deputy-commissioners; why the Penal Code of Lord Macaulay reigns supreme instead of a Code Napoleon; why we are not looking on helplessly from Mahe, Karikal, and Pondicherry, while the French are ruling all over Madras, and spending millions of francs in attempting to cultivate the slopes of the Neilgherries, may be learnt from this modest volume. Colonel Malleson is always painstaking, and generally accurate; his style is transparent, and he never loses sight of the purpose with which he commenced to write."—*Saturday Review.*

"A book dealing with such a period of our history in the East, besides being interesting, contains many lessons. It is written in a style that will be popular with general readers."—*Athenæum.*

"It strikes one as the best thing he has yet done. Searching, yet easy, his pen goes with unflagging power through the military wonders of a hundred years, connecting the accounts of battles by a sufficient historic thread."—*Academy.*

History of Afghanistan, from the Earliest Period to the Outbreak of the War of 1878, with map, demy 8vo, 18s.

"The name of Colonel Malleson on the title-page of any historical work in relation to India or the neighbouring States is a satisfactory guarantee both for the accuracy of the facts and the brilliancy of the narrative. The author may be complimented upon having written a History of Afghanistan which is likely to become a work of standard authority."—*Scotsman.*

The Battle-Fields of Germany, from the Outbreak of the Thirty Years' War to the Battle of Blenheim, with maps and one plan, demy 8vo, 16s.

"Colonel Malleson has shown a grasp of his subject, and a power of vivifying the confused passages of battle, in which it would be impossible to name any living writer as his equal. In imbuing these almost forgotten battle-fields with fresh interest and reality for the English reader, he is re-opening one of the most important chapters of European History, which no previous English writer has made so interesting and instructive as he has succeeded in doing in this volume."—*Academy.*

Ambushes and Surprises, being a Description of some of the most famous instances of the Leading into Ambush and the Surprises of Armies, from the time of Hannibal to the period of the Indian Mutiny, with a portrait of General Lord Mark Ker, K.C.B., demy 8vo, 18s.

Any Bookseller at Home and Abroad.

JAMES IRVIN LUPTON, F.R.C.V.S., author of "The External Anatomy of the Horse," &c.

The Horse: as he Was, as he Is, and as he Ought to Be, with Illustrations. Crown 8vo, 3s. 6d.

"Written with a good object in view, namely, to create an interest in the important subject of horse-breeding, more especially that class known as general utility horses. The book contains several illustrations, is well printed and handsomely bound, and we hope will meet with the attention it deserves."—*Live Stock Journal.*

T. MILLER MAGUIRE, M.A., LL.D.

American War—Campaigns in Virginia, 1861-2, with Maps. Roya 8vo, paper covers, 3s. 6d.

MRS MANNING.

Ancient and Mediæval India. Being the History, Religion, Laws, Caste, Manners and Customs, Language, Literature, Poetry, Philosophy, Astronomy, Algebra, Medicine, Architecture, Manufactures, Commerce, &c., of the Hindus, taken from their Writings. With Illustrations. 2 vols., demy 8vo, 30s.

IRVING MONTAGU (late Special War Correspondent "Illustrated London News").

Camp and Studio. Illustrated by the Author. New Edition. Crown 8vo, 6s.

"His animated pages and sketches have a more than ephemeral interest, and present a moving picture of the romance and the misery of countries and populations ravaged by great opposing armies, and many a picturesque episode of personal experiences; he is pleasant and amusing enough."—*Daily News.*

"Mr Irving Montagu's narrative of his experiences as war artist of the *Illustrated London News* during the Russo-Turkish war, though late in appearing, may be read with interest. War correspondents and artists usually enjoy a fair share of adventure; but Mr Montagu appears to have revelled in dangers which seem anything but desirable when studied in cold blood. Mr Montagu has much that is interesting to tell about the horrors of the siege of Kars and the prowess of the fair young Amazon who commanded a troop of Bashi-Bazuks, and even seduced a Russian general to her side. How he got to the front in spite of Russian prohibition, disguised as a camp follower, how his portmanteau was shelled a few inches behind his back, what he risked and what he saw in the memorable lines before Plevna, will be read with great interest. The book is well illustrated by many vigorous sketches, some of which are exceedingly humorous."—*Athenæum.*

"A bright chatty record of wars, scenes, and adventures in various parts of the world."—*Echo.*

Wanderings of a War Artist. Illustrated by the Author. New Edition. Crown 8vo, 6s.

"Mr Montagu is to be congratulated on an eminently readable book, which, both in style and matter, is above the average of productions in this kind."—*The Morning Post.*

"This is an enchanting book. Equally as writer and as artist, Mr Irving Montagu is a delightful companion. This beautiful and exceptionally interesting volume does not by any means exhaust the literary and artistic achievements of the well-known 'special' of the *Illustrated London News*."—*The Daily News.*

"His own adventures are largely seasoned with stories of other people and anecdotes he picks up. He went through the second siege of Paris under the Commune, and some of the best reading in the book is the picture he gives of the state of poor, beautiful Paris, seen by the eye of an observing, impartial man, who has no object in either exaggerating or under-colouring the work of the Commune."—*The Spectator.*

"The adventures of Mr Montagu are narrated with humour, and are seldom dull reading."—*Glasgow Herald.*

For the Reduced Prices apply to

J. MORRIS, Author of "The War in Korea," &c., thirteen years resident in Tokio under the Japanese Board of Works.

Advance Japan. A Nation Thoroughly in Earnest. With over 100 Illustrations by R. Isayama, and of photographs lent by the Japanese Legation. 8vo, 12s. 6d.

"Mr Morris evidently knows the country well, and is a strong believer in its future; his book will be found a useful summary of recent history, abounding in good character sketches, accompanied with photographs, of the leading men."—*Times.*

"Is really a remarkably complete account of the land, the people, and the institutions of Japan, with chapters that deal with matters of such living interest as its growing industries and armaments, and the origin, incidents, and probable outcome of the war with China. The volume is illustrated by a Japanese artist of repute; it has a number of useful statistical appendices, and it is dedicated to His Majesty the Mikado."—*Scotsman.*

"Mr Morris, who writes, of course, with thorough local knowledge, gives a very complete and eminently readable account of the country, its government, people, and resource... The work, which contains a large number of portraits and other illustrations, is decidedly 'on the nail,' and may be recommended not only as a book to read, but as of value for reference."—*Westminster Gazette.*

"Puts before us a clear view of the point which has been reached. His work is historical, social, and descriptive; we see in it the Japanese of to-day as he really is. Mr Morris has also something to say on the Japanese at home—how he eats, how he dresses, and how he comports himself; while wider issues are discussed in the chapters treating of the administration of the islands, their ports, communications, trades, and armaments."—*Globe.*

"A well-proportioned sketch of the Japanese of to-day, so recent as to include the results of the war... There is much else I should like to quote in this able and interesting book. It has a good chapter on natural history, and an excellent chapter on diet, dress, and manners; it gives just enough of Japanese history to help the ordinary reader who wants to learn his Japan on easy terms; it has also most useful and attractively conveyed information in its brief account of the principal cities of Japan, communications and armament, language and literature, mines and minerals."—*Queen.*

"He summarises clearly, concisely, the existing knowledge on the Japanese Parliamentary system, territorial and administrative divisions, natural history, domestic and national customs, dynastic changes, old feudal institutions, town populations, industries, mineral and other natural resources, railways, armaments, the press, and other subjects too many for enumeration. Even the chapter on language and literature makes an appalling subject interesting. . . . Mr Morris has brought his very useful account of Japan up-to-date. He gives a good summary of the recent war with China, and then proceeds to make some well-considered suggestions on a matter of supreme importance to Europe no less than to the two Empires of the Far East."

CHARLES MARVIN.

The Region of the Eternal Fire. An Account of a Journey to the Caspian Region in 1883. New Edition. With Maps and Illustrations. Crown 8vo, handsomely bound, 6s.

"The leading authority of the English Press on the Central Asian Question is Charles Marvin, a man of iron industry, who has wielded his comprehensive knowledge of the region in such a manner as to render eminent service to his country."—*Opinion of Arminius Vambery.*

"Charles Marvin's services in respect of the Russo-Afghan Question have been invaluable. He has heard with his own ears the opinions expressed on the subject by Russian generals and diplomatists, and, for the love of England, has spent his own money to warn England's people."—*Opinion of Colonel Malleson, "The Russo-Afghan Question," p. 55.*

Any Bookseller at Home and Abroad

W. O'CONNOR MORRIS.

Great Commanders of Modern Times, and the Campaign of 1815. Turenne—Marlborough—Frederick the Great—Napoleon—Wellington—Moltke. With Illustrations and Plans. Royal 8vo, 21s.

"Mr Morris certainly brings to his task vast reading and exhaustive research."—*Athenæum.*

"We gladly welcome this handsome volume by Judge O'Connor Morris, which gives evidence on every page of careful reading and correct judgment. . . . An admirable book to place in the hands of any student who wishes to get some idea of the history of the art of war."—*Academy.*

"To the students of war this book will prove of the utmost interest and the greatest possible service."—*National Observer.*

"Writes vividly and well."—*Times.*

CARDINAL NEWMAN.

Miscellanies from the Oxford Sermons of John Henry Newman, D.D. Crown 8vo, gilt top, 5s.

"All the resources of a master of English style—except, perhaps one, description—were at his command; pure diction, clear arrangement, irony, dignity, a copious command of words, combined with a reserve in the use of them—all these qualities went to make up the charm of Newman's style, the finest flower that the earlier system of a purely classical education has produced."—*Athenæum.*

"The pieces presented to us here are carefully chosen, and answer the purpose of the present volume. The selections which are contained in it happily avoid any of those passages which have been the grounds of controversy. As a general rule we are able to take in the teachings of this book without any *arrière-pensée*, without any feeling that we have here the germ of those theories which estrange their author from us."—*Athenæum.*

COL. F. A. WHINYATES, late R.H.A., formerly commanding the Battery.

Military Regiments—From Corunna to Sevastopol, the History of "C" Battery, "A" Brigade, late "C" Troop, Royal Horse Artillery, with succession of Officers from its formation to the present time. With 3 Maps, demy 8vo, 14s.

EDWARD NEWMAN, F.Z.S.

British Butterflies. With many Illustrations. Super royal 8vo, 7s. 6d.

DEPUTY SURGEON-GENERAL C. T. PASKE, late of the Bengal Army, and Edited by F. G. AFLALO.

Life and Travel in Lower Burmah, with Frontispiece. Crown 8vo, 6s.

"In dealing with life in Burmah we are given a pleasant insight into Eastern life; and to those interested in India and our other Eastern possessions, the opinions Mr Paske offers and the suggestions he makes will be delightful reading. Mr Paske has adopted a very light style of writing in 'Myamma,' which lends an additional charm to the short historical-cum-geographical sketch, and both the writer and the editor are to be commended for the production of a really attractive book."—*Public Opinion.*

For the Reduced Prices apply to

Translation of the famous Passion Play.
Passion Play at Oberammergau, The, with the whole Drama translated into English, and the Songs of the Chorus in German and English; also a Map of the Town, Plan of the Theatre, &c. 4to, cloth, 3s. 6d.; paper, 2s. 6d.

"The author of 'Charles Lowder' has done a real service in publishing a translation of 'The Passion Play at Oberammergau,' with a description of the play and short account of a visit there in 1880. To those who have already seen it, this little book will recall vividly the experience of what must be to all a memorable day, while to those who are going in 1890 it is simply invaluable."—*Guardian.*

MARY A. PRATTEN.
My Hundred Swiss Flowers, with a short account of Swiss Ferns. With 60 Illustrations. Crown 8vo, plain plates, 12s. 6d.; *with plates coloured by hand,* 25s.

"The temptation to produce such books as this seems irresistible. The author feels a want; the want is undeniable. After more or less hesitation he feels he can supply it. It is pleasantly written, and affords useful hints as to localities."—*Athenæum.*

R. A. PROCTOR.
Watched by the Dead, a loving study of Dickens' half-told tale. Crown 8vo, cloth, 1s. 6d.; boards, 1s.

"Mr Proctor here devotes much study and much ingenious conjecture to restoring the plot of 'The Mystery of Edwin Drood.' It would not be fair were we to attempt to give in a small compass the result of his labours. It must suffice to say that those who have occupied themselves with this curious problem will be interested in the solution here offered for their acceptance."—*Spectator.*

WILLIAM PROCTOR, Stud Groom.
The Management and Treatment of the Horse in the Stable, Field, and on the Road. Second Edition, Revised and Enlarged, Illustrated. Crown 8vo, 6s.

"There are few who are interested in horses will fail to profit by one portion or another of this useful work."—*Sportsman.*
"We cannot do better than wish that Mr Proctor's book may find its way into the hands of all those concerned in the management of the most useful quadruped we possess."—*England.*
"There is a fund of sound common sense views in this work which will be interesting to many owners."—*Field.*
"Coming from a practical hand the work should recommend itself to the public."—*Sportsman.*

WILLIAM RAEBURN ANDREW.
Raeburn (Sir Henry, R.A.), Life by his Great-Grandson, William Raeburn Andrew, with an Appendix comprising a list of his works exhibited in the Royal Academy, Edinburgh. 8vo, 10s. 6d.

"Mr Andrew's book, which on this occasion appeals to a wider public, makes no pretence to do more than to bring together the biographical fragments concerning Raeburn gathered out of various publications and to 'make them coherent with a little cement of his own.' Possibly a fuller and more original biography of the greatest of our portrait-painters, who was at the same time one of the greatest ornaments of the Edinburgh Society of the beginning of the century, may yet see the light; and in the meantime we can be grateful to Mr Andrew for bringing together and arranging so rich a store of topographical and personal details connected with his illustrious ancestor. In an appendix is a useful annotated catalogue of the 1876 exhibition of Raeburn's works."—*Scotsman.*

Any Bookseller at Home and Abroad.

R. RIMMER, F.L.S.
The Land and Freshwater Shells of the British Isles. Illustrated with 10 Photographs and 3 Lithographs, containing figures of all the principal Species. Second Edition. Crown 8vo, 5s.

"This handsomely got up little volume supplies a long-felt want in a very ingenious and trustworthy manner. The author is an enthusiastic conchologist, and writes both attractively and well, and in a manner so simple and natural that we have no fear that any ordinarily educated man will easily understand every phrase. But the feature of this book which strikes us most is that every species of British land and freshwater shell has been photographed, and here we have all the photographs, natural size in the albertype process, so that the merest tyro will find no difficulty in identifying any shell he may find."—*Science Gossip.*

ALEXANDER ROGERS (*Bombay Civil Service, Retired*).
The Land Revenue of Bombay, a History of its Administration, Rise, and Progress, with 18 Maps. 2 vols., demy 8vo, 30s.

"Mr Rogers has produced a continuous and an authoritative record of the land changes and of the fortunes of the cultivating classes for a full half-century, together with valuable data regarding the condition and burdens of those classes at various periods before the present system of settlement was introduced. Mr Rogers now presents a comprehensive view of the land administration of Bombay as a whole, the history of its rise and progress, and a clear statement of the results which it has attained. It is a narrative of which all patriotic Englishmen may feel proud. The old burdens of native rule have been lightened, the old injustices mitigated, the old fiscal cruelties and exactions abolished. Underlying the story of each district we see a perennial struggle going on between the increase of the population and the available means of subsistence derived from the soil. That increase of the population is the direct result of the peace of the country under British rule. But it tends to press more and more severely on the possible limits of local cultivation, and it can only be provided for by the extension of the modern appliances of production and distribution. Mr Rogers very properly confines himself to his own subject. But there is ample evidence that the extension of roads, railways, steam factories, and other industrial enterprises, have played an important part in the solution of the problem, and that during recent years such enterprises have been powerfully aided by an abundant currency."—*The Times.*

ROBERT SEWELL.
Analytical History of India, from the earliest times to the Abolition of the East India Company in 1858. Post 8vo, 8s.

"Much careful labour has been expended on this volume."—*Athenæum.*
"The object of the author in compiling the following analytical sketch of Indian history has been to supply a want felt by most students of the more voluminous standard works of Mill, Elphinstone, Thornton, and Marshman, for a condensed outline in one small volume, which should serve at once to recall the memory and guide the eye. At the same time he has attempted to render it interesting to the general reader by preserving a medium between a bare analysis and a complete history; so that, without consulting the eminent authorities mentioned above, the mind may readily grasp the principal outlines of the early condition of India, and the rise and progress of the East India Company. For the more full comprehension of these facts the author has provided, in addition to a table of contents and a chronological index, an index to the geographical position of the places to which reference is made in the text, bearing the latitudes and longitude as given in Thornton's 'Gazetteer of India.' This will be found not only to aid the student who is but partially acquainted with the map of India, but also by means of occasional accents to guide him in the ordinary pronunciation of the names."—*Preface.*

For the Reduced Prices apply to

G. P. SANDERSON.

Thirteen Years among the Wild Beasts of India; their Haunts and Habits, from Personal Observation, with an account of the Modes of Capturing and Taming Wild Elephants. With 21 full-page Illustrations, reproduced for this Edition direct from the original drawings, and 3 Maps. Fifth Edition. Fcap. 4to, 12s.

"We find it difficult to hasten through this interesting book; on almost every page some incident or some happy descriptive passage tempts the reader to linger. The author relates his exploits with ability and with singular modesty. His adventures with man-eaters will afford lively entertainment to the reader, and indeed there is no portion of the volume which he is likely to wish shorter. The illustrations add to the attractions of the book."—*Pall Mall Gazette.*

"This is the best and most practical book on the wild game of Southern and Eastern India that we have read, and displays an extensive acquaintance with natural history. To the traveller proposing to visit India, whether he be a sportsman, a naturalist, or an antiquarian, the book will be invaluable: full of incident and sparkling with anecdote."—*Bailey's Magazine.*

"This—the fifth edition of a work as charming to read as it is instructive—will be welcomed equally by lovers of sport, and of natural history. Though he met with and shot many other kinds of wild beasts, the bulk of the volume, well written, well illustrated, and generally well got up, deals chiefly with the elephant, the tiger, the bison, the leopard, and the bear. Mr Sanderson, with exceptional powers of observation, cultivated friendly intercourse with the natives; and he was consequently able to utilise to the utmost the singularly favourable opportunities enjoyed by him as director of elephant-capturing operations in Mysore and Chittagong. The result is a book which to graphic details of sporting adventures far surpassing the common, adds a correct natural history of the animals chiefly dealt with, and particularly the elephant. From this real king of beasts, Mr Sanderson carefully removes every exaggeration made both for or against him, which had been repeated without any good foundation by one writer after another; he substitutes for fables a description of elephantine anatomy, size, habits, and character which may be said to sum up all that we know for certain about the animal, and nearly all that one can wish to know. We should have wished to see this edition brought up to date. The book is more fascinating than a romance; and we have read it now the third time with as great a zest as when we revelled over the perusal of the first edition."—*Imperial and Asiatic Quarterly Review.*

PROFESSOR SHELDON.

The Future of British Agriculture, how Farmers may best be benefited. Crown 8vo, 2s. 6d.

"Fortunately Prof. Sheldon has no mind to play the part of a prophet, but from the plenitude of a long experience gives sage counsel how to farm abreast of the time and be ready for whatever may ensue. . . . This little book is well worth reading, and it is pleasant to find that the Professor by no means despairs of the future of agriculture in England."—*Academy.*

"We welcome the book as a valuable contribution to our agricultural literature, and as a useful guide to those branches in which the author is especially qualified to instruct."—*Nature.*

"In this beautifully printed and well-bound little book Professor Sheldon, in his usual happy style, surveys the agricultural field, and indicates what he thinks is the prospect in front of the British farmer. Like a watchman he stands upon his tower—and when asked, What of the night? he disavows not that we are in the night, but earnestly declares that the morning cometh apace. The professor is an optimist; he does not believe that the country is done, and still less does he favour the idea that, taking a wide survey, the farmer days were better than these. On the contrary, he urges that the way out of the wilderness is not by any by-path, but by going right ahead; and, ere long, the man who holds the banner high will emerge triumphant."
—*Scottish Farmer.*

J. SMITH, A.L.S.

Ferns: British and Foreign. Fourth Edition, revised and greatly enlarged, with New Figures, &c. Crown 8vo, 7s. 6d.

Any Bookseller at Home and Abroad.

G. BARNETT SMITH, Author of " History of the English Parliament."

Leaders of Modern Industry. Biographical Sketches. Contents :—The Stephensons, Charles Knight, Sir George Burns, Sir Josiah Mason, The Wedgwoods, Thomas Brassey, The Fairbairns, Sir William Siemens, The Rennies. Crown 8vo, 7s. 6d.

"'Leaders of Modern Industry' is a volume of interesting biographical sketches of the pioneers of various phases of industry, comprising the Stephensons, Charles Knight, Sir George Burns, Sir Josiah Mason, the Wedgwoods, Thomas Brassey, the Fairbairns, Sir William Siemens, and the Rennies."—*World.*

Women of Renown. Nineteenth Century Studies. Contents :—Frederika Bremer, Countess of Blessington, George Eliot, Jenny Lind, Mary Somerville, George Sand, Mary Carpenter, Lady Morgan, Rachel, Lady Hester Stanhope. Crown 8vo, 7s. 6d.

Mr Barnett Smith continues his biographical activity. It is not many weeks since a volume appeared from his pen on "Christian Workers of the Nineteenth Century"; now we have " Women of Renown : Nineteenth Century Studies." The later is the larger and more elaborate work of the two, but in design and execution it is not greatly dissimilar from the earlier volume. Desirous of showing what the women of eminence whom he has chosen for delineation really were—how they lived, moved, and acted—the author has presented them wherever he could "as painted by themselves or their contemporaries." Autobiographies and biographies are thus, as far as available, laid under contribution. In the hands of so capable a compiler as Mr Barnett Smith such materials have been skilfully utilised, and the result is a series of brightly written sketches.

The Life and Enterprises of Ferdinand de Lesseps—The only full and Complete English Account of. New Edition. Revised, and brought up to the time of his death, with Portrait. Crown 8vo, 7s. 6d.

"A great part of M. de Lesseps' career already belongs to history, and is invested with a lustre which nothing can obscure. Mr G. Barnett Smith makes this clear in his useful and painstaking compilation. . . . It is skilfully executed, and illustrates aptly and not altogether inopportunely, both the poetry and the prose of M. de Lesseps' extraordinary career."—*The Times.*

"A very comprehensive life of Ferdinand de Lesseps has been produced by G. Barnett Smith, who has already proved his ability as a faithful and painstaking biographer. The career of M. de Lesseps was one of great achievements and great vicissitudes. This biographer lauds his achievements. The facts of the prosecution in connection with the Panama Canal project are elaborately set forth in this volume, to which all readers interested in the question should refer for information on a matter which to people not resident in France must have appeared unusually complicated."—*Westminster Review.*

ARTHUR PENRHYN STANLEY, D.D. (Dean of Westminster).

Scripture Portraits and other Miscellanies collected from his Published Writings. By Arthur Penrhyn Stanley, D.D. Crown 8vo, gilt top, 5s.

"In virtue of his literary genius, his solid acquirements, his manly sense, and his sympathetic and generous piety, he ranks among the most eminent and estimable of Christian teachers."—*Chambers's Encyclopædia.*

"These essays range over a period of twenty years (1850-1870), and they furnish a series of singularly interesting illustrations of the great controversies which have agitated that time. . . . Every one, indeed, of his essays has achieved in its day a success which makes a recommendation unnecessary."—ALLIBONE.

For the Reduced Prices apply to

E. Œ. SOMERVILLE and MARTIN ROSS, THE AUTHORS OF "AN IRISH COUSIN."

Through Connemara in a Governess Cart. Illustrated by W. W Russell, from Sketches by Edith Œ. Somerville. Crown 8vo, 3s. 6d.

"The quaint seriousness, the free and hearty fun, the sly humour of this narrative, are charmingly bright and attractive."—*World*.

"A bright and breezy narrative of two ladies in Connemara who preferred independence and a mule to society and a mail car. Their simple story is divertingly told."—*Times*.

"The delightful wilderness of mountain, peat bog, and heather, and all that they said and did, are graphically described in this chatty and extremely readable volume."—*Daily Telegraph*.

"Sketches of Irish Life, the eccentricities of wandering Saxons, and descriptions of local scenery, are worked up in a manner which makes the book a pleasant companion. Mr Russell has in his illustration ably supported the writers."—*Morning Post*.

By the same Authors

In the Vine Country—Bordeaux and its Neighbourhood, Illustrated. Crown 8vo, 3s. 6d.

"The genuine fund of wit and humour which sparkles throughout will be enjoyed by all."—*Glasgow Herald*.

"The authors have the knack of putting their readers in the situation in which they themselves were, and so the book, light and smart as it is, is heartily enjoyable."—*Scotsman*.

"A bright, artless narrative of travel."—*Times*.

"There is not a dull line in the volume from the first page to the last."—*Lady's Pictorial*.

J. E. TAYLOR, F.L.S., F.G.S., &c.

For fuller notices of Dr Taylor's Works, see *Scientific*, pp. 33, 34.

Flowers: Their Origin, Shapes, Perfumes, and Colours. Illustrated with 32 Coloured Figures by Sowerby, and 161 Woodcuts. Second Edition. Crown 8vo, 7s. 6d.

The Aquarium: Its Inhabitants, Structure, and Management. Second Edition, with 238 Woodcuts. Crown 8vo, 3s. 6d.

Half-Hours at the Seaside. Illustrated with 250 Woodcuts. Fourth Edition. Crown 8vo, 2s. 6d.

Half-Hours in the Green Lanes. Illustrated with 300 Woodcuts. Fifth Edition. Crown 8vo, 2s. 6d.

E. THORNTON.

A Gazetteer of the Territories under the Government of the Viceroy of India. Last Edition. Revised and Edited by Sir Roper Lethbridge, C.I.E., and A. N. Wollaston, C.I.E. Demy 8vo, 1,070 pp., 28s.

PERCY M. THORNTON.

Harrow School and its Surroundings. With Maps and Plates. Demy 8vo, 15s.

Any Bookseller at Home and Abroad

W. M. TORRENS.

History of Cabinets. From the Union with Scotland to the Acquisition of Canada and Bengal. 2 vols. Demy 8vo, 36s.

"It is almost impossible—and, alas! now useless as regards the writer—to praise this book too highly. It is a clever, sincere, and painstaking contribution to the making of modern history, and all students of constitutional and parliamentary history will find much to interest and instruct them in these able volumes. In all the minor matters of references, indexing, and printing every care has been taken. Indeed, all is praiseworthy, and the pity is that the writer should have passed away without receiving the thanks of students."—*St James's Budget.*

"'A History of Cabinets' from the beginning of the Eighteenth Century down to the death of George II., which the late Mr M'Cullagh Torrens regarded as 'the work of his life,' was published yesterday. It consists of two volumes of considerable bulk, showing at once that something more than the origin and progress of the Cabinet system had occupied the attention of the author. In fact, a history of Cabinets is a history of Governments, and a history of Governments is, in a great measure, a history of England."—*The Standard.*

A. J. WALL.

Indian Snake Poisons. Their Nature and Effects. Crown 8vo, 6s.

CONTENTS.

The Physiological Effects of the Poison of the Cobra (Naja Tripudians).—The Physiological Effects of the Poison of Russell's Viper (Daboia Russellii).—The Physiological Effects produced by the Poison of the Bungarus Fasciatus and the Bungarus Coeruleus.—The Relative Power and Properties of the Poisons of Indian and other Venomous Snakes.—The Nature of Snake Poisons.—Some practical considerations connected with the subject of Snake-Poisoning, especially regarding prevention and treatment. The object that has been kept in view, has been to define as closely as possible, the conditions on which the mortality from Snake-bite depends, both as regards the physiological nature of the poisoning process, and the relations between the reptiles and their victims, so as to indicate the way in which we should best proceed with the hope of diminishing the fearful mortality that exists.

JOHN WATSON, F.L.S.

Ornithology in Relation to Agriculture and Horticulture, by various writers, edited by John Watson, F.L.S., &c. Crown 8vo, 3s. 6d.

LIST OF CONTRIBUTORS.—Miss Eleanor A. Ormerod, late Consulting Entomologist to the Royal Agricultural Society of England; O. V. Alpin, F.L.S., Member of the British Ornithologists' Union; Charles Whitehead, F.L.S., F.G.S., &c., author of "Fifty Years of Fruit Farming"; John Watson, F.L.S., author of "A Handbook for Farmers and Small Holders"; the Rev. F. O. Morris, M.A., author of "A History of British Birds"; G. W. Murdoch, late editor of *The Farmer;* Riley Fortune, F.Z.S.; T. H. Nelson, Member of the British Ornithologists' Union; T. Southwell, F.Z.S.; Rev. Theo. Wood, B.A., F.L.S.; J. H. Gurney, jun., M.P.; Harrison Weir, F.R.H.S.; W. H. Tuck.

"Will form a textbook of a reliable kind in guiding agriculturists at large in their dealings with their feathered friends and foes alike."—*Glasgow Herald.*

"This is a valuable book, and should go far to fulfil its excellent purpose. . . . It is a book that every agriculturist should possess."—*Land and Water.*

"It is well to know what birds do mischief and what birds are helpful. This book is the very manual to clear up all such doubts."—*Yorkshire Post.*

"In these days of agricultural depression it behoves the farmer to study, amongst other subjects, ornithology. That he and the gamekeeper often bring down plagues upon the land when they fancy they are ridding it of a pest is exceedingly well illustrated in this series of papers."—*Scotsman.*

For the Reduced Prices apply to

of Messrs W. H. Allen & Co.'s Publications. 27

SAMUEL WILBERFORCE, D.D. (*Bishop of Winchester*).
Heroes of Hebrew History. Crown 8vo, gilt top, 5s.

"The tales which he relates are all good, and have a moral aim and purpose."—*Athenæum.*
"It is written with a natural and captivating fervour."—*London Quarterly Review.*
"An interesting historical account."—*London Lit. Gaz.*
"Using his influence as a man of the world for the purpose of modifying those about him for good, and making them serve as his instruments for the furtherance of the objects which he had at heart. He was the most delightful of companions, and the wittiest talker of his time. Of his extraordinary versatility and extraordinary powers of work, it is impossible to speak at length here, but both qualities are abundantly illustrated in his life by Canon Ashwell."—*Celebrities of the Century.*

S. WELLS WILLIAMS, LL.D., *Professor of the Chinese Language and Literature at Yale College.*
China—The Middle Kingdom. A Survey of the Geography, Government, Literature, Social Life, Arts, and History of the Chinese Empire and its Inhabitants. Revised Edition, with 74 Illustrations and a New Map of the Empire. 2 vols. Demy 8vo, 42s.

Dr S. Wells Williams' *Middle Kingdom* has long occupied the position of a classic. It is not only the fullest and most authoritative account of the Chinese and their country that exists, but it is also the most readable and entertaining. This issue is practically a new work—the text of the old edition has been largely re-written and the work has been expanded so as to include a vast amount of new material collected by Dr Williams during the late years of his residence in China—as well as the most recent information respecting all the departments of the Empire. Many new illustrations have been added and the best of the old engravings have been retained. An important feature of this edition is a large map of the Chinese Empire from the best modern authorities, more complete and accurate than any map of the country hitherto published.

HARRY WILLIAMS, R.N. (*Chief Inspector of Machinery*).
Dedicated, by permission, to Admiral H.R.H. the Duke of Edinburgh.
The Steam Navy of England. Past, Present, and Future.
Contents:—Part I.—Our Seamen; Part II.—Ships and Machinery; Part III.—Naval Engineering; Part IV.—Miscellaneous, Summary, with an Appendix on the Personnel of the Steam Branch of the Navy. Third and enlarged Edition. Medium 8vo, 12s. 6d.

"It is a series of essays, clearly written and often highly suggestive, on the still unsolved, or only partially and tentatively solved, problems connected with the manning and organisation, and propulsion of our modern war-ships, . . . being laudably free from technicalities, and written in a not unattractive style, they will recommend themselves to that small, but happily increasing, section of the general public which concerns itself seriously and intelligently with naval affairs."—*Times.*
"Mr Harry Williams, a naval engineer of long experience and high rank, discusses the future requirements of the fleet. He is naturally most at home when dealing with points which specially affect his own branch of the service, but the whole book is well worth study."—*Manchester Guardian.*
"Must be pronounced a technical book in the main, although its author expressly states that he wrote it 'not so much for professional as non-professional men.' Its manifest object is to promote the efficiency of our steam navy in times to come, keeping which aim steadfastly in view Mr Williams has brought great knowledge and ability to bear upon the endeavour to forecast what provision it would be well to make in order to meet the full naval requirements of the British nation. His highly instructive work is divided into four parts, under the respective titles of 'Our Seamen,' 'Ships and Machinery,' 'Naval Engineering,' and 'Miscellaneous,' which again are carefully summarised in some fifty pages of eminently readable matter. The three chapters of miscellanea deal principally with the coal endurance, engine-room complements, electric lighting, and steam-steering machinery of Her Majesty's ships."—*Daily Telegraph.*

Any Bookseller at Home and Abroad.

Professor H. H. WILSON, author of the " Standard History of India."
Glossary of Judicial Terms, including words from the Arabic, Persian, Hindustani, Sanskrit, Hindi, Bengali, Uriya, Marathi, Guzarathi, Telugu, Karnata, Tamil, Malayalam, and other languages. 4to, cloth, 30s.

Wynter's Subtle Brains and Lissom Fingers. Crown 8vo, 3s. 6d.

CONTENTS.

- The Buried Roman City in Britain.
- "Silvertown."
- Advertising.
- Vivisection.
- The New Hotel System.
- The Restoration of our Soil.
- Half-Hours at the Kensington Museum.
- Mudie's Circulating Library.
- Fraudulent Trade Marks.
- Superstition : Where does it End?
- The New Counterblast to Tobacco.
- Air Traction.
- Illuminations.
- Boat-Building by Machinery.
- The Effects of Railway Travelling upon Health.
- The Working-Men's Flower Show.
- Messages under the Sea.
- Town Telegraphs.
- The Bread We Eat.
- Early Warnings.
- Dining Rooms for the Working Classes.
- Railway and City Population.
- A Day with the Coroner.
- The English in Paris.
- The *Times* Newspaper in 1798.
- The Under-Sea Railroad.
- Oh, the Roast Beef of Old England.
- Physical Education.
- Advice by a Retired Physician.
- The Clerk of the Weather.
- Portsmouth Dockyard.
- Village Hospitals.
- Railways, the Great Civilisers.
- On taking a House.
- Photographic Portraiture.
- Doctor's Stuff.
- Smallpox in London.
- Hospital Dress.
- Excursion Trains.

"Altogether 'Subtle Brains and Lissom Fingers' is about the pleasantest book of short collected papers of chit chat blending information with amusement, and not overtasking the attention or the intelligence, that we have seen for a good while."—*London Reader.*

LIEUT. G. J. YOUNGHUSBAND, Queen's Own Corps of Guides.
Eighteen Hundred Miles in a Burmese Tat, through Burmah, Siam, and the Eastern Shan States. Illustrated. Crown 8vo, 5s.

"There is a good deal of jocular description in this book, which, as the reader will easily see, has been introduced with an eye rather to amusement than to accuracy; but after all the volume will have repaid the reader for the few hours which may be spent in its perusal if it conveys to him, as it is calculated to do, a fair impression of the difficulties which beset the wayfarer in a strange land who, when in search of the pleasures of travel, begins his journey where he should leave off, and ends it where he should have started."—*Athenæum.*

"Mr Younghusband's account of his adventures is written simply and without exaggeration, but on the whole we would rather read about the Shan country than travel in it."—*Literary World.*

For the Reduced Prices apply to

Scientific Works: including Botany, Natural History, &c.

E. BONAVIA, M.D., Brigade-Surgeon, Indian Medical Service.

The Cultivated Oranges and Lemons of India and Ceylon. Demy 8vo, with oblong Atlas Volume of Plates, 2 vols. 30s.

R. BRAITHWAITE, M.D., F.L.S., &c.

The Sphagnaceæ, or Peat Mosses of Europe and North America. Illustrated with 29 Plates, **coloured by hand**. Imp. 8vo, 25s.

"All muscologists will be delighted to hail the appearance of this important work. ... Never before has our native moss-flora been so carefully figured and described, and that by an acknowledged authority on the subject."—*Science Gossip.*

"Mosses, perhaps, receive about as little attention from botanists as any class of plants, and considering how admirably mosses lend themselves to the collector's purposes, this is very remarkable. Something may be due to the minuteness of the size of many of the species, and something perhaps to the difficulties inherent in the systematic treatment of these plants; but we fancy the chief cause of comparative neglect with which they are treated is to be sought in the want of a good illustrated English treatise upon them. In the work which is now before us, Dr Braithwaite aims at placing the British mosses on the same vantage-ground as the more favoured classes of the vegetable kingdom; and judging from the sample lately issued, he will succeed in his endeavours."—*Popular Science Review.*

B. CARRINGTON, M.D., F.R.S.

British Hepaticæ. Containing Descriptions and Figures of the Native Species of Jungermannia, Marchantia, and Anthoceros. Imp. 8vo, sewed, Parts 1 to 4, plain plates, 2s. 6d. each; **coloured plates**, 3s. 6d. each.

M. C. COOKE, M.A., LL.D.

The British Fungi: A Plain and Easy Account of. **With Coloured Plates of 40 Species.** Fifth Edition, Revised. Crown 8vo, 6s.

"Mr Cooke writes for those whose education and means are limited, and with preeminent success. It is really a pleasure to read the manuals which he has published, for they are up to the mark, and so complete as to leave hardly anything to be desired. The new work on the fungi appears to be equally valuable with those which he has already printed. It contains descriptions of the esculent fungi, the manner in which they are prepared for the table, how to discriminate the nutritious from the poisonous species, details of the principles of their scientific classification, and a tabular arrangement of orders and genera."

Handbook of British Hepaticæ. Containing Descriptions and Figures of the Indigenous Species of Marchantia, Jungermannia, Riccia, and Anthoceros, Illustrated. Crown 8vo, 6s.

"It is very creditable to Mr Cooke that the drawings in his book are all sketches from nature made by his own pencil. This shows work, and is more respectable than the too common practice of copying engravings from the authorities in the particular branch of science. This little book is valuable, because in some respects it is certainly a good guide-book to a number of edible fungi unknown to the public."—*Popular Science Review.*

"Probably no group in the British flora has received so little attention as the Hepaticæ. Dr M. C. Cooke has now filled up the gap by producing a 'Handbook of the British Hepaticæ,' containing full descriptions of all the species, about two hundred in number, known to inhabit the British Islands."—*Nature.*

M. C. Cooke's Books continued.

Any Bookseller at Home and Abroad.

M. C. COOKE, M.A., LL.D.—continued.

Our Reptiles and Batrachians. A Plain and Easy Account of the Lizards, Snakes, Newts, Toads, Frogs, and Tortoises indigenous to Great Britain. New and Revised Edition. **With original Coloured Pictures of every Species**, and numerous Woodcuts. Crown 8vo, 6s.

CONTENTS.

Reptiles and Snake-stones.	The Blind Worm.	The Common Frog.
The Common Lizard.	The Common Snake.	The Edible Frog.
The Sand Lizard.	The Smooth Snake.	The Common Toad.
The Green Lizard.	The Viper, or Adder.	Common Smooth Newt or Eft.
The Natterjack.	Great Water Newt.	
Palmate Newt.	Gray's Banded Newt.	The Hawk's-Bill Turtle.
The Leathery Turtle.	Amphibia or Batrachians.	Appendix.

" Mr Cooke has especially distinguished himself as a student of the fungi and the fresh-water algæ, his works on these orders being the standard treatises in English. He has also paid some attention to zoology and chemistry, his education in these as in other sciences being obtained by persistent self-instruction."—*Celebrities of the Century.*

Rust, Smut, Mildew, and Mould. An Introduction to the Study of Microscopic Fungi. **Illustrated with 269 Coloured Figures by J. E. Sowerby.** Fifth Edition, Revised and Enlarged, with Appendix of New Species. Crown 8vo, 6s.

Those of our readers who are the happy possessors of microscopes would welcome this book with delight, as opening the way to a definite study of a most interesting branch of plant life. The minute fungi, here so faithfully depicted by Mr Sowerby, and so carefully described by Dr Cooke, have not only beauty of form and colour, but wonderful life-histories. Every hedge or lane or piece of waste ground, even in the suburbs of large towns, will provide specimens, which may be easily preserved on the plants which they attack or mounted as microscope slides.

Important to Botanists and Students of Natural History.

European Fungi (Hymenomycetum) — Synoptical Key to. Cooke (M. C.) and Quelet (L., M.D., &c.)—Clavis Synoptica Hymenomycetum Europæorum. Fcap. 8vo, 7s. 6d. ; or, interleaved with ruled paper, 8s. 6d.

" Without pretending to high scientific quality, the work throughout is well fitted to instruct and to attract a class of readers who might shrink from grappling with a scientific text-book."—*Saturday Review.*

BARON CUVIER.

The Animal Kingdom. With considerable Additions by W. B. Carpenter, M.D., F.R.S., and J. O. Westwood, F.L.S. New Edition, Illustrated with 500 Engravings on Wood and **36 Coloured Plates.** Imp. 8vo, 21s.

J. HUNTER, late Hon. Sec. of the British Bee-keepers' Association.

A Manual of Bee-keeping. Containing Practical Information for Rational and Profitable Methods of Bee Management. Full Instructions on Stimulative Feeding, Ligurianising and Queen-raising, with descriptions of the American Comb Foundation, Sectional Supers, and the best Hives and Apiarian Appliances on all systems. Fourth Edition. With Illustrations. Crown 8vo, 3s. 6d.

" We cordially recommend Mr Hunter's neat and compact Manual of Bee-keeping. Mr Hunter writes clearly and well."—*Science Gossip.*

" We are indebted to Mr J. Hunter, Honorary Secretary of the British Bee-keepers' Association. His Manual of Bee-keeping, just published, is full to the very brim of choice and practical hints fully up to the most advanced stages of Apiarian Science, and its perusal has afforded us so much pleasure that we have drawn somewhat largely from it for the benefit of our readers."—*Bee-keepers' Magazine (New York).*

For the Reduced Prices apply to

G. H. KINAHAN.
A Handy Book of Rock Names. Fcap. 8vo, 4s.

"This will prove, we do not doubt, a very useful little book to all practical geologists, and also to the reading student of rocks. When a difficulty is incurred as to a species of deposit, it will soon vanish. Mr Kinahan's little book will soon make it all clear. The work is divided into three parts. The first is a classified table of rocks, the second part treats of the *Ingenite* rocks, and the third part deals with those rocks which are styled *Derivate*. Dana's termination of *yte* has been most generally used by the author, but he has also given the *ite* terminations for those that like them. The book will be purchased, for it must be had, by every geologist; and as its size is small, it will form a convenient pocket companion for the man who works over field and quarry."—*Popular Science Review.*

Professor E. LANKESTER.
The Uses of Animals in Relation to the Industry of Man. New Edition. Illustrated. Crown 8vo, 4s.

Silk, Wool, Leather, Bone, Soap, Waste, Sponges, and Corals, Shell-fish, Insects, Furs, Feathers, Horns and Hair, and Animal Perfumes, are the subjects of the twelve lectures on "The Uses of Animals."

"In his chapter on 'Waste,' the lecturer gives startling insight into the manifold uses of rubbish. . . . Dr Lankester finds a use for everything; and he delights in analysing each fresh sample of rejected material, and stating how each of its component parts can be turned to the best account."—*Athenæum.*

Practical Physiology: A School Manual of Health. With numerous Woodcuts. Sixth Edition. Fcap. 8vo, 2s. 6d.

CONTENTS.

Constitution of the Human Body.
Nature of the Food supplied to the Human Body.
Digestion, and the Organs by which it is performed.
Nature of Blood and its Circulation by the Heart.
Breathing, or the Function of Respiration.
The Structure and Functions of the Skin.
The Movements of the Human Body.
The Brain and Nerves.
The Organs of the Senses.

"Writing for schoolboys, Dr Lankester has been careful to consult their tastes. There are passages in this little work which will make it popular, and the instructor will probably be hailed by a name which is new to people of his class, that of a 'regular brick.'"—*Athenæum.*

MRS LANKESTER.
Talks about Health: A Book for Boys and Girls. Being an Explanation of all the Processes by which Life is Sustained. Illustrated. Small 8vo, 1s.

The Late EDWARD NEWMAN, F.Z.S.
British Butterflies. With many Illustrations. Super royal 8vo, 7s. 6d.

"The British butterflies have found a good friend in Mr Newman, who has given us a history of their lives—from *larva* to *imago*, their habits and their whereabouts—which is one of the most perfect things of the kind. And we are glad to read the author's statement that his work has attained, while in progress, a sale that is almost unattainable in English scientific works. Firstly, the work consists of a series of notices to the young who may be disposed to go butterfly-hunting. And in them we find the author's great experience, and we commend this part of his work to our readers. The next part deals with the subjects of anatomy, physiology, and embryology of the insects; and finally we come to the separate account of each species. This latter is admirably given. First comes a capital engraving, life size, of the species, and then follows in order the life, history, time of appearance and locality, occupying from a page to a page and a half or two pages of a large quarto (or nearly so) volume. All this is done well, as we might expect from the author; it is clear, intelligible, and devoid of much of the rubbish which abounds in books of this kind generally. We must conclude by expressing the hope that all who are interested in insects will make themselves aquainted with the volume."—*Popular Science Review.*

Any Bookseller at Home and Abroad.

MARY A. PRATTEN.

My Hundred Swiss Flowers. With a Short Account of Swiss Ferns. With 60 Illustrations. Crown 8vo, plain plates, 12s. 6d.; coloured plates, 25s.

"The temptation to produce such books as this seems irresistible. The author feels a want; the want is undeniable. After more or less hesitation he feels he can supply it. It is pleasantly written, and affords useful hints as to localities."—*Athenæum.*

S. L. PUMPHREY.

A Little Brown Pebble, with 10 full-page cuts. Fcap. 4to, 3s. 6d.

"In the story of 'A Little Brown Pebble,' its writer endeavours to introduce geological science into the nursery, showing what strange creatures lived in the ancient seas, what monsters inhabited the primeval forests, and how our country alternated between torrid heats and an arctic cold. The accuracy of the information is guaranteed by competent authorities, and the illustrations are spirited. There is no reason why the attempt should not succeed."—*Academy,* 21st December 1889.

R. RIMMER, F.L.S.

The Land and Freshwater Shells of the British Isles. Illustrated with 10 Photographs and 3 Lithographs, containing figures of all the principal Species. Second Edition. Crown 8vo, 5s.

"This handsomely got up little volume supplies a long-felt want in a very ingenious and trustworthy manner. The author is an enthusiastic conchologist, and writes both attractively and well, and in a manner so simple and natural that we have no fear that any ordinarily educated man will easily understand every phrase. But the feature of this book which strikes us most is that every species of British land and freshwater shell has been photographed, and here we have all the photographs, natural size in the albertype process, so that the merest tyro will find no difficulty in identifying any shell he may find."—*Science Review.*

J. SMITH, A.L.S.

Ferns: British and Foreign. Fourth Edition, revised and greatly enlarged, with many illustrations. Crown 8vo, 7s. 6d.

"Each genus is described, and the technical characters upon which it is founded are shown in the accompanying illustrations, and the indispensable technical terms are explained by examples. The meaning and derivations of the botanical names of ferns are also given in sufficient detail and with sufficient accuracy to meet the wants of amateurs, if not of scholars. But perhaps the most valuable part of the work is that devoted to instruction in the cultivation of ferns, which occupies some seventy pages of the book. A bibliography of the subject and an excellent index make up the remainder of this useful volume, which we recommend to all persons desirous of knowing something more about ferns than being able to recognise them by sight."—*Field.*

"Mr Smith's work entitles him to admiration for his industry and for the manifest care with which he has studied his subject; and his present enlarged work will certainly become and be a standard library book of reference for all pteridologists and ornamental gardeners (whether professional or amateur) who devote attention to filiculture. And there really is no family of plants which is more elegant than are ferns. Indigenous British ferns alone afford a most interesting scope of research and collection."—*Whitehall Review.*

"This is a new and enlarged edition of one of the best extant works on British and foreign ferns which has been called for by the introduction, during the interval of ten years which has elapsed since the issue of the first edition, of a number of exotic species which have been collected and arranged under their respective genera and tribes as an appendix. There are thus introduced 234 entirely new species. The sixty pages devoted to a treatise on the cultivation of ferns are invaluable to the fern-grower, professional or amateur, describing the conditions under which ferns grow in their native country—knowledge which is essential to their really successful cultivation in this."—*Rural World.*

For the Reduced Prices apply to

J. E. TAYLOR, F.L.S., F.G.S.

Flowers: Their Origin, Shapes, Perfumes, and Colours, Illustrated with 32 Coloured Figures by **Sowerby,** and 161 Woodcuts. Second Edition. Crown 8vo, cloth gilt, 7s. 6d.

CONTENTS

The Old and New Philosophy of Flowers—The Geological Antiquity of Flowers and Insects—The Geographical Distribution of Flowers—The Structure of Flowering Plants—Relations between Flowers and their Physical Surroundings—Relations between Flowers and the Wind—The Colours of Flowers—The External Shapes of Flowers—The Internal Shapes of Flowers—The Perfumes of Flowers—Social Flowers—Birds and Flowers—The Natural Defences of Flowering Plants.

"This is an altogether charming book, full of wisdom, cheerful, simple, attractive, and informed throughout with a high purpose. Its object is to place within reach of the general public in an agreeable form the results of the most recent and comprehensive botanical research. The author is so bold as to ask why flowers were made, and is not without means to answer the question reverently and truthfully. He connects them by the aids that science supplies with the history of creation, and with the records of the rocks, and with the history of man, and the progress of the agricultural and horticultural arts. He tells us how they are influenced by soil and climate, how changed and multiplied by insects and other agencies, how their seeds are blown about the world, and how by innumerable divine appointments it at last comes about that the life of a man is environed and beautified with flowers. The work is rich in the results of travel, and it happily connects the vegetable products of the globe with the conditions that favour them and the wants they satisfy. It is therefore a book for all ages, and for botanists and gardeners, as well as for such as rather too gladly confess they know nothing about plants. We should like to see it on every family table in the whole length and breadth of the United Kingdom."—*Gardeners' Magazine.*

The Aquarium: Its Inhabitants, Structure, and Management. Second Edition, with 238 Woodcuts. Crown 8vo, 3s. 6d.

"Few men have done more to popularise the natural history science than the late Dr Taylor. The work before us, while intended as a handbook to public aquaria, is responsible for many attempts, successful and otherwise, at the construction of the domestic article. The book is replete with valuable information concerning persons and things, while the directions for making and managing aquaria are very clear and concise. The illustrations are numerous, suitable, and very good."—*Schoolmaster.*

"The ichthyologist, be it known, is not such a fearful or horrific 'sort of wildfowl' as his name would seem to argue him. The prevalence of the breed, the extent of its knowledge, the zeal of its enthusiasm, and the number of the aquaria it has built for itself in town or country, are all part and parcel of that 'march of science' which took its impetus from Darwin and the 'Origin of Species.' Those who do not already know that useful book, 'The Aquarium,' by Mr J. E. Taylor, Ph.D., F.L.S., &c., should procure this new edition (the sixth). It forms a convenient handbook or popular manual to our public aquaria. The aquarium, its inhabitants, its structure and its management, are the author's especial care And with the help of well-known works and a wide experience he has managed to put together a most praiseworthy book."—*Science Siftings.*

Half-Hours in the Green Lanes. Illustrated with 300 Woodcuts. Fifth Edition. Crown 8vo, 2s. 6d.

"A book which cannot fail to please the young, and from which many an older reader may glean here and there facts of interest in the field of nature. Mr Taylor has endeavoured to collect these facts which are to be recorded daily by an observant country gentleman with a taste for natural history; and he has attempted to put them together in a clear and simple style, so that the young may not only acquire a love for the investigation of nature, but may also put up (by reading this little book) an important store of knowledge. We think the author has succeeded in his object. He has made a very interesting little volume, not written above the heads of its readers as many of those books are, and he has taken care to have most of his natural history observations very accurately illustrated."—*Popular Science Review.*

J. E. Taylor's Books continued.

Any Bookseller at Home and Abroad.

J. E. TAYLOR, F.L.S., F.G.S.—continued.

Half-Hours at the Seaside. Illustrated with 250 Woodcuts. Fourth Edition. Crown 8vo, 2s. 6d.

"The love of natural history has now become so prevalent, at least among purely English readers, that we hardly meet a family at the seaside one of whose members has not some little knowledge of the wonders of the deep. Now, of course, this love of marine zoology is being vastly increased by the existence of the valuable aquaria at the Crystal Palace and at Brighton. Still, however, notwithstanding the amount of admirable works on the subject, more especially the excellent treatises of Gosse and others, there was wanted a cheap form of book with good illustrations which should give a clear account of the ordinary creatures one meets with on the sands and in the rock pools. The want no longer exists, for the excellent little manual that now lies before us embraces all that could be desired by those who are entirely ignorant of the subject of seaside zoology, while its mode of arrangement and woodcuts, which are carefully drawn, combine to render it both attractive and useful."—*Popular Science Review.*

Riding, Veterinary, and Agriculture.

EDWARD L. ANDERSON.

How to Ride and School a Horse. With a System of Horse Gymnastics. Fourth Edition. Revised and Corrected. Crown 8vo, 2s. 6d.

"He is well worthy of a hearing."—*Bell's Life.*
"Mr Anderson is, without doubt, a thorough horseman."—*The Field.*
"It should be a good investment to all lovers of horses."—*The Farmer.*
"There is no reason why the careful reader should not be able, by the help of this little book, to train as well as ride his horses."—*Land and Water.*

JAMES IRVINE LUPTON, F.R.C.V.S.

The Horse, as he Was, as he Is, and as he Ought to Be. Illustrated. Crown 8vo, 3s. 6d.

"Written with a good object in view, namely, to create an interest in the important subject of horse-breeding, more especially that class known as general utility horses. The book contains several illustrations, is well printed and handsomely bound, and we hope will meet with the attention it deserves."—*Live Stock Journal.*

WILLIAM PROCTOR, Stud Groom.

The Management and Treatment of the Horse in the Stable, Field, and on the Road. New and Revised Edition. Crown 8vo, 6s.

"There are few who are interested in horses will fail to profit by one portion or another of this useful work. Coming from a practical hand the work should recommend itself to the public."—*Sportsman.*
"There is a fund of sound common-sense views in this work which will be interesting to many owners."—*Field.*

GEORGE GRESSWELL.

The Diseases and Disorders of the Ox. Second Edition. Demy 8vo, 7s. 6d.

"This is perhaps one of the best of the popular books on the subject which has been published in recent years, and demonstrates in a most unmistakable manner the great advance that has been made in Bovine and Ovine Pathology since the days of Youatt. . . . To medical men who desire to know something of the disorders of such an important animal—speaking hygienically—as the Ox, the work can be recommended."—*The Lancet.*
"It is clear, concise, and practical, and would make a very convenient handbook of reference."—*Saturday Review.*

For the Reduced Prices apply to

PROFESSOR SHELDON.

The Future of British Agriculture. How Farmers may best be Benefited. Crown 8vo, 2s. 6d.

"Fortunately Prof. Sheldon has no mind to play the part of a prophet, but from the plenitude of a long experience gives sage counsel how to farm abreast of the time and be ready for whatever may ensue. . . . This little book is well worth reading, and it is pleasant to find that the professor by no means despairs of the future of agriculture in England."—*Academy*.

"We welcome the book as a valuable contribution to our agricultural literature, and as a useful guide to those branches in which the author is especially qualified to instruct."—*Nature*.

"In this beautifully printed and well-bound little book of 158 pp., Professor Sheldon, in his usual happy style, surveys the agricultural field, and indicates what he thinks is the prospect in front of the British farmer. Like a watchman he stands upon his tower—and when asked, What of the night? he disavows not that we are in the night, but earnestly declares that the morning cometh apace. The professor is an optimist; he does not believe that the country is done, and still less does he favour the idea that, taking a wide survey, the former days were better than these. On the contrary, he urges that the way out of the wilderness is not by any by-path, but by going right ahead; and, ere long, the man who holds the banner high will emerge triumphant."—*Scottish Farmer*.

JOHN WATSON, F.L.S.

Ornithology in Relation to Agriculture and Horticulture, by various writers, edited by John Watson, F.L.S., &c. Crown 8vo. 3s. 6d.

LIST OF CONTRIBUTORS.—Miss Eleanor A. Ormerod, late Consulting Entomologist to the Royal Agricultural Society of England; O. V. Aplin, F.L.S., Member of the British Ornithologists' Union; Charles Whitehead, F.L.S., F.G.S., &c., author of "Fifty Years of Fruit Farming"; John Watson, F.L.S., author of "A Handbook for Farmers and Small Holders"; the Rev. F. O. Morris, M.A., author of "A History of British Birds"; G. W. Murdoch, late editor of *The Farmer;* Riley Fortune, F.Z.S.; T. H. Nelson, Member of the British Ornithologists' Union; T. Southwell, F.Z.S.; Rev. Theo. Wood, B.A., F.I.S.; J. H. Gurney, jun., M.P.; Harrison Weir, F.R.H.S.; W. H. Tuck.

"Will form a textbook of a reliable kind in guiding agriculturists at large in their dealings with their feathered friends and foes alike."—*Glasgow Herald*.

"This is a valuable book, and should go far to fulfil its excellent purpose. . . . It is a book that every agriculturist should possess."—*Land and Water*.

"It is well to know what birds do mischief and what birds are helpful. This book is the very manual to clear up all such doubts."—*Yorkshire Post*.

"In these days of agricultural depression it behoves the former to study, among other subjects, ornithology. That he and the gamekeeper often bring down plagues upon the land when they fancy they are ridding it of a pest is exceedingly well illustrated in this series of papers."—*Scotsman*.

Any Bookseller at Home and Abroad.

India, China, Japan, and the East.

SURGEON-MAJOR L. A. WADDELL, M.B., F.L.S., F.R.G.S.,
Member of the Royal Asiatic Society, Anthropological Institute, &c.

The Buddhism of Tibet, with its Mystic Cults, Symbolism, and Mythology, and in its Relation to Indian Buddhism, with over 200 Illustrations. Demy 8vo, 31s. 6d.

SYNOPSIS OF CONTENTS:—Introductory. *Historical:* Changes in Primitive Buddhism leading to Lamaism—Rise, Development, and Spread of Lamaism—The Sects of Lamaism. *Doctrinal:* Metaphysical Sources of the Doctrine—The Doctrine and its Morality—Scriptures and Literature. *Monastic:* The Order of Lamas—Daily Life and Routine—Hierarchy and Reincarnate Lamas. *Buildings:* Monasteries—Temples and Cathedrals—Shrines (and Relics and Pilgrims). *Mythology and Gods:* Pantheon and Images—Sacred Symbols and Charms. *Ritual and Sorcery:* Worship and Ritual—Astrology and Divination—Sorcery and Necromancy. *Festivals and Plays:* Festivals and Holidays—Mystic Plays and Masquerades and Sacred Plays. *Popular Lamaism:* Domestic and Popular Lamaism. *Appendices:* Chronological Table—Bibliography—Index.

" By far the most important mass of original materials contributed to this recondite study."—*The Times.*

"Dr Waddell deals with the whole subject in a most exhaustive manner, and gives a clear insight into the structure, prominent features, and cults of the system ; and to disentangle the early history of Lamaism from the chaotic growth of fable which has invested it, most of the chief internal movements of Lamaism are now for the first time presented in an intelligible and systematic form. The work is a valuable addition to the long series that have preceded it, and is enriched by numerous illustrations, mostly from originals brought from Lhasa, and from photographs by the author, while it is fully indexed, and is provided with a chronological table and bibliography."—*Liverpool Courier.*

" A book of exceptional interest."—*Glasgow Herald.*

"A learned and elaborate work, likely for some time to come to be a source of reference for all who seek information about Lamaism. . . . In the appendix will be found a chronological table of Tibetan events, and a bibliography of the best literature bearing on Lamaism. There is also an excellent index, and the numerous illustrations are certainly one of the distinctive features of the book."—*Morning Post.*

"Cannot fail to arouse the liveliest interest. The author of this excellently produced, handsomely illustrated volume of nearly six hundred pages has evidently spared no pains in prosecuting his studies. . . . The book is one of exceptional value, and will attract all those readers who take an interest in the old religions of the far East."—*Publishers' Circular.*

SIR EDWIN ARNOLD, M.A., Author of " The Light of Asia," &c.

The Book of Good Counsels. Fables from the Sanscrit of the Hitopadésa. With Illustrations by Gordon Browne. Autograph and Portrait. Crown 8vo, antique, gilt top, 5s.

A few copies of the large paper Edition (limited to 100 copies), bound in white vellum, 25s. each net.

"' The Book of Good Counsels,' by Sir Edwin Arnold, comes almost as a new book, so long has it been out of print. Now, in addition to being very tastefully and prettily reissued, it contains numerous illustrations by Mr Gordon Browne. As some few may remember, it is a book of Indian stories and poetical maxims from the Sanskrit of the Hitopadésa. The book is almost a volume of fairy tales, and may pass for that with the younger generation, but it is a little too heavily overlaid with philosophy to be dismissed wholly as such. In fact, like all that Sir Edwin Arnold has brought before us, it is full of curious fancies, and that it is a charming little book to look at is its least merit."—*Daily Graphic.*

For the Reduced Prices apply to

CAPTAIN JAMES ABBOTT.

Narrative of a Journey from Herat to Khiva, Moscow, and St Petersburgh during the late Russian invasion at Khiva. With Map and Portrait. 2 vols., demy 8vo, 24s.

The real interest of the work consists in its store of spirited anecdote, its entertaining sketches of individual and national character, its graphic pictures of Eastern life and manners, its simply told tales of peril, privation, and suffering encountered and endured with a soldier's courage. Over the whole narrative, the *naiveté* and frankness of the writer cast a charm that far more than covers its occasional eccentricities of style and language. It has seldom fallen to our lot to read a more interesting narrative of personal adventure. Rarely, indeed, do we find an author whose constant presence, through almost the whole of two large volumes, is not only tolerable, but welcome. Few readers will rise from a perusal of the narrative without a strong feeling of personal sympathy and interest in the gallant Major; even though here and there unable to repress a smile at some burst of ecstasy, some abrupt apostrophe, such as would never have been perpetrated by a practical writer, and a man of the world.

SIR E. C. BAYLEY.

The Local Muhammadan Dynasties, Gujarat. Forming a Sequel to Sir H. M. Elliott's "History of the Muhammadan Empire of India." Demy 8vo, 21s.

"The value of the work consists in the light which it serves to throw upon disputed dates and obscure transactions. As a work of reference it is doubtless useful. Regarding the way in which its learned translator and editor has acquitted himself of his task it is scarcely necessary to write; a profound scholar and painstaking investigator, his labours are unusually trustworthy, and the world of letters will doubtless award him that meed of praise, which is rarely withheld from arduous and conscientious toil, by assigning him, in death, a niche in the temple of fame, side by side with his venerated master, Sir Henry Elliott."—*Academy*.

"This book may be considered the first of a series designed rather as a supplement than complement to the 'History of India as Told by its own Historians.' Following the Preface, a necessarily brief biographical notice—written in the kindly and appreciative spirit which ever characterises the style of the learned editor of Marco Polo, whose initials are scarcely needed to confirm his identity—explains how on Professor Dowson's death, Sir Edward Clive Bayley was induced to undertake an editorship for which he was eminently qualified by personal character and acquaintance with the originator of the project which constituted his *raison d'être*. But the new editor did not live to see the actual publication of his first volume. Scarcely had he completed it for the press, when his career was brought to a close. A singular fatality seems to have attended the several able men who have taken the leading part in preserving this particular monument of genuine history. Henry Elliott, John Dowson, Edward Clive Bayley, and more recently still (during the current year), Edward Thomas, the high-class numismatist, all have passed away, with hands upon the plough in the very field of Oriental research. Without asking to whose care the preparation of any future volumes may be entrusted, let us be thankful for the work, so far completed and—at this time especially—for the instalment which has just appeared."—*Athenæum*.

SIR GEORGE BIRDWOOD, M.D.

Report on the Old Records of the India Office, with Maps and Illustrations. Royal 8vo, 12s. 6d.

"Those who are familiar with Sir George Birdwood's literary method will appreciate the interest and the wealth of historical illustration with which he invests these topics."—*Times, Feb. 26, 1891*.

"Sir George Birdwood has performed a Herculean task in exploring, sorting, and describing the masses of old India Office records, which Mr Danvers has now got into a state of admirable arrangement, so that, with the help of Sir George's Index, they may be readily and profitably consulted by students."—*Scotsman*.

Any Bookseller at Home and Abroad.

E. BONAVIA, M.D., Brigade-Surgeon, Indian Medical Service.
The Cultivated Oranges and Lemons of India and Ceylon. Demy 8vo, with Atlas of Plates, 30s.

"The amount of labour and research that Dr Bonavia must have expended on these volumes would be very difficult to estimate, and it is to be hoped that he will be repaid, to some extent at least, by the recognition of his work by those who are interested in promoting the internal industries of India."—*Home News.*

"There can be no question that the author of this work has devoted much time and trouble to the study of the Citrus family in India. That the preparation of the book has been a labour of love is evident throughout its pages."—*The Englishman.*

F. C. DANVERS, Registrar and Superintendent of Records, India Office, London.
Report to the Secretary of State for India in Council on the Portuguese Records relating to the East Indies, contained in the Archivo da Torre de' Tombo, and the Public Libraries at Lisbon and Evora. Royal 8vo, sewed, 6s. net.

"The whole book is full of important and interesting materials for the student alike of English and of Indian history."—*Times.*

"It is more than time that some attention was paid to the history of the Portuguese in India by Englishmen, and Mr Danvers is doing good service to India by his investigation into the Portuguese records."—*India.*

"We are very grateful for it, especially with the gratitude which consists in a longing for more favours to come. The Secretary of State spends much money on worse things than continuing the efforts of which the book under review is only the first result."—*Asiatic Quarterly Review.*

The visits of inspection into the records preserved in Portugal bearing on the history of European enterprise in Eastern seas, which were authorised by the Secretary of State for India in 1891 and 1892, have resulted in the production of a most interesting report, which shows that a vast store of historical papers has been carefully preserved in that country, which deserves more thorough investigation. Mr Danvers, whose devotion to the duties of the Record Department is well known, hastened to carry out his instructions, and his report fully attests the earnestness with which he pursued his task. The documents range in date from 1500 to the present date, and contain clusters of documents numbering 12,465 and 5,274, and 1,783 in extent, besides many other deeply interesting botches of smaller bulk. It seems that no copies exist of most of these documents among our own records, a fact which invests them with peculiar interest.

GEORGE DOBSON.
Russia's Railway Advance into Central Asia. Notes of a Journey from St Petersburg to Samarkand, Illustrated. Crown 8vo, 7s. 6d.

"The letters themselves have been expanded and rewritten, and the work contains seven additional chapters, which bring the account of the Transcaspian Provinces down to the present time. Those of our readers who remember the original letters will need no further commendation of our correspondent's accuracy of information and graphic powers of description."—*Times.*

"Offers a valuable contribution to our knowledge of this region. The author journeyed from St Petersburg to Samarkand by the Russian trains and steamers. He wonders, as so many have wondered before, why the break in the line of railway communication which is made by the Caspian Sea is allowed to continue. His book is eminently impartial, and he deals with the question of trade between India and Central Asia in a chapter full of the highest interest, both for the statesman and the British merchant."—*Daily Telegraph.*

For the Reduced Prices apply to

REV. A. J. D. D'ORSEY, B.D., K.C., P.O.C.

Portuguese Discoveries, Dependencies, and Missions in Asia and Africa, with Maps. Crown 8vo, 7s. 6d.

CONTENTS.

Book I.
Introductory.
The Portuguese in Europe and Asia.
Portugal and the Portuguese.
Portuguese Discoveries in the Fifteenth Century.
Portuguese Conquests of India in the Sixteenth Century.
The Portuguese Empire in the Sixteenth Century.

Book II.
The Portuguese Missions in Southern India.
Early History of the Church in India.
First Meeting of the Portuguese with the Syrians.
Pioneers of the Portuguese Missions.
The Rise of the Jesuits.
The Jesuits in Portugal.
St Francis Xavier's Mission in India.
Subsequent Missions in the Sixteenth Century.

Book III.
The Subjugation of the Syrian Church.
Roman Claim of Supremacy.
First Attempt, by the Franciscans.
Second Attempt, by the Jesuits.
The Struggle against Rome.

Book III.—*continued.*
The Archbishop of Goa.
The Synod of Diamper.
The Triumph of Rome.

Book IV.
Subsequent Missions in Southern India, with special reference to the Syrians.
Radiation of Mission of Goa.
The Madura Mission.
Portuguese Missions in the Carnatic.
Syrian Christians in the Seventeenth Century.
Syrian Christians in the Eighteenth Century.

Book V.
The Portuguese Missions, with special reference to Modern Missionary efforts in South India.
The First Protestant Mission in South India.
English Missions to the Syrians 1806-16.
English Missions and the Syrian Christians.
The Disruption and Its Results.
Present State of the Syrian Christians.
The Revival of the Romish Missions in India.

GENERAL GORDON, C.B.

Events in the Taeping Rebellion. Being Reprints of MSS. copied by General Gordon, C.B., in his own handwriting; with Monograph, Introduction, and Notes. By A. Egmont Hake, author of "The Story of Chinese Gordon." With Portrait and Map. Demy 8vo, 18s.

"A valuable and graphic contribution to our knowledge of affairs in China at the most critical period of its history."—*Leeds Mercury.*

"Mr Hake has prefixed a vivid sketch of Gordon's career as a 'leader of men,' which shows insight and grasp of character. The style is perhaps somewhat too emphatic and ejaculatory—one seems to hear echoes of Hugo, and a strain of Mr Walter Besant—but the spirit is excellent."—*Athenæum.*

"Without wearying his readers by describing at length events which are as familiar in our mouths as household words, he contents himself with giving a light sketch of them, and fills in the picture with a personal narrative which to most people will be entirely new."—*Saturday Review.*

F. V. GREENE, Military Attaché to the U.S. Legation at St Petersburg.

Sketches of Army Life in Russia. Crown 8vo, 9s.

Any Bookseller at Home and Abroad.

M. GRIFFITH.

India's Princes. Short Life Sketches of the Native Rulers of India, with 47 Portraits and Illustrations. Demy 4to, gilt top, 21s.

LIST OF PORTRAITS.

THE PUNJAUB.
H.H. the Maharaja of Cashmere.
H.H. the Maharaja of Patiala.
H.H. the Maharaja of Kapurthalla.

RAJPUTANA.
The Maharaja of Oudipur.
The Maharaja of Jeypore.
The Maharaja of Jodhpur.
The Maharaja of Ulware.
The Maharaja of Bhurtpur.

CENTRAL INDIA.
H.H. the Maharaja Holkar of Indore.
H.H. the Maharaja Scindia of Gwallor.
H.H. the Begum of Bhopal.

THE BOMBAY PRESIDENCY.
H.H. the Gaikwar of Baroda.
H.H. the Rao of Cutch.
H.H. the Raja Kolhapur.
H.H. the Nawab of Junagarh.
H.H. the Thakore Sahib of Bhavnagar.
H.H. the Thakore Sahib of Dhangadra.
H.H. the Thakore Sahib of Morvi.
H.H. the Thakore Sahib of Gondal.

SOUTHERN INDIA.
H.H. the Nizam of Hyderabad.
H.H. the Maharaja of Mysore.
H.H. the Maharaja of Travancore.

"A handsome volume containing a series of photographic portraits and local views with accompanying letterpress, giving biographical and political details, carefully compiled and attractively presented."—*Times*.

C. HAMILTON.

Hedaya or Guide. A Commentary on the Mussulman Laws. Second Edition. With Preface and Index by S. G. Grady. 8vo, 35s.

"A work of very high authority in all Moslem countries. It discusses most of the subjects mentioned in the Koran and Sonna."—MILL'S *Muhammadanism*.

The great Law-Book of India, and one of the most important monuments of Mussulman legislation in existence.

"A valuable work."—ALLIBONE.

SYNOPSIS OF CONTENTS.

Of Zakat.
Of Nikkah or Marriage.
Of Rizza or Fosterage.
Of Talak or Divorce.
Of Ittak or the Manumission of Slaves.
Of Eiman or Vows.
Of Hoodood or Punishment.
Of Saraka or Larceny.
Of Al Seyir or the Institutes.
Of the Law respecting Lakeets or Foundlings.
Of Looktas or Troves.
Of Ibbak or the Absconding of Slaves.
Of Mafkoods or Missing Persons.
Of Shirkat or Partnership.
Of Wakf or Appropriations.
Of Sale.
Of Serf Sale.
Of Kafalit or Bail.
Of Hawalit or the Transfer of the Kazee.
Of the Duties of the Kazee.
Of Shahadit or Evidence.
Of Retractation of Evidence.
Of Agency.
Of Dawee or Claim.
Of Ikrar or Acknowledge.
Of Soolb or Composition.
Of Mozaribat or Co-partnership in the Profits of Stock and Labour.

Of Widda or Deposits.
Of Areeat or Loans.
Of Hibba or Gifts.
Of Ijaro or Hire.
Of Mokatibes.
Of Willa.
Of Ikrah or Compulsion.
Of Hijr or Inhibition.
Of Mazoons or Licensed Slaves.
Of Ghazb or Usurpation.
Of Shaffa.
Of Kissmat or Partition.
Of Mozarea or Compacts of Cultivation.
Of Mosakat or Compacts of Gardening.
Of Zabbah or the Slaying of Animals for Food.
Of Uzheea or Sacrifice.
Of Kiraheeat or Abominations.
Of the Cultivation of Waste Lands.
Of Prohibited Liquors.
Of Hunting.
Of Rahn or Pawns.
Of Janayat or Offences against the Person.
Of Deeayat or Fines.
Of Mawakil or the Levying of Fines.
Of Wasaya or Wills.
Of Hermaphrodites.

For the Reduced Prices apply to

HOWARD HENSMAN, Special Correspondent of the "Pioneer" (Allahabad) and the "Daily News" (London).

The Afghan War, 1879-80. Being a complete Narrative of the Capture of Cabul, the Siege of Sherpur, the Battle of Ahmed Khel, the March to Candahar, and the defeat of Ayub Khan. With Maps. Demy 8vo, 21s.

"Sir Frederick Roberts says of the letters here published in a collected form that 'nothing could be more accurate or graphic.' As to accuracy no one can be a more competent judge than Sir Frederick, and his testimony stamps the book before us as constituting especially trustworthy material for history. Of much that he relates Mr Hensman was an eye-witness: of the rest he was informed by eye-witnesses immediately after the occurrence of the events recorded. We are assured by Sir Frederick Roberts that Mr Hensman's accuracy is complete in all respects. Mr Hensman enjoyed singular advantages during the first part of the war, for he was the only special correspondent who accompanied the force which marched out of Ali Kheyl in September 1879. One of the most interesting portions of the book is that which describes the march of Sir Frederick Roberts from Cabul to Candahar. Indeed, the book is in every respect interesting and well written, and reflects the greatest credit on the author."—*Athenæum.*

Sir H. HUNTER.

A Statistical Account of Bengal. 20 vols. Demy 8vo, £6.

1. Twenty-four Parganas and Sundarbans.
2. Nadiya and Jessor.
3. Midnapur, Hugli, and Hourah.
4. Bardwan, Birbhum, and Bankhura.
5. Dacca, Bakarganj, Faridpur, and Maimansinh.
6. Chittagong Hill Tracts, Chittagong, Noakhali, Tipperah, and Hill Tipperah State.
7. Meldah, Rangpur, Dinajpur.
8. Rajshahi and Bogra.
9. Murshidabad and Pabna.
10. Darjiling, Jalpaigurf, and Kutch Behar State.
11. Patna and Saran.
12. Gaya and Shahabad.
13. Tirhut and Champaran.
14. Bhagalpur and Santal Parganas.
15. Monghyr and Purniah

Bengal MS. Records, a selected list of Letters in the Board of Revenue, Calcutta, 1782-1807, with an Historical Dissertation and Analytical Index. 4 vols. Demy 8vo, 30s.

"This is one of the small class of original works that compel a reconsideration of views which have been long accepted and which have passed into the current history of the period to which they refer. Sir William Wilson Hunter's exhaustive examination of the actual state of the various landed classes of Bengal during the last century renders impossible the further acceptance of these hitherto almost indisputable *dicta* of Indian history. The chief materials for this examination have been the contemporary MS. records preserved in the Board of Revenue, Calcutta, of which Sir William Hunter gives a list of 14,136 letters dealing with the period from 1782 to 1807. Nothing could be more impartial than the spirit in which he deals with the great questions involved. He makes the actual facts, as recorded by these letters, written at the time, speak for themselves. But those who desire to learn how that system grew out of the pre-existing land rights and land usages of the province will find a clear and authoritative explanation. If these four volumes stood alone they would place their author in the first rank of scientific historians; that is, of the extremely limited class of historians who write from original MSS. and records. But they do not stand alone. They are the natural continuation of the author's researches, nearly a generation ago, among the District Archives of Bengal, which produced his 'Annals of Rural Bengal' in 1868 and his 'Orissa' in 1872. They are also the first-fruits of that comprehensive history of India on which he has been engaged for the last twenty years, for which he has collected in each province of India an accumulation of tested local materials such as has never before been brought together in the hands, and by the labours, of any worker in the same stupendous field, and which, when completed, will be the fitting crown of his lifelong services to India. These volumes are indeed an important instalment towards the projected *magnum opus*; and in this connection it is of good augury to observe that they maintain their author's reputation for that fulness and minuteness of knowledge, that grasp of principles and philosophic insight, and that fertility and charm of literary expression which give Sir William Hunter his unique place among the writers of his day on India."—*The Times.*

Any Bookseller at Home and Abroad.

REV. T. P. HUGHES.

A Dictionary of Islam, being a Cyclopædia of the Doctrines, Rites, Ceremonies, and Customs, together with the Technical and Theological Terms of the Muhammadan Religion. With numerous Illustrations. Royal 8vo, £2 2s.

"Such a work as this has long been needed, and it would be hard to find any one better qualified to prepare it than Mr Hughes. His 'Notes on Muhammadanism,' of which two editions have appeared, have proved decidedly useful to students of Islam, especially in India, and his long familiarity with the tenets and customs of Moslems has placed him in the best possible position for deciding what is necessary and what superfluous in a 'Dictionary of Islam.' His usual method is to begin an article with the text in the Koran relating to the subject, then to add the traditions bearing upon it, and to conclude with the comments of the Mohammedan scholiasts and the criticisms of Western scholars. Such a method, while involving an infinity of labour, produces the best results in point of accuracy and comprehensiveness. The difficult task of compiling a dictionary of so vast a subject as Islam, with its many sects, its saints, khalifs, ascetics, and dervishes, its festivals, ritual, and sacred places, the dress, manners, and customs of its professors, its commentators, technical terms, science of tradition and interpretation, its superstitions, magic, and astrology, its theoretical doctrines and actual practices, has been accomplished with singular success; and the dictionary will have its place among the standard works of reference in every library that professes to take account of the religion which governs the lives of forty millions of the Queen's subjects. The articles on 'Marriage,' 'Women,' 'Wives,' 'Slavery,' 'Tradition,' 'Sufi,' 'Muhammad,' 'Da'wah' or Incantation, 'Burial,' and 'God,' are especially admirable. Two articles deserve special notice. One is an elaborate account of Arabic 'Writing' by Dr Steingass, which contains a vast quantity of useful matter, and is well illustrated by woodcuts of the chief varieties of Arabic script. The other article to which we refer with special emphasis is Mr F. Pincott's on 'Sikhism.' There is something on nearl every page of the dictionary that will interest and instruct the students of Eastern religion, manners, and customs."—*Athenæum*.

Dictionary of Muhammadan Theology.
Notes on Muhammadanism. By Rev. T. P. Hughes. Third Edition, revised and enlarged. Fcap. 8vo, 6s.

"Altogether an admirable little book. It combines two excellent qualities, abundance of facts and lack of theories. . . . On every one of the numerous heads (over fifty) into which the book is divided, Mr Hughes furnishes a large amount of very valuable information, which it would be exceedingly difficult to collect from even a large library of works on the subject. The book might well be called a 'Dictionary of Muhammadan Theology,' for we know of no English work which combines a methodical arrangement (and consequently facility of reference) with fulness of information in so high a degree as the little volume before us."—*The Academy*.

"It contains *multum in parvo*, and is about the best outline of the tenets of the Muslim faith which we have seen. It has, moreover, the rare merit of being accurate; and, although it contains a few passages which we would gladly see expunged, it cannot fail to be useful to all Government employés who have to deal with Muhammadans; whilst to missionaries it will be invaluable."—*The Times of India*.

"The main object of the work is to reveal the real and practical character of the Islam faith, and in this the author has evidently been successful."—*The Standard*.

For the Reduced Prices apply to

MRS GRACE JOHNSON, Silver Medallist, Cookery Exhibition.
Anglo-Indian and Oriental Cookery. Crown 8vo, 3s. 6d.

H. G. KEENE, C.I.E., B.C.S., M.R.A.S., &c.
History of India. From the Earliest Times to the Present Day. For the use of Students and Colleges. 2 vols. Crown 8vo, with Maps, 16s.

" The main merit of Mr Keene's performance lies in the fact that he has assimilated all the authorities, and has been careful to bring his book down to date. He has been careful in research, and has availed himself of the most recent materials. He is well known as the author of other works on Indian history, and his capacity for his self-imposed task will not be questioned. We must content ourselves with this brief testimony to the labour and skill bestowed by him upon a subject of vast interest and importance. Excellent proportion is preserved in dealing with the various episodes, and the style is clear and graphic. The volumes are supplied with many useful maps, and the appendix include notes on Indian law and on recent books about India."—*Globe*.

"Mr Keene has the admirable element of fairness in dealing with the succession of great questions that pass over his pages, and he wisely devotes a full half of his work to the present century. The appearance of such a book, and of every such book, upon India is to be hailed at present. A fair-minded presentment of Indian history like that contained in Mr Keene's two volumes is at this moment peculiarly welcome."—*Times*.

" In this admirably clear and comprehensive account of the rise and consolidation of our great Indian Empire, Mr Keene has endeavoured to give, without prolixity, 'a statement of the relevant facts at present available, both in regard to the origin of the more important Indian races and in regard to their progress before they came under the unifying processes of modern administration.' To this undertaking is, of course, added the completion of the story of the 'unprecedented series of events' which have led to the amalgamation of the various Indian tribes or nationalities under one rule. In theory, at least, there is finality in history. Mr Keene traces the ancient Indian races from their earliest known ancestors and the effect of the Aryan settlement. He marks the rise of Buddhism and the great Muslim Conquest, the end of the Pathans, and the advent of the Empire of the Mughals. In rapid succession he reviews the Hindu revival, the initial establishment of English influence, and the destruction of French power. The author records the policy of Cornwallis, the wars of Wellesley, and the Administration of Minto—the most important features in Indian history before the establishment of British supremacy. It is a brilliant record of British prowess and ability of governing inferior races that Mr Keene has to place before his readers. We have won and held India by the sword, and the policy of the men we send out year by year to assist in its administration is largely based on that principle. The history of the land, of our occupation, and our sojourning, so ably set forth in these pages, is inseparable from that one essential point."—*Morning Post*.

An Oriental Biographical Dictionary. Founded on materials collected by the late Thomas William Beale. New Edition, revised and enlarged. Royal 8vo, 28s.

"A complete biographical dictionary for a country like India, which in its long history has produced a profusion of great men, would be a vast undertaking. The suggestion here made only indicates the line on which the dictionary, at some future time, could be almost indefinitely extended, and rendered still more valuable as a work of reference. Great care has evidently been taken to secure the accuracy of all that has been included in the work, and that is of far more importance than mere bulk. The dictionary can be commended as trustworthy, and reflects much credit on Mr Keene. Several interesting lists of rulers are given under the various founders of dynasties."—*India*.

The Fall of the Moghul Empire. From the Death of Aurungzeb to the Overthrow of the Mahratta Power. A New Edition, with Corrections and Additions. With Map. Crown 8vo, 7s. 6d.

This work fills up a blank between the ending of Elphinstone's and the commencement of Thornton's Histories.

Fifty-Seven. Some Account of the Administration of Indian Districts during the Revolt of the Bengal Army. Demy 8vo, 6s.

Any Bookseller at Home and Abroad.

G. B. MALLESON.

History of the French in India. From the Founding of Pondicherry in 1674, to the Capture of that place in 1761. New and Revised Edition, with Maps. Demy 8vo, 16s.

"Colonel Malleson has produced a volume alike attractive to the general reader and valuable for its new matter to the special student. It is not too much to say that now, for the first time, we are furnished with a faithful narrative of that portion of European enterprise in India which turns upon the contest waged by the East India Company against French influence, and especially against Dupleix."—*Edinburgh Review.*

"It is pleasant to con'rast the work now before us with the writer's first bold plunge into historical composition, which splashed every one within his reach. He swims now with a steady stroke, and there is no fear of his sinking. With a keener insight into human character, and a larger understanding of the sources of human action, he combines all the power of animated recital which invested his earlier narratives with popularity."—*Fortnightly Review.*

"The author has had the advantage of consulting French Archives, and his volume forms a useful supplement to Orme."—*Athenæum.*

Final French Struggles in India and on the Indian Seas. New Edition. Crown 8vo, 6s.

"How India escaped from the government of prefects and sub-prefects to fall under that of Commissioners and Deputy-Commissioners; why the Penal Code of Lord Macaulay reigns supreme instead of a Code Napoleon; why we are not looking on helplessly from Mahe, Karikal, and Pondicherry, while the French are ruling all over Madras, and spending millions of francs in attempting to cultivate the slopes of the Neilgherries, may be learnt from this modest volume. Colonel Malleson is always painstaking, and generally accurate; his style is transparent, and he never loses sight of the purpose with which he commenced to write."—*Saturday Review.*

"A book dealing with such a period of our history in the East, besides being interesting, contains many lessons. It is written in a style that will be popular with general readers."—*Athenæum.*

History of Afghanistan, from the Earliest Period to the Outbreak of the War of 1878. With map. Demy 8vo, 18s.

"The name of Colonel Malleson on the title-page of any historical work in relation to India or the neighbouring States, is a satisfactory guarantee both for the accuracy of the facts and the brilliancy of the narrative. The author may be complimented upon having written a History of Afghanistan which is likely to become a work of standard authority."—*Scotsman.*

The Battlefields of Germany, from the Outbreak of the Thirty Years' War to the Battle of Blenheim. With Maps and 1 Plan. Demy 8vo, 16s.

"Colonel Malleson has shown a grasp of his subject, and a power of vivifying the confused passages of battle, in which it would be impossible to name any living writer as his equal. In imbuing these almost forgotten battlefields with fresh interest and reality for the English reader, he is reopening one of the most important chapters of European history, which no previous English writer has made so interesting and instructive as he has succeeded in doing in this volume."—*Academy.*

Ambushes and Surprises, being a Description of some of the most famous instances of the Leading into Ambush and the Surprises of Armies, from the time of Hannibal to the period of the Indian Mutiny. With a portrait of General Lord Mark Ker, K.C.B. Demy 8vo, 18s.

For the Reduced Prices apply to

MRS MANNING.
Ancient and Mediæval India. Being the History, Religion, Laws, Caste, Manners and Customs, Language, Literature, Poetry, Philosophy, Astronomy, Algebra, Medicine, Architecture, Manufactures, Commerce, &c., of the Hindus, taken from their Writings. With Illustrations. 2 vols. Demy 8vo, 30s.

J. MORRIS, Author of " The War in Korea," &c., thirteen years resident in Tokio under the Japanese Board of Works.
Advance Japan. A Nation Thoroughly in Earnest. With over 100 Illustrations by R. Isayama, and of Photographs lent by the Japanese Legation. 8vo, 12s. 6d.

"Is really a remarkably complete account of the land, the people, and the institutions of Japan, with chapters that deal with matters of such living interest as its growing industries and armaments, and the origin, incidents, and probable outcome of the war with China. The volume is illustrated by a Japanese artist of repute; it has a number of useful statistical appendices, and it is dedicated to His Majesty the Mikado."—*Scotsman.*

DEPUTY SURGEON-GENERAL C. T. PASKE, late of the Bengal Army, and Edited by F. G. AFLALO.
Life and Travel in Lower Burmah, with frontispiece. Crown 8vo, 6s.

"In dealing with life in Burmah we are given a pleasant insight into Eastern life; and to those interested in India and our other Eastern possessions, the opinions Mr Paske offers and the suggestions he makes will be delightful reading. Mr Paske has adopted a very light style of writing in 'Myamma,' which lends an additional charm to the short historical-cum-geographical sketch, and both the writer and the editor are to be commended for the production of a really attractive book."—*Public Opinion.*

ALEXANDER ROGERS, Bombay Civil Service Retired.
The Land Revenue of Bombay. A History of its Administration, Rise, and Progress. 2 vols, with 18 Maps. Demy 8vo, 30s.

"These two volumes are full of valuable information not only on the Land Revenue, but on the general condition and state of cultivation in and aspects of the Bombay Presidency. Each collectorate is described separately, and an excellent map of each is given, showing the divisional headquarters, market-towns, trade centres, places of pilgrimage, travellers, bungalows, municipalities, hospitals, schools, post offices, telegraphs, railways, &c."—*Mirror of British Museum.*

"Mr Rogers has produced a continuous and an authoritative record of the land changes and of the fortunes of the cultivating classes for a full half-century, together with valuable *data* regarding the condition and burdens of those classes at various periods before the present system of settlement was introduced. Mr Rogers now presents a comprehensive view of the land administration of Bombay as a whole, the history of its rise and progress, and a clear statement of the results which it has attained. It is a narrative of which all patriotic Englishmen may feel proud. The old burdens of native rule have been lightened, the old injustices mitigated, the old fiscal cruelties and exactions abolished. Underlying the story of each district we see a perennial struggle going on between the increase of the population and the available means of subsistence derived from the soil. That increase of the population is the direct result of the peace of the country under British rule. But it tends to press more and more severely on the possible limits of local cultivation, and it can only be provided for by the extension of the modern appliances of production and distribution. Mr Rogers very properly confines himself to his own subject. But there is ample evidence that the extension of roads, railways, steam factories, and other industrial enterprises, have played an important part in the solution of the problem, and that during recent years such enterprises have been powerfully aided by an abundant currency."—*The Times.*

Any Bookseller at Home and Abroad.

G. P. SANDERSON, *Officer in Charge of the Government Elephant Keddahs.*

Thirteen Years among the Wild Beasts of India; their Haunts and Habits, from Personal Observation. With an account of the Modes of Capturing and Taming Wild Elephants. With 21 full-page Illustrations, Reproduced for this Edition direct from the original drawings, and 3 Maps. Fifth Edition. Fcap. 4to, 12s.

"We find it difficult to hasten through this interesting book; on almost every page some incident or some happy descriptive passage tempts the reader to linger. The author relates his exploits with ability and with singular modesty. His adventures with man-eaters will afford lively entertainment to the reader, and indeed there is no portion of the volume which he is likely to wish shorter. The illustrations add to the attractions of the book."—*Pall Mall Gazette.*

"This is the best and most practical book on the wild game of Southern and Eastern India that we have read, and displays an extensive acquaintance with natural history. To the traveller proposing to visit India, whether he be a sportsman, a naturalist, or an antiquarian, the book will be invaluable; full of incident and sparkling with anecdote."—*Bailey's Magazine.*

ROBERT SEWELL, Madras Civil Service.

Analytical History of India. From the Earliest Times to the Abolition of the East India Company in 1858. Post 8vo, 8s.

"Much labour has been expended on this work."—*Athenæum.*

EDWARD THORNTON.

A Gazetteer of the Territories under the Government of the Viceroy of India. New Edition, Edited and Revised by Sir Roper Lethbridge, C.I.E., late Press Commissioner in India, and Arthur N. Wollaston, H.M. Indian (Home) Civil Service, Translator of the "Anwar-i-Suhaili." In one volume, 8vo, 1,000 pages, 28s.

Hunter's "Imperial Gazetteer" has been prepared, which is not only much more ample than its predecessor, but is further to be greatly enlarged in the New Edition now in course of production. In these circumstances it has been thought incumbent, when issuing a New Edition of Thornton's "Gazetteer" corrected up to date, to modify in some measure the plan of the work by omitting much of the detail and giving only such leading facts and figures as will suffice for ordinary purposes of reference, a plan which has the additional advantage of reducing the work to one moderate-sized volume.

It is obvious that the value of the New Edition must depend in a large measure upon the care and judgment which have been exercised in the preparation of the letterpress. The task was, in the first instance, undertaken by Mr Roper Lethbridge, whose literary attainments and acquaintance with India seemed to qualify him to a marked degree for an undertaking demanding considerable knowledge and experience. But in order further to render the work as complete and perfect as possible, the publishers deemed it prudent to subject the pages to the scrutiny of a second Editor, n the person of Mr Arthur Wollaston, whose lengthened service in the Indian Branch of the Civil Service of this country, coupled with his wide acquaintance with Oriental History, gives to his criticism an unusual degree of weight and importance. The joint names which appear on the title-page will, it is hoped, serve as a guarantee to the public that the "Gazetteer" is in the main accurate and trustworthy, free alike from sins of omission and commission. It will be found to contain the names of many hundreds of places not included in any former edition, while the areas and populations have been revised by the data given in the Census Report of 1881.

*** The chief objects in view in compiling this Gazetteer are:—

1st. To fix the relative position of the various cities, towns, and villages with as much precision as possible, and to exhibit with the greatest practicable brevity all that is known respecting them; and

2ndly. To note the various countries, provinces, or territorial divisions, and to describe the physical characteristics of each, together with their statistical, social, and political circumstances.

For the Reduced Prices apply to

of Messrs W. H. Allen & Co.'s Publications. 47

DR C. EDWARD SACHAU.
Athâr-Ul-Bâkiya of Albírûní: The Chronology of Ancient Nations, an English Version of the Arabic Text Translated and Edited with Notes and Index. Imp. 8vo (480 pp.), 42s.
A book of extraordinary erudition compiled in A.D. 1000.

A. J. WALL.
Indian Snake Poisons: Their Nature and Effects. Crown 8vo, 6s.
CONTENTS.
The Physiological Effects of the Poison of the Cobra (Naja Tripudians).—The Physiological Effects of the Poison of Russell's Viper (Daboia Russellii).—The Physiological Effects produced by the Poison of the Bungarus Fasciatus and the Bungarus Coeruleus. —The Relative Power and Properties of the Poisons of Indian and other Venomous Snakes.—The Nature of Snake Poisons.—Some practical considerations connected with the subject of Snake-Poisoning, especially regarding Prevention and Treatment.—The object that has been kept in view, has been to define as closely as possible the conditions on which the mortality from Snake-bite depends, both as regards the physiological nature of the poisoning process, and the relations between the reptiles and their victims, so as to indicate the way in which we should best proceed with the hope of diminishing the fearful mortality that exists.

S. WELLS WILLIAMS, LL.D., Professor of the Chinese Language and Literature at Yale College.
China—The Middle Kingdom. A Survey of the Geography, Government, Literature, Social Life, Arts, and History of the Chinese Empire and its Inhabitants. Revised Edition, with 74 Illustrations and a New Map of the Empire. 2 vols. Demy 8vo, 42s.
" Williams' ' Middle Kingdom' remains unrivalled as the most full and accurate account of China—its inhabitants, its arts, its science, its religion, its philosophy— that has ever been given to the public. Its minuteness and thoroughness are beyond all praise."—*North American Review.*
" The standard work on the subject."—*Globe.*

PROFESSOR H. H. WILSON.
Glossary of Judicial and Revenue Terms, including words from the Arabic, Teluga, Karnata, Tamil, Persian, Hindustani, Sanskrit, Hindi, Bengali, Marathi, Guzarathi, Malayalam, and other languages. 4to, 30s.
" It was the distinguishing characteristic of our late director that he considered nothing unworthy of his labours that was calculated to be useful, and was never influenced in his undertakings by the mere desire of acquiring distinction or increasing his fame. Many of his works exhibit powers of illustration and close reasoning, which will place their author in a high position among the literary men of the age. But it is as a man of deep research and as a Sanskrit scholar and Orientalist, as the successor of Sir Wm. Jones and H. T. Colebrooke, the worthy wearer of their mantles and inheritor of the pre-eminence they enjoyed in this particular department of literature, that his name will especially live among the eminent men of learning of his age and country."—H. T. PRINSEP.
" A work every page of which teems with information that no other scholar ever has or could have placed before the public. . . . The work must ever hold a foremost place not only in the history of India but in that of the human race."—*Edinburgh Review.*

LIEUT. G. J. YOUNGHUSBAND, Queen's Own Corps of Guides.
Eighteen Hundred Miles in a Burmese Tat, through Burmah, Siam, and the Eastern Shan States. Illustrated. Crown 8vo, 5s.

Any Bookseller at Home and Abroad.

www.ingramcontent.com/pod-product-compliance
Lightning Source LLC
Chambersburg PA
CBHW051723300426
44115CB00007B/440